Act Like A Man

By Peter Parris

Library of Congress Catalog Card Number TXu 686-994

Published by Peter Parris
2213 Tiffany Glenn Ct.
Bedford, Texas 76021
Printed in the United States of America

ISBN# 0-9648902-0-8

Cover photograph of Peter and his son David.
By Andy Moys in 1976.

Contents

Dedication

In loving memory of my father, Charles E. Parris, who received Christ as his Lord and Savior just before he died. Despite his lack of biblical knowledge and Christian experience, he was an example of manhood in responsibility, industry and affection. Although during his life he was only a nominal Christian, he was used of God to point me in the direction of God from my earliest recollections.

In affectionate memory of Theo M. Bamber, our Baptist minister whose godly life and teaching opened me up to the truth of the gospel, the majesty of Christ and the glory of God. Such a rich beginning in the Scriptures founded my wife and me in a relationship with the Lord that caused us to appreciate His closeness but would not permit flippancy or overfamiliarity.

In grateful memory of Dr. D. Martyn Lloyd-Jones, whose Friday-evening Bible studies and Sunday services were a source of inspiration and revelation. With great gifting he systematically expounded the doctrines of God and rooted us in the foundational revelation of the sovereignty of God. That foundation has put all our woes and trials in the perspective of God's rule and His will for our lives.

To G.W. North, an itinerant teacher whose insights into the indwelling Christ and our union with the Lord expanded our appreciation and experience. His teaching of life in the Spirit gave us an awareness of the inner witness by which we now live.

To Bryn Jones, whose measure of the gift of Christ enabled him to become the obvious leader of a team of ministry of which I was a part. He stretched me into scenes nationally and internationally. He pioneered the magazine "Restoration" and what were to become the famous Bible weeks in the Dales. We merged the groups we had along with a third in Bradford, Yorkshire, and had an expression of an apostolic team that became an accepted norm for which to aim.

In cherished memory of W.J.Ern.Baxter, who many in Britain first met at the Lakes and subsequent Dales Bible weeks. His prophetic teaching was pregnant with revelation. We waited with baited breath as he unfolded the Scriptures with clarity, sensitivity and balance. I am thankful for the years of close relationship I had with him after coming to America.

These are the men among many who in the hand of God are outstanding in my personal growth in the Lord. They have helped shape my life and thinking, an influence for which I am profoundly grateful. I am honored if any vestige of reflection from these men is discernible in me.

Special Thanks

To Mark Mueller, who gave his time and tireless efforts to edit these writings. I greatly appreciate his fellowship as a brother and friend. His grammatical corrections and suggestions make this material more readable.

To Robert Moeller, for his labor of love in formatting so expertly this book page by page.

Special Acknowledgment

Brenda was introduced to me in 1953 at the Baptist church youth club, just two years after I was converted. I was fifteen, and she was almost thirteen. I asked her out shortly after, on the night she was converted, and we have been together ever since.

I cannot thank God enough for the singular blessing Brenda has been through the years. Her love and trust in God have always made her a dependable source of encouragement. Her discernment has often been the necessary caution that has adjusted my judgment. Her convictions have been used as an extension of my conscience, when by her words or by the way she looked I have added strength to my will to do what I knew was right anyway. Her ingenuity as a wife has kept our relationship vital and full of fun. Her devotion as a mother has been an example and a formative influence from which our children have richly benefited. Being like their mother is to be godly in character.

Brenda has enhanced my manhood and stood with me through years of development in trial and error. The favor of the Lord was surely mine when He gave me such a "good thing." Above all the God-given influences upon my life, Brenda has been the most consistent in her profound effect for godliness.

Foreward

There's a fresh wind blowing across America. On the one hand we are seeing hundreds of thousands of men trekking to Promise Keepers' conferences to learn what it means to be a biblical man. On the other hand, we are seeing renewal and signs of revival sweeping thousands of churches not only in other parts of the world, but also, finally, here at home. Coupled with this wind is a growing trend among Charismatics and Evangelicals to learn from each other—the Charismatics in their need for the stability and safety of sound doctrine, the Evangelicals in their need to be released from dead orthodoxy—something to which Dr. Martin Lloyd-Jones dedicated his influential ministry.

Peter Parris' book can best be appreciated in light of these exciting developments. As one on the cutting edge of what God is doing, Peter teaches us, day by day, to "Act Like a Man", i.e. as Spirit-filled men of God deeply steeped in the Word and deeply committed to be faithful husbands and fathers. You can feel the wind blowing across these pages.

The reader should be aware that the insights of this book, flowing from the Spirit and Word, reflect a vital and personal walk with God. When Peter was ministering in the San Diego area, we were introduced by a mutual friend, Dr. Alexander De Jong of Chicago. We immediately struck up a friendship and enjoyed considerable time together over lunches at Denny's and in prayer. I have been impressed and refreshed by Peter as one who not only "knows" what it means to be a man of God, but also beautifully models what these 365 devotionals teach.

My hope and prayer is that this wonderful book will receive a wide audience for years to come. I have grown from reading and meditating on its contents in my personal Quiet Time. It is my conviction that he who prayerfully makes use of this on a daily basis, and implements its divine principles, will certainly learn to "Act Like a Man" and experience something of the fresh wind that is blowing across our land.

Dr. David Schuringa
Senior Pastor,
Wellspring Christian Fellowship;
Professor of Practical Theology,
Westminister Theological Seminary

Introduction

Our generation is witnessing the eroding of the God-ordained roles of male and female. We now have a mixture and a perversion that cries out for redefinition and clarity. Only a recovery of God-given directives will pave the way for a return to true manhood. Feminized men and masculinized women have become an acceptable expression of the sexes. God will hold women accountable for their violation of His clearly recorded order, but men bear the brunt of the responsibility. God created man first and made woman from man, for man. The order of man and woman is creational not cultural or the result of sin. The divine order is most clearly set forth and established in the new covenant. God has a mystery to be revealed through the relationship between a man and a woman, the mystery of Christ and the church. The headship of the man speaks of the headship of Christ and the submission of the woman to the man speaks of the submission of the church to Christ. It was God who created man to be the glory of God and woman the glory of the man; this order was not the result of the fall. Becoming a Christian does not abrogate the creational order, nor does the new covenant nullify its own teaching.

Man has emerged in a broad spectrum of types that equally oppose manhood as instituted by God. Man has become characterized by feminine traits and unmanliness, as well as homosexuality. The other extreme, male chauvinism, is manifested in wife and child abuse and self-indulgences that spurn his God-ordained headship in the family.

God-rejecting philosophies have produced a travesty of manhood, which has in turn caused problems with women and children. It can be said that the trouble with the women is the men. The abortion issue highlights the fact that men have abdicated their responsibility for what they have fathered. No thought or care is taken for their offspring. This irresponsibility is taken into marriage, with many fathers abandoning their wives and children. This practice not only denies wives headship and security, but deprives children of the right to be fathered and loved.

There is a promise from God which is yet to be totally ful-filled. It gives hope in what otherwise is a hopeless state of af-fairs. He will turn the hearts of the fathers to the children and the hearts of the children to the fathers. The implications of this promise are far reaching. It is inconceivable that wives and mothers would be unaffected by the reversal of rebellious trends. The promise poses a picture of restored family life. Men will once again be loving and responsible in discharging their role as head. Husbands and wives will provide a secure haven for the nurturing of children. The church will lead the way, because Jesus will build His church. The judgment that begins with the house of God will purge it from every vestige of carnal philosophy and practice. There will be glory in the church through Jesus Christ, and every family in the earth will be blessed by testimony of Jesus in His church.

There will be God's men, men of God who live by the power of the Holy Spirit revealing God's intentions for men. With the role models of true manhood will be the corresponding display of godly women. Many times the phrase "but God" occurs in the Scriptures to change the course of events. It can be confidently affirmed that in the chaotic climate of God-rejecting ways there will be another "but God," and He will turn the hearts of fathers to the children and the children to the fathers. Man may pursue his hellish course, but God will raise up a standard against the flood of evil that will bring about the restoration of which our Lord spoke.

Although this book is focused towards men, it will have its application for both men and women. God made man in His image, and woman (who was made from the man) inherently pos-sesses an aspect of the image of God, although displayed in a different role than that of a man. The beautiful order of God has been marred by the foolish philosophies of men. The word of God is the only source of recovery from the grotesque caricature to the true image of God. The time has come to act like men, men of God.

Be on the alert, stand firm in the faith, act like men. 1 Cor.16:13

Act Like Men

Man was made in the image of God, but the noble creature that represented God in image fell from his created state. Sin marred the image and what began to emerge represented indwelling sin. Death came upon Adam and all his offspring.

It was not until the coming of the second man, the last Adam, the Lord Jesus, that life was to be communicated. Jesus was God manifested in flesh and blood, our supreme example of manhood. He was a life-giving spirit who came to give us life abundantly. "Learn of Me," Jesus said. To act like men we must be instructed by the life of Jesus. His actions and reactions, His motives and goals, His unswerving obedience, love, and zeal, His relationship with His Father—these are all recorded for our instruction.

What parades as man in our society today is a far cry from what we see in the Lord Jesus. Feminized men, unmanly men, homosexuals and proud macho men are all a product of God-rejecting ways. True repentance includes turning from what sort of men we were, for we were all in need of being saved. Receiving Jesus Christ as our Redeemer and Lord inseparably joins us to Him and enables us to live as sons of God. Christ in us gives us the authority and capacity to be to our wives what Christ is to the church. We act as true men when we love, honor, nourish and cherish our wives. We represent our heavenly Father when our hearts are towards our children. We must resist the pressure of being conformed to the men of this world. We will succeed by demonstrating a higher degree of manhood as sons of God.

Act like men, be strong. 1 Cor.16:13

Be Strong

A man should excel in fortitude, which is defined as strength and courage in pain or adversity. God charged Joshua to be strong and courageous, not to be fearful, to tremble or be to be dismayed, nor turn to the left, to the right, or waver. David and his men displayed qualities of valor, stamina and determination. They were warriors and heroes who left us examples of true manhood in boldness and bravery. They attempted great things and were admired for their achievements and noble deeds. What a contrast to the feminized men of our generation who imbibe the characteristics that should be found in the weaker vessels.

Many men have contravened God's image and have become emotionally and temperamentally effeminate. The strength to be displayed is not the strength of the bigot, but the strength of character that is in Jesus, the strength of love. Such loving strength emanating from one who has been designed to be a head would produce a security in his role as leader.

The strength of a natural man makes him obstinate; the strength of a spiritual man enables him to be steadfast and resolute. If such a standard appears too high to attain, remember that Christ is your strength. The power of His might will transform you from within until what you are in Christ overtakes what you were in Adam.

Your grace is according to your gift. If God has given you to be a man, then He will provide the necessary grace for you to fulfill your manhood.

Let all that you do be done in love. 1 Cor.16:14

Men of Love

This *all* is a fully embracing all—from our spirits and intentions through our thoughts and desires, into the expressions of our bodies. The new commandment for those in the new covenant is that we love as Christ loved. We are to testify to the fact that we have been born of God who is love. We are to walk in love, serve by love and speak the truth in love. Love is the most excellent way without which we are nothing. Love goes beyond mere duty and obligation. It is greater than faith or hope.

The love of God that has been shed abroad in our hearts is the same love that conceived our redemption and was commended to us while we were sinners. To be loved by God and to love God with all our hearts is the highest experience afforded to man. Our love for the Lord will express itself in the way we love others. Jesus prayed that the love with which God loved Him might be in us.

If we are to love our enemies, how much more our friends, our wives and our children. This love lays down its life for others. It is patient and kind. It is not jealous and does not brag, act unbecomingly or seek its own. It is not easily provoked and does not take into account a wrong suffered. Can you imagine what a difference we would make in our homes if we lived according to what is in us in Christ?

To be the man that God has created you to be, to be fulfilled in a way that satisfies God and yourself, you must love in deed and in truth. All the wonder of love waits to be expressed and experienced in those born of God.

Then we cried to the Lord, the God of our fathers. Deut. 26:7

The God of My Fathers

All fatherhood is derived from God the Father. He has expressed something of His own being in the family, which is the basic unit in the structure of society. Everyone is involved with the relationships that make up a family, even though those relationships may not be functioning properly.

God has instructed us that a child is to be the outcome of a union between a husband and his wife. When that instruction is violated, then all three parties, particularly the child, suffer.

God has given headship to the man; therefore, the man's responsibility is greater. His role is the most crucial to the harmonious structure of the family. For this reason, the waywardness of the fathers in abdicating their responsibilities, not only towards their wives, but also towards their children, is the biggest cause of the collapse of the family.

A child, because of its nature, has to be taught and cared for. It is dependent upon its father and mother for love, security, provisions and instruction, along with loving discipline. A child has inbuilt needs and is a responder. Where those needs are not met, the child is provoked. The resulting frustration combines with sinful nature in producing antisocial responses. Outrageous input into a child will produce outrage.

To father is to represent our heavenly Father. It is not difficult for children to honor their parents when they feel loved and respected. A loving father can also inspire children to want the God of their father.

I ascend to My Father and your Father, and My God and your God. John 20:17

My Father God

Jesus came to introduce us to the Father. As a son He understood the relationship between a son and a father. He saw the fulfillment of His own identity in submitting to the will of His Father. Jesus came to glorify the name of His Father, and in so doing He was perfected. In His prayer in John 17 He affirms that He had manifested His Father's name to His disciples and had given them His word. He told them over and over again that He did nothing of His own initiative, even as far as speaking only those things He had received from the Father.

After fulfilling redemption and rising from the dead, He spoke a wonderful mystery to His disciples: "I ascend to My Father and your Father, to My God and your God." We too can be born of the Holy Spirit and cry "Abba Father" to God our Father. Jesus taught us to pray "our Father" to His Father and informed us that our heavenly Father knows and supplies all our needs.

The world is to see our good works and be convinced that our natural parents could not be responsible for such a life. The world will glorify our heavenly Father for what we do. There needs to be a radical change in the standard of Christianity to bring about such an impact. The Holy Spirit is convicting the church as well as the world. Wherever the substandard prevails, God will judge as a Father chastening His children whom he loves. He will purify His sons and thoroughly purge His people. The true standard, which is the life of Jesus, will be manifested by those sons of God who prove their love for their Father by doing His will.

I press on toward the goal for the prize of the upward call of God in Christ Jesus. Phil. 3:14

Are God's Goals Our Goals?

To be without definite goals is to be indefinite in our direction. Satan capitalizes on wanderers and those who are ignorant of God's goals. Satan is the master of viable alternatives. He can make the wrong way seem palatable and attractive, logical and personally comfortable. If we are not aimed in the direction that God is taking things, then we are on the wrong path. God's goals give us life, purpose and fulfillment.

Jesus set His face like a flint. He was sharp in His focus and rock hard in determination as He set Himself in the direction of His Father's will. Those who sought to dissuade Him hit against an immovability that sent them away stunned by the impact of the collision. The collision was the violent encounter of clashing wills. He knew who He was, who had sent Him, what He had come for and where He was going. Whatever the cost He was going to achieve His appointed goal.

The adversary, who stands against, withstands us as we pursue God's goals. Perhaps that is why it appears easier to do the wrong thing. The illusion is deceptive because it will lead to despair and ultimately to death. What a sad commentary about Israel when God gave them their desires but also leanness of soul.

Greater is He that is in you than he that is in the world; therefore, the yoke of Jesus is easy and His burden light. Through Christ you can not only resist, but you can attack and overcome the adversary. Although you may have to wrestle, it is a good fight. Time and eternity will reveal that reaching God's goals is worth the fight.

For there is one God, and one mediator between God and men, the man Christ Jesus. 1 Tim. 2:5

Christ Alone

It was difficult for the early Jewish believers to comprehend that all the Old Testament types were taken up and fulfilled in one man, Jesus of Nazareth. Centuries of ceremonial traditions, rituals, washings, incense, temple, priests, feasts, sabbaths and so on were hard for many to relinquish.

Likewise, many Gentile Christians still hold to varying forms of religious trappings. There are countless so-called Christians who have never received Jesus as the one mediator between God and man and are ignorant of the fact that there is only one name whereby we must be saved. Mary, saints, angels, days, touch not, taste not, handle not, candles, images, money, rosaries, crosses, vicars, priests and prelates—all are more than useless as mediators. They are all an affront to the sufficiency of the sacrifice and high priestly mediation of Christ Jesus, the only Mediator, Savior and Lord.

The letter to the Hebrews addresses this problem by showing the excellency and supremacy of Jesus over and above all that went before. In stating that Jesus cannot be excelled, the new covenant renders the old covenant ceremonies and ritual obligations obsolete. The letters to the Galatians and to the Colossians address a similar problem, that of the commandments and teachings of men who try to bring us back into bondage. These letters point us away from such teachings to Jesus the Head.

Hold fast to the Head, sup with Him, know Him, love Him and suffer with Him. There is no other mediator or Savior except Jesus. Separate Jesus from all others as Lord in your heart.

He is also the Head of the body, the church...so that He Himself might come to have first place in everything. Col.1:18

The Supremacy of Christ

In the book of Hebrews, the outstanding patriarchs of Israel are shown to be inferior to Jesus Christ in that He has a more excellent name and function. When angels, Abraham, Moses, Aaron and Melchizedek are all surpassed, not only individually but collectively, it is a persuasive argument for the supremacy of Jesus.

We are to look to Jesus and consider Him, the author and finisher of faith. In Jesus we have a better covenant, a better hope, better promises, a better sacrifice and an unfading, everlasting glory. Jesus had a glory with the Father before the world was, and after He had purged our sins He was glorified with that same glory. We do not yet see all things in subjection to man, but we see Jesus crowned with glory and honor.

Jesus is the Lord of glory, and we have been called to obtain the glory of Christ. He has given to us the glory that His Father gave Him, that we might be one. The challenge of our status as sons of God is that the world might now see our glory. Isaiah speaks of the glory of God being seen upon us and actually attributed to us.

"Nations shall see your righteousness and all kings your glory" (Isa.62:2). This glory is not apart from Jesus. If the Lord of glory indwells the church and is head of the church, then there will be glory in the church. He will build His church, and nothing will stop Him. He already is the conqueror. All power and authority have been given to Him in heaven and on earth. His enemies will be put beneath His feet. Reveal the supremacy of Christ in your life.

To Him be the glory in the church and in Christ Jesus to all generations...amen. Eph.3:21

Glory in the Church

The challenge for us in our generation is to declare God's glory in the church. The church's glory will be determined by the glory that is revealed in and through each of us personally. Glory is the radiant manifestation of the presence of God. Jesus revealed the glory of God in His flesh, and He will manifest this same glory in His body, the church. This is not to be confused with the final glorifying when we get to heaven. It is a glory that the world around us sees. Isaiah tells us that His glory shall be seen upon us and nations will come to the brightness of our rising.

Glory is also practical righteousness. When we suffer for His sake, the Spirit of God and of glory rests upon us. Glory is the outcome of obedience that declares to the world what being saved is all about. Our righteousness is to shine like brightness and our salvation as a lamp that burns. It is God who is at work in us both to will and to do His good pleasure. He is able to do exceeding abundantly above all that we ask or think, according to His power that works in us. Do you desire to manifest His glory? What are you willing to do to be a glorious testimony of Jesus? The Lord has said that His people will be willing in the day of His power. When your willingness corresponds to His, then there will be a display of His glory in you.

The measure of your obedience is the measure of your love. Doing what you know to be right and abstaining from what you know to be wrong are what will please the Lord and produce the Lord of glory in your mortal body.

The God of our Lord Jesus Christ, the Father of Glory. Eph. 1:17

The Father of Glory

God is the God of glory. He is glorious, and His glory is above the heavens and fills the earth. Of the many words which are translated *glory* in the Old Testament, the most frequently used mean weight, heaviness, worthiness, honor and reputation. Glory is also used to indicate wealth and substance. Solomon in all his glory was breathtaking. The queen of Sheba was overwhelmed by what she saw. Creation itself displays the glory of the Creator, whether in the constant sunrises, sunsets, rainbows, and lightnings, or in the beauty of form and substance of matter in their unlimited variety.

Glory is revealed in its brilliance on those occasions when the invisible breaks in on the visible, as when the announcement of Messiah's birth came to the shepherds. "The glory of the Lord shone round about them."

A greater than Solomon has come. The radiance of God's glory was beheld in Jesus. Words fail to convey what majesty, beauty and holiness are intrinsic in Jesus, the Lord of glory. Paul prayed for the Ephesians that the Father of glory would give them a spirit of revelation in the true knowledge of Jesus. Such a revelation is an utter necessity for every individual.

God is to be desired above all the tangible glory of His creation. No wonder that all idols and efforts of man to portray Him are a contemptible abomination. Longing for Him and counting all else as rubbish is the only reasonable response to give to the Lord of glory. As sons of our glorious Father, let us "father" gloriously.

Wives be subject to your husbands, as to the Lord. For the husband is the head of the wife, as Christ also is the Head of the church. Eph.5:22,23

God's Order for Relationships

To become a Christian is to be born again by the Holy Spirit. Being crucified and buried with Christ means the end of a value system that was contrary to God's. The word of God becomes the basis on which we live. We were dead in trespasses and sins, and therefore blind and deaf; but having been made alive, we see things differently. The Holy Spirit becomes our teacher, and we find ourselves listening to wisdom that is not of this world. The contrast of philosophies is particularly marked in the relationship between husband and wife. Feminism and humanism are the sources of our modern manifestation of the roles of male and female. Man's alternatives to God's order have led to disaster in human relations.

God, the creator of male and female, knows best how the creature should live. We must relearn, be reeducated and start to appreciate God's wisdom in how to relate as men and women. God's word is truth, and the truth shall set us free from the bondage of deceitful philosophies, free to enjoy what God has designed for our fulfillment.

When the roles are confused, then perverseness and ultimate dissatisfaction will ensue. Your fulfillment is wrapped up in your God-given identity. Millions of men and women are deceived into unfulfillment by the contrary voice of Satan. When you adjust to the wisdom of God, then your personality will also adjust into wholeness and fulfillment. Most importantly, embracing God's beautiful order will cause you to please Him, instead of grieving Him.

Not having become a forgetful hearer but an effectual doer, this man shall be blessed in what he does. James 1:5

Family: Theory or Practice?

We must be not forgetful hearers, but effectual doers. The truth may open the door of the dark dungeon of ignorance and lies, but only obedience will take us through the door into the experience of freedom.

Please allow me to be personal and practical. Are you motivated from your heart to please God in all your ways? Are you a loving, caring, affectionate, faithful husband, giving godly leadership and security to your wife and children? The Holy Spirit is producing such men today. God has historically been the restorer of waste places. When we offer true repentance to God, then His grace for recovery becomes available.

The rewards of giving ourselves as testimonies of Jesus are priceless. There must be diligent application in practical ways. Simply be nicer, more loving and more innovative. Rearrange priorities for the success of the family, and prove God's wisdom to be relevant. It is never too late to stop living below God's ordained level for His children. The truth can either set us free or be a source of condemnation if we know what to do and fail to do it. God can bring order out of chaos. He is not a God of confusion. He can exalt every valley of deficiency, bring low every mountain of obstacle, straighten out the crookedness of years of deviation and make the roughness of our character like a polished shaft in His hand. He is at work in us; all we have to do is work it out.

All power in heaven and earth is given to Jesus. That power and all necessary grace are available for those who have a will to practice the will of God.

Let marriage be held in honor among all, and let the marriage bed be undefiled; for fornicators and adulterers God will judge. Heb.13:4

The Perils of Dishonoring Marriage

All relational problems could find a resolution if love were exercised by participating parties. Marriage is to be honored by the husband and the wife. *God will judge* is the solemn warning given as the ultimate prohibition to anyone engaged in or contemplating adultery or fornication. Marriages are a prime target of satanic assault, and many Christians are instruments in Satan's hand to effect the breakdown of their own marriages. Are you one of them?

The first responsibility is to the husband to love his wife as Christ loved the church and gave Himself for her. Many women have no such husband. However, women also are responsible for marriage failures. The mental and physical cruelty that is inflicted upon partners is disgraceful (without grace) and does not go unnoticed or unpunished.

The deception of sin abounds, nullifying the most fulfilling of relationships. In place of fulfillment many couples experience condemnation, pain, anguish and heartbreak. Children are plunged into fear and frustration as they experience the terror of being deprived of God-given relationships. As their feelings of helplessness increase, their already fragile personalities further warp and twist in inward despair. The Judge stands at the door. Judgment must begin at the house of God. Judge yourself so that you may not be judged. God is giving time to repent, but He will come and wage war against all who dishonor marriage and defile the bed.

To sum up, let all be harmonious, sympathetic, brotherly, kindhearted, and humble in spirit. 1 Pet.3:8

Married Life

The old saying "life is what you make it" is not without some merit. It is typical of man to make a mess of things, and marriage is no exception. Even Satan was created perfect until he made a wrong decision and made his life a fearful example of lost heaven. *Marriage is hell* is a frequently used expression. How could something inaugurated by God to serve as a sign of our union with Christ become such a failure?

Divorce is one tragic commentary on how we can ruin what God has given for our good. But of the marriages that remain intact, how many enjoy the good life that was designed to be realized in that union? The church is by no means exempt from the ravages of incompatibility and separation. Yet God, through what He has done in Christ's coming in the flesh, has totally and successfully made provision for us to have abundant life. In order to make something, one has to do something. In order to make a mess of a marriage, one has to be doing just that.

God, by the power of His Spirit, enables us to make marriage work. You are making what you are doing. What are you doing to your wife and your children? If you are not pleasing God, then you are certainly pleasing Satan. Many Christian marriages are a declaration of willful rebellion, carnal selfishness, satanic control and downright disregard for God and His will. "To sum up...not returning evil for evil, or insult for insult, but giving a blessing instead; for you were called for the very purpose that you might inherit a blessing."

But I want you to understand that Christ is the head of every man, and the man is the head of a woman. 1 Cor.11:3

A Question of Headship

One integral element of truth that is being left out in the ongoing controversy over the role of a woman is that of headship. The new covenant does not nullify headship; it establishes it. Although Jesus is one with His Father, God the Father is still the head of Christ. The unity of the church with Christ does not negate the fact that He is the head. The fact that the head of a woman is the man is for our instruction as new covenant believers.

While we are in the body, the absoluteness of our mortal and physical bodies cannot intelligently be denied. God is declaring a mystery in the role of man and woman when they come together in marriage; it is concerning Christ and the church. A time will come when sexual differences will be done away with, but it is important to remember that we are not there yet. There are many provisions in our redemption that are not yet available, including the redemption of our bodies. When we see Him we shall be like Him. Then shall this mortal put on immortality, but NOT YET. We do NOT YET see all things subjected to man, and it does NOT YET appear what we shall be.

The role of a man as opposed to the role of a woman still has significance and should not be abnegated. Whatever our view of women's ministry, it must not deny the new covenant provision of what God wants demonstrated in the headship of man. Christ was in submission to His head. The church should be in submission to her head. The woman is exhorted to be in submission to her head, the man. It is error to introduce into this age what is reserved for the age to come.

Because the Lord has been a witness between you and the wife of your youth, against whom you have dealt treacherously. Mal.2:14

Fulfillment or Frustration?

When God made the woman and presented her to the man, it was to fulfill him, for it was not good that Adam was alone. From the beginning, monogamy was to be the source of mutual completion and shared consummation. The satisfaction that God designed through the union of a man and a woman was to be a lifetime experience of love, both given and received. Two becoming one is a mystery. It brought together individually exquisite expressions of God, blending them into a single, powerfully vivid manifestation.

God is the God of fun! Marriage was not intended to spoil the fun. Pleasure, gratification, humor and every agreeable sensation were conceived by God to enhance the joy of marriage. God laughed before anyone else did, and with us being made in His image, He desires for us to laugh together.

Felicitous is defined as skillful or pleasantly ingenious. With this in mind, what fortunate horizons open up when two hearts join and two personalities mingle in felicity. What scope there is for genius and expertise. Happiness was intended to grow into bliss. God is blessed forever, and as marriage expresses divine life, it is blessed.

Fidelity means to adhere to marriage vows eagerly and with warmth of passion. Fidelity brings to a marriage the pervasive ingredients of cohesion and spice. When frustration is experienced instead of fulfillment, then fantasy takes the place of reality. With all the sensational promise of what can be experienced in marriage, failure to apprehend it becomes nothing less than a fiasco.

The thief comes only to steal, kill, and destroy. John 10:10

The Family under Fire

The old adage that it takes two to make an argument is not necessarily true. When Israel fell out with God, He was not to blame. There are innocent parties in some breakdowns, but whether it be one or both who are guilty, the cause can always be attributed to sin. Pride is a prominent cause of conflict and expresses itself in various ways. One form of pride is unfaithfulness. It is self-gratification at the expense of the feelings of the other partner and the vows made to God.

What God wants to demonstrate through the family as a testimony to Him makes it a prime target for satanic assault. Satan has many different strategies for breaking up marriages. He influences the media to constantly barrage the minds of people with unreal and illicit images of glamor and seduction that appeal to the carnal self and cause an underlying dissatisfaction with one's own marriage. The deception of sin finally gives the opposite of what it promised. Ruin, heartache and death are never promised, yet thousands of Christians fall foul to satanic pressure.

God also has a strategy and is not bankrupt of an policy to carry out His purposes. He has conclusively defeated Satan, sin, the world and death in Jesus Christ. His salvation works! In the place of indwelling sin, His Spirit comes and indwells us. The power of the cross triumphs over our old self, and the power of the resurrection produces our new self. Despite the failure of many Christians to remain faithful, there will be God-honoring marriages and families that testify of His love. Jesus is building His church. The grace and power necessary to build Christian marriages into the envy of the world are available. Take them!

For this cause a man shall leave his father and his mother, and shall cleave to his wife, and they shall become one flesh. Gen. 2:24

God's Plan for the Family

The monogamous relationship between a man and a woman is God's intention, and it is the exclusive relationship that He designed as the basis of the family. Our text embodies the biblical view of marriage and was quoted by our Lord, who further said that what God has joined together let no man put asunder. *Joined together* defines the nature of the coming together. "Let no man put asunder" defines the duration.

When the two become one flesh, a completeness is realized, one that God ordained to give mutual fulfillment for the rest of their life together. The Lord Jesus makes His bride secure by telling her that He will never leave or forsake her. We also should give such assurances of our love to each other—often.

God is love, and we were created in His image with a capacity to love. What the fall ruined, our new birth has renewed. When a man directs his love towards a woman and receives a corresponding love directed towards him, the unfolding of a wonderful mystery begins.

The mingling of minds, emotions and bodies in the environment of exclusive love is a fitting relationship that typifies Christ and the church. In order to enjoy all the latent fulfillment that a marriage holds, single-hearted love and total adherence to marriage vows are necessary. Despite all pressures to the contrary, happiness and growing satisfaction are still the experience of many people within the bonds of matrimony. God-given directives have been provided for true happiness and for an increasing experience of pleasure. The choice of blessing or cursing is yours.

And in the middle of the lampstands one like a son of man.
Rev.1:13

Jesus in the Churches

One vitally important lesson to learn from the verdict of Jesus concerning the churches of Asia is the necessity of keeping current with His assessment of ourselves. Despite commendable features of each church in particular areas, the contrast between where the churches thought they were and where Jesus knew them to be is alarming. Hearing the voice of the Shepherd is the only guarantee of a true appraisal.

The causes of overriding the voice of the Spirit are many and varied. Self-indulgence in its multifaceted forms causes compromise with the conviction of the Spirit. Vested carnal interests rationalize away the cautions of the Spirit. Halfhearted attempts at obedience result in a searing of the conscience and a deception concerning our state. The Lord Jesus gave us clear instructions in how to bear fruit: abiding in Him, letting His word abide in us, and obeying that word. Allowing a contrary voice to persuade us to disobey interrupts our walk with the Lord.

The church is full of the appalling contradiction of carnal Christians. The clamoring seductions of the flesh find little resistance in the double-minded, because mixed with belief is unbelief. So often our insecurity and need for acceptance can weigh heavily on the wrong side of the scales of our judgment. We are susceptible to the intimidation of peer pressure when we are not secure in the Lord.

Does the Lord's verdict of your condition require repentance? Why wait for the shame of exposure when you can rightly judge yourself and live to receive the ultimate commendation of "Well done."

Shepherd the church of God which He purchased with His own blood. Acts 20:28

The Blood of God

The blood that was shed for our redemption was the blood of God. God was manifested in the flesh, and Emmanuel, God with us, was also called Jesus. The flesh of Jesus was the bread that He gave for the life of the world. His flesh was the true food and His blood the true drink (John 6:55). When those who are dead in trespasses and sins eat and drink of Jesus, they live. His blood was shed for the remission of our sins, and we have peace with God through the blood of the everlasting covenant. We are given the peace that God enjoys with us because the ransom has been paid in full. Peace at last, peace because we are made holy, peace that passes understanding—His peace He gives to us. The power of the death of His body when He poured out His life blood is the power that puts our old man to death and loosens us from our sins. Charles Wesley wrote, "He breaks the power of cancelled sin and sets the prisoner free. His blood can make the foulest clean, His blood availed for me." No habit, no natural trait or emotional dilemma caused by genetic root, no addiction (we are all addicted to sin) is any match for the crucified Son of God to overpower conclusively. He even overpowered death and rose from the dead because His blood was accepted for our justification. Let the word of truth bring faith and liberty. Hear, and you shall live. Your inheritance is confirmed by the death of your Benefactor. Your life is assured because He was raised from the dead ever to live unto God. Let the redeemed say so, and live accordingly.

For John baptized with water, but you shall be baptized with the
Holy Spirit not many days from now. Acts 1:5

Good News of the Holy Spirit

The Lord Jesus told His disciples about "the promise of
the the Father" which was to come, and He told them to wait
until they had received power from on high. Jesus had been
conceived by the Spirit and was born the Son of God. He was
not without the Spirit, but thirty years later the Holy Spirit descended **upon** Him in the likeness of a dove; and at that point,
He began His ministry. He was **filled** with the Spirit, and having received His anointing, went forth in the **power** of the Spirit
(Luke 3:22,23; 4:1).

After His resurrection Jesus breathed on His disciples and
said, "Receive the Spirit", which obviously they did. This was
their new birth. Then Jesus told them that they were yet to receive
the promise of the Father: the coming of the Holy Spirit upon
them. The same terminology found in Luke's narrative of what
happened to Jesus at the beginning of His ministry is used concerning His disciples. The Holy Spirit came **upon** them. They
were **filled** with the Spirit and testified in the **power** of the Spirit.

Peter testified that God had done the same to the Gentiles.
Joel's prophecy that the Holy Spirit would be poured out upon all
flesh was being fulfilled. They spoke in tongues and prophesied
as the Spirit gave them utterance.

As the New Testament era unfolds, we see the Holy Spirit
distributing diverse gifts as He wills. There are varieties of gifts,
ministries and effects, but the same Spirit, Lord and God. The
baptism of the Holy Spirit is still an unresolved issue in the
church at large. However, the experience clearly expressed in the
Scriptures is the doctrinal basis of today's experience.

In whom you also are being built together into a dwelling of God in the Spirit. Eph. 2:22

More Good News about the Holy Spirit

Man becomes the dwelling place of God by the Holy Spirit. Power—great power, exceeding great power, exceeding great and mighty power—is at work in those who have been born again and baptized by the Holy Spirit. The physical body may be an earthen vessel, but the excellency of the power within is of God. God can, by the power that works in us, do far beyond anything that we can ask or think.

Through repentance we experience the power of the cross that overpowers the power of sin and Satan, and puts to death the old man. Being quickened in our mortal bodies by the same Spirit that raised Christ from the dead brings us to new birth. Then we are to receive our anointing: the baptism of the Spirit that endues us with power from on high; power to be witnesses of Jesus, to do the works that He did and greater works; power to be transformed into His likeness, to be as He is in this world.

This world will come under the impact of a people of power, millions of members of the body of Christ properly working and relating under the direction of their Head—by the power of the Spirit. To think that the Bible takes the place of the multifarious gifted body of Christ is to misunderstand the purpose of both the body and the Bible.

Those who deny the experience of the baptism of the Spirit will not prevail. To deny the gifts of the Spirit is to deny the Giver. To deny the functions of the body is to deny the Head. Jesus is still the one who baptizes with the Holy Spirit and fire. Through the proper working of each individual part His church will be built and will be powerfully glorious.

And because you are sons, God has sent forth the Spirit of His son into our hearts, crying,"Abba! Father!" Gal.4:6

The Spirit of Life

All men are born under the law of sin and death. The spirit now working in the disobedient has worked in us all. Jesus, the Son of God, was born of a woman, under the law, yet in order to redeem those who were under the law that they might receive the adoption as sons, He never sinned. To all who receive Him He gives the power to become the sons of God, and God sends the spirit of His Son into their hearts, whereby they cry, "Abba! Father!"

To be born again is to receive a new heart and a new spirit and to become a new creature. A new law, the law of the Spirit of life in Christ Jesus, sets us free from the law of sin and death. Jesus overcame and is able to liberate those who come to God through Him. No one else was God manifested in the flesh. No one else overcame sin, the world and the devil. For this reason there is salvation in no other. Jesus alone sets us truly free.

He changed the reign. Sin and death once reigned, but since Jesus prevailed in righteousness, grace and life now reign. By the power of the Holy Spirit we can now live and walk by the Spirit, demonstrating our new root. The wonderful qualities of divine life that were so visible in Jesus are now to be manifested in those who walk by the same Spirit.

This is how righteousness will spring up before all nations and men will see our good works and glorify our heavenly Father. When the cross crucifies us to the world and the world to us, the root of our fallen Adamic nature is cut off, and we are engrafted into a new root, Christ. Only then are we free to live by the Spirit and bear fruit unto God.

But the fruit of the Spirit is love, joy, peace, patience, kindness, goodness, faithfulness. Gal.5:22

The Fruit of the Spirit

"You shall know them by their fruit," said Jesus. He was speaking of not only the variety, but also the quality. We were all bad trees. No one was righteous or good, not even one. Apart from the grace of God we were destined to keep on bearing fruit unto death, but God in His mercy provided a Savior and cut us off from our old root. New birth engrafts us into our new root, Christ. Having been rooted and grounded in Christ, we can now bear fruit to God.

All the works of the flesh are natural to man, while none of the fruit of the Spirit is natural to man. To produce the fruit of the Spirit, one must be born of the Spirit. He who is joined to the Lord is one spirit with Him. Because our root is holy, the tree and the fruit can be holy. How else could we be holy as He is holy?

God hates a mixture. The old covenant did not permit a mixture of seeds nor the yoking of the ox with the ass. The new covenant enables us to live without the mixture of the old and the new man. Jesus instructed the Laodicean church to be either hot or cold, but if they remained lukewarm He would spew them out of His mouth. Let the tree be either good or evil, one or the other, not a mixture of both.

If we profess to be trees of righteousness, the planting of the Lord, then let us not deny Him by our behavior, which is our fruit. We were in the flesh and did the works of the flesh, but now, by contrast, we are not in the flesh but in the Spirit. If we walk in the Spirit, we shall bear His fruit.

Gentleness, self-control; against such things there is no law.
Gal. 5:23

More Fruit

The fruit of the Spirit is defined in contrast to the deeds of the flesh. What power is it that can take a body that expresses such depravity and transform it to express divine nature? Just consider the first three works of the flesh—sexual immorality, impurity and sensuality—then, by contrast, the first fruit of the Spirit—love. These qualities are mutually exclusive and cannot operate at the same time.

It is all a matter of the root. In the death of Christ we have been cut off from our old Adamic root, and through His resurrection we have been born again and grafted into our new root, Christ. As surely as it was natural for us to be depraved, it is now natural for us to be righteous. We are now partakers of the divine nature, having been given everything that pertains to life, abundant life and godliness. We are not waiting to become God's sons; we are **now** the sons of God. As He is so are we, not only in the world to come, but in **this** world.

Our new birth makes us the light of the world and the salt of the earth. God pours His love into our new hearts, giving us a new capacity to walk in the Spirit and not fulfill the lusts of the flesh. The exhortation not to be overcome by evil, but to overcome evil with good, implies the truth that we have the ability to overcome evil. There are many similar references to our new man being able to resist the dominance of sin.

Your union with the Lord Jesus is demonstrated in your mortal body by your likeness to Him. What was tried and proved in the Lord Jesus can be evidenced in you.

Gentleness, self-control; against such things there is no law.
Gal.5:23

Against Such There Is No Law

Life without prohibitive restrictions would be utterly disastrous in the natural, but not in the Spirit. There is no law against the fruit of the Spirit. We have the freedom to express love and all the other evidences of the Spirit in our lives, with an unrestricted horizon. The very nature of God is before us to explore and possess. God will never pass a law restricting us in our pursuit of Him or limiting our expression of Him. We are the offenders in providing our own limitations, drawing lines where we go no further, withdrawing into self-imposed boundaries and stagnation.

There is something sad about a dried up river that once flowed, maintaining and sustaining all manner of life. When Jesus referred to the coming of the Holy Spirit He said that the result would be rivers of living water flowing from our innermost being. The awesome sight of a river in full spate, overflowing its boundaries and bringing life to an otherwise arid terrain, is a picture of what the church is to be in the world: ordinary men and women, who through their unswerving obedience to their root, Christ, fill the earth with the knowledge and the glory of God. We will blossom and bud and fill the face of the world with fruit.

The Lord will pour water opon him who is thirsty and floods upon the dry ground, until the desert blossoms like a rose and the fruitful field becomes a forest. Whatever analogy is used, it all speaks of a time of unrestricted growth. As a kind of firstfruit of a final harvest, you can flourish in the Spirit and fulfill your true liberty to be like Jesus.

But now abide faith, hope, love, these three; but the greatest of these is love. 1 Cor.13:13

The Greatest Is Love

The fact that God is love reveals the origin of love. Before creation, before anything else, love existed in God Himself. It was this same love that predestined us to be conformed to the image of His Son. In love He chose us in Him before the foundation of the world and adopted us. He first loved us. Even while we were sinners and His enemies, He commended His love to us.

The infinite nature of God gives love its boundless dimensions. God told Israel that He loved them with an everlasting love and that His whole heart and soul were involved. The all-embracing sweep of God's love is capable of saving to the uttermost and encompassing the chief of sinners. Love is the way of life that excels and transcends all others. We must desire the gifts of the Spirit, but we must pursue love above all.

Love gives such value to other gifts that without it, however gifted, we are nothing. The qualities that are expressed in true love are listed for us so that we might compare our motives and responses. We should use this standard from time to time as a gauge to check out our lifestyle. If without love we are nothing, then it is of paramount importance that we practice love and grow in it. There is no substitute for love. Faith, knowledge and martyrdom count for nothing, if we have not love.

God has given us the ability to love as He loved. Whether under pressure of enemies who curse us and despitefully use us or of Christians who treat us wrongfully, we can express love until it permeates our whole being. Let us love.

Love never fails. 1 Cor.13:8

The Greatest Commandment

When asked which commandment is foremost of all, Jesus said, "you shall love the Lord your God with all your heart and with all your soul and with all your mind and with all your strength...you shall love your neighbor as yourself." This whole-hearted love must be perfected in us. Patient obedience to His word is the path to perfection. Keeping His word enables us to abide in His love, and love is thereby perfected in us.

The new commandment is that we love one another as Christ loved us. We lie if we say that we love God and hate our brother. Love covers a multitude of sins, and we should above all keep fervent love for each other in our hearts. Love is not blind, but it has the capacity to shut out from present consideration what would otherwise be a glaring hindrance to fellowship. Compassion and forgiveness are part of the generous and accommodating nature of love.

Love confronts as well as covers. Confrontation is the other side of the tension of love's true nature, for love faces issues and addresses them. Bearing grudges is often a result of cowardice that will not confront in love. Chastisement is a vehicle of love. Expect to be chastened because of God's love.

Love also conquers. He commended his love to us while we were yet sinners and conquered all that was separating us from Him. Now we can overwhelmingly conquer through Him who loves us. We love Him because He first loved us. His love motivates us to respond by demonstrating our love for Him.

For God has not given us a spirit of timidity, but of power and love and discipline. 2 Tim.1:7

The Spirit of Love

Love conforms, and God has designed that we be conformed to the image of His Son. Jesus told His disciples that just as the Father had loved Him He had loved them, and that they ought to love each other. He prayed that the love with which the Father loved Him may be in us. This love has been shed into our hearts by the Holy Spirit who was given to us. We have received the Spirit of love and now partake of the divine nature, which is love.

The love that is in our spirits by reason of our new birth and our union with the Lord is to motivate our souls and be expressed through our bodies. Love is not stagnant. It needs to be communicated, first to Him who loves us, then to each other and even to our enemies. Not only can we love, but we can love with God's love. The new commandment teaches us to love each other as He loved us. Everyone who loves is born of God and knows God. Love convicts, as Jesus explained in the parable of the two who were forgiven their debt. One owed much and loved much, while one owed little and loved little. When we understand the enormity of our iniquity, we can appreciate the immensity of God's great love in forgiving us of all our sins. If God so loved us, we ought also to love and forgive one another.

Love controls those who know what it is to be loved and owned of God. The goodness of God in loving us leads us to repentance. Make love your aim until, with the hateful Saul of Tarsus who was transformed by the one who loved him and gave Himself for him, you can say that the love of God controls you.

Peace I leave with you; My peace I give you. John 14:27

Have You Got Peace?

God is the God of peace. He is the true source of peace. He is not the author of confusion, but of peace. Adam lost his peace when he fell from the way of peace. Disobedience caused him to inherit *dispeace*. He chose discord rather than accord with God and was turned out of the way of peace. Fallen man is but a shell of the image of God in which he was first created. Man's peace is a poor shadow of the peace he once had with God.

There is a peace that the world knows in a corrupted and fragile form, but true peace, which is a fruit of the Spirit, only Jesus can give. The world cannot give peace like Jesus gives. The angels who heralded the birth of Jesus declared that there was to be peace on earth. The Prince of peace had come to re-store peace with God. Jesus is our peace. He said that our peace would be in Him. Through our redemption in Jesus we have been reconciled to God.

We now have harmony instead if enmity. Peace is restored. We cannot be peacemakers unless we have peace in our own hearts and minds. The outworking of our individual peace is the peace we have with each other. The infighting of Christians is a lie against the truth. We are to be at peace among ourselves.

There must be peace between Christians and God, between husbands and wives and between members of families before it can be communicated to the world at large. To be spiritually minded is life and peace, not the peace of a stagnant pool, but the living, vital peace that rules our hearts as we walk at peace with God. The world cannot give it, and the world cannot take it away.

And He came and preached peace to you who were far away, and peace to those who were near. Eph. 2:17

Peace: Cessation of War

Sin caused our separation from God and replaced peace with hostility. Ever since the fall, man has been at war with his Maker. The powers of darkness that man aligned himself with are not for him, but against him. Even creation itself became a hostile environment.

When men die, R.I.P.(rest in peace) is often inscribed on their tombstones because it is said that the troubles of life have come to an end. For many, troubles begin there in earnest because the wrath and judgment of God is unleashed upon them in eternal damnation. God in His great love, although rejected by man, had compassion on man's plight. He sent His only Son, Jesus, to purchase, at the colossal price of His own lifeblood, our peace. He came to preach peace to all men and to extend peace to us like a river, ever flowing, never to dry up. We were not even at peace within ourselves, for our consciences disallowed so much of our behavior. Our bodies suffered from intruding influences that robbed us of our peace. We were at war in our own members and at war with one another, not only race against race and nation against nation, but open hostility within families, proving we had lost our peace.

God has made peace for us through the blood of Jesus. When we receive Jesus, we receive peace, a penetrating peace that permeates our hearts, minds and consciences. We can breathe a great sigh of relief as we leave our old ways and reckon ourselves crucified with Jesus. Sins are forgiven. There is no condemnation, fear or dread because God has come and spoken peace to His people.

Strengthened with all power, according to His glorious might, for the attaining of all steadfastness and patience; joyously. Col.1:11

Patience

Patience and its close companions of long-suffering, forbearance and endurance are evidences of the Holy Spirit. God is the God of patience. We surely thank the Lord that He has exercised long-suffering patience towards us. His patient Spirit brings us to new birth and indwells us as our life. When the old man rears his ugly head we can overcome by expressing the patience of Christ, and by so doing we become changed into His likeness.

We live in an impatient environment, in an *instant* generation. "I want it now," "urgent," and the like are common expressions of impatience. Fast foods, quick relief, and get-rich-quick schemes are hallmarks of our generation. To be patient runs against the grain of the trends and demands placed upon us, but the Lord knows what patience works in and out of us.

Patience works perfection in us. Patience honors the sovereignty of God in our lives. Patience has an element of trust in God's timing that is content to leave the outworking to Him. It takes us out of our timetable into His and teaches us to wait. It enables us to receive the word of the Lord, "Not yet," without frustration. When we are in danger of folding under the pressures of various trials, we are encouraged to look unto Jesus and consider Him. Faith and patience are in Him. He endured and will strengthen us to endure to the end.

We have tried the Lord's patience for so long. The least we can do is be patient with each other, with all humility and gentleness, forbearing one another in love.

What is desirable in a man is his kindness. Prov.19:22

Kindness

Kindness is desirable in a man. God is wonderfully kind, and He has supremely revealed it in giving up His Son, the Lord Jesus, for us. Throughout the history of the world, He has openly displayed His loving kindness. Even in the face of rejection, rebellion and unfaithfulness, He has remained faithful in not removing His kindness from us. He promised that with everlasting kindness He will have mercy on us and that His kindness will not depart from us.

God's kindness, along with the rest of His image, was marred and even lost to man in the fall of Adam into sin. Ever since, we have been alienated from the life of God. Man's gentle, benevolent nature was corrupted to where its affections became indifferent to other's pain and distress.

Jesus came as a man and restored the spirit of kindness in flesh and blood. Men who profess Christ must recover kindness in all its gentle compassion. To be a kind man is not what the world portrays as manly. Yet the world longs for kindness: kind husbands, kind fathers and kind neighbors. Kindness is an expression of true manhood. It is a quality of greatness because it testifies to Christ, who made known to us the kindness of God.

Make known your kindness by being kind. Be kind to your wife. React differently than the old self-centered man. Absorb her weaknesses. Encourage her with an outgoing, giving heart. Comfort her and your children with the security you can build in them through your kindness. Freely you have received the kindness of God; freely give.

*And concerning you, my brethren, I myself am convinced that
you yourselves are full of goodness. Rom.15:14*

Goodness

With the modern overuse of many superlatives, things that
are good are looked upon as *merely* good in almost a derogatory
way. If it is not fantastic, incredible or marvelous, it is viewed as
inferior. Good has been reduced to being ordinary and commonplace, but it is more than that. God is good. Jesus said that there
is none good but God. Jesus went about doing good and exhorting His disciples to let their light so shine before men that men
would see their good works and glorify their heavenly Father.
Acts of self-denial for the sake of others and heroic or brave
behavior are good works. Paying the bills and giving generously,
considering the poor and disadvantaged and alleviating their distress are also good works.

Paul reminds us of what our Lord said when he states that
there is none who does good (Rom.3:10-18). Goodness is a
divine attribute, and it exists only through His grace. God wants
good men, men who are testimonies of Jesus. This fruit of the
Spirit is to be evidenced by being good at and in all we do.

Christian men should be good men, good husbands, good
fathers, good employers and good employees. Barnabas was an
encourager. He was full of the Holy Spirit and faith. The
description of him in Acts 11:24 starts with the observation that
He was a good man.

How will you be remembered? How are you considered
now? Goodness is one facet of Jesus that the Holy Spirit desires
to produce in us. Proverbs tells us that a good name is better than
a good ointment. You are to convey the aroma of goodness.

And as he was discussing righteousness, self-control and the judgment to come, Felix became frightened. Acts 24:25

Self-Control

When Adam sinned he lost control, not only of creation, which God had put under his rule to subdue, but of himself. He became driven by various lusts and impulses as Satan and sin took dominion over him and brought him into bondage.

Unexpected consequences became the bitter and terrifying experience of fallen man. The unknown sensation of fear ravaged his consciousness as the fear of death brought him into a lifetime of bondage. He was in the bondage of corruption from which there was no escape. We are born into that state naturally. Even when we know what we should do we find ourselves without the power to do it, leaving us doing the very things we know we should not do.

Jesus came to a world of men who were out of control. He did not come to bring control back to God, for God never lost it, but He came to bring control back to man. Jesus demonstrated what man had been created for, man in union with God with God-given control.

Christ's self-control defeated the world, the flesh and the devil. We too can know deliverance from all that has ruled us and can overwhelmingly conquer through Him. Man was created to rule himself as well as all the works of God's hand. Without Christ we are doomed to frustration, because we were built for dominion but are incapable of it. Receiving Jesus Christ as our deliverer and Lord reinstates us to where we can have self-control. Any habit or substance that controlled us is subject to the far superior power of Jesus. Christ in you enables you to regain control and reign with Him.

These things I have spoken to you, that My joy may be in you, and that your joy may be made full. John 15:11

His Joy, Our Joy

This basic ingredient of the nature of God was forfeited by Adam when he fell. Joy is an expression of the kingdom of God and is unknown in the kingdom of darkness. Joy is in the Holy Spirit, and when the Spirit makes us alive and indwells us, He brings the vivid emotional pleasure of the joy of the Lord. Man has sought many and varied means to fill up the void that cries out for joy. Sin replaced joy with despair. Guilt, condemnation, insecurity and dread filled the gaping void as death started to ravage the being that was created to live and enjoy God.

Angels appeared to the shepherds announcing the birth of Jesus Christ and the ensuing joy to all people. He was the Savior who came to redeem and liberate us and fill us with His joy. Knowing our Savior releases within us a rejoicing of unspeakable joy. He fills our mouths with laughter and our tongues with shouts of joy. No wonder we want to shout for joy, leap for joy, sing for joy and dance for joy—we have been restored to His presence. In His presence is fulness of joy. We can measure our awareness of His presence by our joy.

It is His will that our joy might be full. That same joy of the Lord is our strength. Sin robs us of our joy and compounds our lack of strength. Many Christians live without joy because they walk in defeat and guilt. If we confess and forsake our sin we can cry with David, "Restore to me the joy of Thy salvation." If we fight a good fight, finish the course and keep the faith, then we will be welcomed into eternal bliss with the commendation "Well done good and faithful slave...enter into the joy of your Lord."

Who also made us adequate as servants of a new covenant, not of the letter, but of the Spirit. 2 Cor. 3:6

The New Covenant

As glorious as the old covenant was, we are told that it has no glory compared with the glory of the new covenant. One might as well compare the blood of animals with the blood of the Son of God. The old covenant could not make anyone perfect, but the new covenant—which is based on better sacrifices, better promises and a more excellent ministry—perfects forever those who are sanctified. Under the old, the ceremonial washings cleansed the outward flesh; whereas, the new provides a cleansing of the conscience and heart.

Enlightened men under the old covenant had a continual consciousness of sin because they had no power within to free them and give them dominion over sin. How many Christians live like Old Testament Jews, never experientially knowing the power of the resurrected Christ in them? The cross, burial and resurrection of Christ are the vehicles that convey us from Mount Sinai to Mount Zion. There, we can dwell in acceptance rather than condemnation.

True repentance and faith in all that Jesus has accomplished for us enable us to become partakers of the new covenant in the blood of Christ. The new covenant takes us out of the flesh and into the Spirit. It brings us into a living and vital union with God, where we are joined inseparably as one spirit.

Newness is the theme: a new heart, a new spirit, a new name and nature, a new creature. In fact all things become new and are of God. The revelation and experience of the new covenant brings us into the unlimited boundaries of the discovery and enjoyment of God.

Who shall separate us from the love of Christ? Rom. 8:35

Nothing Can Separate Us

Shall tribulation or distress separate us from God's love? Jesus told us that in the world we would have tribulation. Paul strengthened the souls of the disciples and encouraged them to continue in the faith, telling them that through much tribulation we must enter the kingdom of God. Tribulation is defined as pressure, affliction, severe suffering and trial. Paul actually gloried in tribulation, knowing what it worked in him. Patience, perseverance and proven character all stem from tribulation, if we approach it as something that works in our favor.

James tells us to count it all joy when we encounter various trials. Paul remarks that he was exceedingly joyful in all tribulation. Such teachings prove that there is a place of maturity to reach where tribulation is experienced as an instrument of blessing. However distressing our circumstances, God is able to sanctify them to us. George Keith's old hymn captures the sovereignty of God in our lives:

> *When through the deep water I cause thee to*
> *go, The rivers of grief shall not thee overflow,*
> *For I will be with thee in trouble to bless,*
> *And sanctify to thee thy deepest distress.*

Jesus Himself learned obedience from the things that He suffered and was made perfect by them. His relationship with the Father was the key to take Him through His tribulation as the great conqueror. If we truly love the Lord, that love will surmount and survive all opposition, and we will more than conquer through Him who loves us.

And He gave some as apostles, and some as prophets, and some as evangelists, and some as pastors and teachers. Eph. 4:11

The Work of the Ministry

When Jesus ascended He gave gifts to men who would in turn equip the saints for the work of the ministry. He gave measures of Himself and His own ministry. "To each one of us grace was given according to the measure of Christ's gift." Jesus identified the nature of His ministry when He read from Isaiah, "The Spirit of the Lord is upon Me, because He has anointed Me to proclaim release to the captives, the recovery of sight to the blind, to set free those that are downtrodden, to proclaim the favorable year of the Lord."

The work of the ministry for all born-again Christians must in some measure include this ministry of Christ. Our effectiveness depends upon our living according to Christ's ministry in us. We cannot offer ourselves in redemption as a sacrifice for sin, but through the anointing of the Holy Spirit we have the ability to minister our particular measure of Christ. To some degree we must be bringing good news to the poor, binding up the brokenhearted and proclaiming liberty to the captives.

Having received this ministry we must not faint or lose heart in functioning in it. We have this treasure of Jesus in our earthen vessel, not to be hidden there, but to be manifested in our mortal bodies to the world around us. All the conditions of poverty that hold man in bondage, naturally and spiritually, can be addressed by the treasure within us. We become equipped for our particular facet of Christ's ministry through the influence of apostles, prophets, evangelists, pastors and teachers. God has not changed his mind about how He equips us.

For there must also be factions among you, in order that those who are approved may have become evident among you.
1 Cor.11:19

The Necessity of Some Divisions

The word *heresy*, which is also translated *faction*, means choice and opinion. A heretic is a self-opinionated person, that is, someone who against the broad consensus of community life both in leadership and congregation causes division with his own personal opinion. We must be on the lookout for those who cause such divisions, while making sure that we ourselves maintain a right attitude, judging ourselves to make sure we are not the guilty party.

On our way to the unity of the faith, there will of necessity be divisions—necessary, not only because of the carnality and ignorance of believers, but also to serve the purpose of manifesting the "approved." God approves of those whose responses represent Him throughout contentions. Time is on the side of truth.

The secrets of all hearts will be manifested, but until then a poor response from us, to what appears to be a bad attitude in others, could highlight something that needs attention in ourselves. If our prayer is to be like our Lord's, then we will be given enemies to love, cursers to bless and those who despitefully use us to pray for. To be conformed to Christ necessitates being led by the Spirit the way Christ was led. Suffering and accusations were the lot of our Lord who is our example to follow.

As unavoidable as offenses are, we are responsible for the offenses we cause. In the process of our refining, there will be divisions, but in them remember that God looks at the heart, seeking for those He can approve.

And this is eternal life, that they may know Thee, the only true God, and Jesus Christ whom Thou hast sent. John 17:3

Knowing God

Jesus said that eternal life was to know the only true God and the one He sent. Our priority, at all costs, should be to know Him. Nothing is more important than knowing God and being known of Him. Paul counted everything but loss for the excellency of the knowledge of Christ Jesus. He then revealed his insatiable thirst for Jesus with the declaration, "That I may know Him" (Phil.3:10). One of the final goals of God for the church is that we might come to the knowledge of the Son of God, unto a perfect man, to the measure of the stature that belongs to the fulness of Christ (Eph.4:13).

There are those who profess to know Him, but by their works deny Him. Jesus confronted the religious leaders with the indictment that they said that God was their God, yet they had not known Him. Those who truly know Him long for more of Him and display by their actions their love for Him.

We can love someone we have never seen, but we cannot love someone we have never known. Peter says that though we have not seen Him, we love Him. God has made Himself known through creation, through angels, through prophets, in our own consciences by His Spirit and supremely through His Son, the Lord Jesus. He longs for us to know Him.

Jesus came and introduced us to God as Father, then sent the Holy Spirit to continue to make known to us the things of God. Knowing Him, loving Him and obeying Him open us up to a continuous revelation of Him. Knowing Him will affect the way we live. "Those who know their God will display strength and take action" (Dan. 11:22).

Because that which is known about God is evident within them; for God made it evident to them. Rom.1:19

God Makes Himself Known

Since the beginning of creation, God has communicated Himself through the visible universe. His invisible attributes, even His eternal power and Godhead, have been clearly seen and understood through what He has made. That is why Paul writes to the Romans that man is without excuse in his ignorance of God. Man has chosen to ignore the evidence externally in creation, and internally, even though God has made it evident. "For even though they knew God, they did not honor Him as God, or give thanks" (Rom.1:21).

The challenge for Christians is great because we have had a revelation of God in His Son and in our hearts by the Holy Spirit. We who have come to know Him in such an intimate way ought to be grateful and glorify Him. One of the signs of the last days is that men will be ungrateful and unthankful. Knowing God and glorifying Him should be the motivation behind our lifestyle. It should be all embracing, all consuming. To be able to know Him and enjoy Him is the supreme privilege.

Our growth as His children is dependent upon the increase of our knowledge of Him and our willingness to glorify Him. How can we glorify God? Jesus said that if we bear much fruit His Father will be glorified. To be fruitful is to be joined to our new root, Christ, and to let His life become evident in our mortal bodies. Under the old covenant He took His people by the hand; under the new covenant He unites us to Himself. "But the one who joins himself to the Lord is one spirit with Him" (1 Cor.6:17). He purchased our unity at a great price. Let Him be satisfied to see in you that for which He travailed.

But no one can tame the tongue; it is a restless evil and full of deadly poison. James 3:8

The Power of the Tongue

The ability to communicate with words is a wonder of God's creativity. What and how we communicate is an awesome responsibility. The tongue is a weapon of construction or destruction, consolation or condemnation, building or blasting. Jesus said that by our words we would be justified or by our words we would be condemned. This is so because out of the abundance of the heart the mouth speaks. We may say that we did not mean to say something, but it is too late. The fact that it came out of our mouth betrays that it was in the heart.

We will have to give an account for every idle word. Jesus was able to say that the words He spoke were spirit and life, because in Him was life. He spoke only those things He received from the Father. James gives serious cautions about the tongue, cautions that should make us slow to speak and quick to listen. The innate power of the tongue should put us constantly on our guard against its unruly tendencies. We can verbally destroy someone by communicating the venom of hatred and malice. Jealousy and envy produce gossip that in turn creates rumors that cause hurt and division devised by Satan himself.

Where do all the false stories and accusations about Christians come from? Often Christians devour one another and become instruments of Satan to destroy the body. Our speech is to be seasoned with salt, ministering grace to the hearers. Love in the heart is the key. We can speak the truth in love because love edifies. Represent Christ with your words, and bless the hearers.

For we all stumble in many ways. If anyone does not stumble in what he says, he is a perfect man, able to bridle the whole body as well. James 3:2

Taming the Tongue

It has been said that the pen is mightier than the sword. However, the tongue is more powerful than both of them. The pen is only an instrument to convey what is being said. Jesus knew what to speak and how to say it. The inflection of His voice interpreted exactly what and how the Father was speaking. The fact that His tongue never ran out of control proved Him to be a perfect man. It also proved Him to have a perfect heart, because out of the abundance of the heart the mouth speaks. He actually cleansed others by the words He spoke.

James tells us that the tongue is a fire, the very world of iniquity. It defiles the whole body, sets on fire the course of our life and is set on fire by hell. It is a restless evil and full of deadly poison (James 3:6,8). We should be aware of its potential and speak accordingly. "Let no unwholesome word proceed from your mouth, but only such a word as is good for edification" (Eph.4:29). This and many similar exhortations direct our attention to the importance of how and what we speak.

Remember, it is what comes out of the mouth that defiles. Some speak because they have to say something; others speak when they have something to say. Things that are rare are valued; things that are plentiful and common are often cheap. Let your words be choice, thought over and selected, direct and to the point, in truth and love. Speak peace where you can. Do not be found guilty of separating the saints. In the multitude of words there is bound to be error. When you speak, speak the oracles of God.

And the glory that Thou hast given Me I have given to them; that they may be one, just as We are one. John 17:22

Pray for Unity

From early in its history, the church has been ravaged by division. Although initially, through the baptism of the Holy Spirit, they were of one heart and soul, schism and separation soon occurred. Prejudice, (judgement) or judging the present through previous convictions was one of the causes. It is always harder to relearn something than to learn for the first time. It was hard for many Jews to stop being legalistic about the law, even though Christ had set them free from the law. The same spirit of prejudice rules many Christians, who cannot enter into what the Spirit is doing today because of previous convictions.

Elevating the messenger beyond the message was another cause of schism. The message was Christ, but as Paul, Peter and Apollos preached Christ, Christians attached themselves to the messengers, identifying themselves as of Paul, or of Peter, or of Apollos. Teachings were emphasized and became central, displacing Christ. Competitive attitudes led to factions that justified themselves at the expense of others. They indulged in gossip with its accompanying exaggeration. Biting, devouring, condemning and despising one another became common. The apostles focused on these maladies, which were the subject of many of their writings.

The challenge for us today is whether we will prolong the sad and destructive course of division or promote its antidote. Let us not use the past as a hindrance to the future, neither give place to the devil, but reinstate Christ as our aim and receive one another as in Christ, with the same love of God.

So the church...enjoyed peace, being built up; and, going on in the fear of the Lord and in the comfort of the Holy Spirit, it continued to increase. Acts 9:31

The Fear of God

Fear is a neglected aspect in contemporary preaching on the new covenant and is often completely missing. The word for fear is erroneously translated as *reverence*, because it means to shake or tremble. The fear of God under the new covenant is not to be confused with the fear of God that Israel had. They feared because of their consciousness of sin, while we fear the prospect of the consequences of sin.

Did Jesus fear God? Isaiah prophesied that the spirit of the fear of the Lord would be upon Him and that He would delight in the fear of the Lord (Isa.11:1-3). If Jesus delighted in the fear of the Lord then so should we. Jeremiah records three reasons why God promised to put His fear in our new hearts: to do us good, to do our children good and to keep us from departing from Him.

Love casts out the old fear of guilt and accountability for our sins. We have not received that spirit again, but God gives His fear as the beginning of wisdom. If we fail to obey out of love, then when contemplating sin, at least the fear of God should make us depart from evil. The fear of God is a safeguard that will keep us from sinning. We are commanded to work out our salvation with fear and trembling.

The early church feared the Lord, sometimes greatly. They went on in the fear of the Lord and in the comfort of the Holy Spirit. Jesus taught us to fear God, and Paul and Peter reiterate the directive. If you have lost the fear of the Lord, then pray that God will resensitize your conscience, and read Prov.1:24-2:5.

Now He who establishes us with you in Christ and anointed us is God. 2 Cor.1:21

The Nature of Our Anointing

Jesus declared openly that He was anointed when He read from Isaiah, "The Spirit of the Lord is upon Me, because He has anointed Me." He knew what He was anointed to do, listing the things Isaiah 61:1-3 records. He knew who He was, who sent Him, what He was to do and where He was going. His strength shone through His confidence, and He was not intimidated. He was always in control. He could have called legions of angels to deliver Him from the cross, but He knew He was anointed to die and endured it for the joy that was before Him.

It is a tragic fact that thousands of Christians live and die having never known their spiritual identity. Our identity and function is determined by our anointing. In order to give ourselves to our ministry we must know what it is. Ignorance of identity causes Christians to be passengers rather than participants. God has provided for the proper working of each individual part, but very few know their function, and they therefore lack confidence. The work is not attempted because the laborers are unidentified.

Fulfillment is dependent upon being what you have been created to be. How many Christians, including ministers, struggle with frustration because they are employed in doing things for which they were never anointed?

The analogy of the body is used to demonstrate how we relate to each other as members one of another. What the Holy Spirit has made you He will witness within you in the context of the body. Your identity as a particular member of Christ's body will also be confirmed by other members affected by your function.

The Spirit of the Lord God is upon Me, because He anointed Me to preach the gospel to the poor. Luke 4:18

Anointed of God

Jesus was the Christ, which means the anointed. The two anointed offices are king and priest: Jesus fulfilled both offices and is the King of kings and the Great High Priest. We, as His brethren, a kingdom of priests, have received of His fulness and anointing. Those who receive the baptism of the Holy Spirit have been anointed of God, as Jesus was anointed when the Holy Spirit descended upon Him. Each one of us is given a measure of faith, a measure of grace according to our gift, when we become partakers of His anointing. The anointing we have received abides in us and tells us that we abide in Him.

Do you know whether you have been anointed? Our function as individuals is a manifestation of Christ, because He is our life. The Holy Spirit sovereignly and individually gives each one of us both gift and grace as He wills. Our function is the expression of the Spirit which has been shed abroad in our hearts by our anointing.

We rob God and each other when we fail to function in our anointing. Out of our innermost being the river of living water is to flow. Jesus spoke of the Spirit which had not yet been given, but was to be poured out. Unstop the well and remove any cause of stagnation. Let the impact of your anointing be felt in the heavens to tear down principalities and powers, and in the earth to do the works that He did and greater works.

If you lack the assurance of your anointing, then ask of Him who is the baptizer and receive from Him who promised to give the Holy Spirit to those who ask.

And since we have gifts that differ according to the grace given to us, let each exercise them accordingly. Rom.12:6

Christ's Gifted Body

The subject of spiritual gifts incorporates our calling and our identity. It is not limited to a fanatic fringe or a pentecostal minority. It deals with the ascended Christ and what He distributed to men and what the Holy Spirit designates according to His will. The gifts are aspects of Jesus in which we as members function. We do not all have the same gifts, either in placement or in measure.

What we have been given to be is for the common good. That is why we should be together as often as possible. We rob the body when we keep from the body what we have been given to be to the body. We must also recognize the spiritual nature of the body, that we never stop ministering to the body at any given moment. The nature of the life that we feed into the body is our responsibility, whether it is poison or health. No Christian is spiritually apart from the body, and everyone has a gift.

Being members one of another takes us beyond friendship and even kinship: we are one spirit and body, one heart and soul. However feeble we may feel, God has so ordered the body that the more feeble the member, the more necessary. If our physical body were only fifty-percent functioning, what a horrid spectacle we would present: dragging one leg, having a withered arm, blind in one eye, half deaf, with serious internal problems. How do you think the body of believers appears?

Are you functioning properly in your gift to the body? The body of Christ on the earth is to function until He appears, not until the Bible appeared. The Bible teaches us that each member of Christ is gifted.

But to each one of us grace was given according to the measure of Christ's gift. Eph. 4:7

Grace Is Given to Each One

The corporate maturity of the church is the collective maturity of individuals. The proper working of each individual part is the goal towards which the Lord is bringing the church. It was Paul's goal to produce love from a pure heart, a good conscience and a sincere faith in those he instructed. He proclaimed Jesus, admonishing and teaching every man so that he might present every man complete in Christ.

The Lord gives apostles, prophets, evangelists, pastors and teachers to equip the saints to become workers in the ministry. Proclaiming, teaching, admonishing, instructing, reproving and rebuking are all necessary to produce a chaste virgin for Christ.

The body builds itself up in love when the individual members, by love, serve one another. Every member of Christ's body receives a measure of Christ in his particular gift, as well as the corresponding grace to function in that gifting. No one is excused from working properly. Then comes the warning that we be no longer children, but grow up. Being childlike is not to be confused with being childish. Such infantile behavior plagues the church. Such selfishness is the antithesis of serving.

Christians in the early church were upbraided for being babes and carnal. They had the best teachers, the apostles themselves. Probably the trio of Paul, Peter and Apollos as teachers could not be surpassed, but the Corinthian church had not grown up. Immaturity is the plague of the church. Those who neglect or deny their gifts or the need for them deny the Baptizer and Giver.

Devote yourselves to prayer, keeping alert in it with an attitude of thanksgiving. Col.4:2

Be Devoted to Prayer

To be devoted is to be zealously loyal. It has the overtones of enthusiastic addiction. Jesus was often found in prayer, sometimes praying all night. He taught His disciples how to pray, asserting the supreme importance of prayer. He said that men ought always to pray and not faint, denoting the constant attitude of fellowship we should sustain with the Lord.

He also said that when we pray we should enter into our private room, shut the door and pray to our Father in secret, thereby stressing the necessity of times of intimacy when everyone else and everything else is shut out.

The early church continually devoted themselves to prayer, and Paul exhorts the Colossians to that same devotion. Disciplining ourselves to give time to prayer is not optional. Prayer has its own rewards. Experiencing God's presence, having heaven opened, and hearing His voice are incentives that make the effort worthwhile. These intimate encounters with the Lord are proof enough of the priority of time we should give to this essential spiritual exercise.

The distractions are endless, from weariness and entertainment to the pressing demands of things that must be done. Satan throws every possible hindrance in our path to prevent us from praying. If we total the amount of time spent in "private room" prayer, we will know whether we have fallen to his wiles and schemes.

Start the day with prayer. Lead your wife and children in prayer. God's house is called a house of prayer. Make prayer a vital aspect of your house, and enjoy the marvelous results of such devotion.

But you, when you pray, go into your inner room, and when you have shut your door, pray to your Father who is in secret. Matt.6:6

When You Pray

Our Lord Jesus is the supreme example in the subject of prayer. His concentrated times of prayer sometimes took Him through the night, even to where He agonized, as in the garden of Gethsemane. He maintained an attitude of constant prayer, speaking only those things He heard from the Father and doing only the works He saw the Father doing.

His instructions to us include both negative and positive approaches. He teaches us how not to pray, citing the Pharisees, and then how to pray, in secret. His model for prayer instructs us about the priorities of worship, His kingdom and His will, as well as the necessities of provision, forgiveness and protection. He emphasizes the importance of importunity, of persevering until the answer comes. Fainting and growing weary cause the abandoning of and the neglecting of prayer, but we are to keep on the alert in prayer.

Prayer has many different forms: supplication, requests, petitions, intercessions, crying, warring and giving thanks. Jesus bids us to pray without ceasing, while He ever lives to make intercession for us. Even when we do not know how to pray as we ought, the Holy Spirit makes intercession for us according to the will of God. God has chosen to use our prayers in the outworking of His purposes. Through prayer we can be directly involved in the overthrow of the kingdom of darkness and the establishing of Christ's kingdom. My old Baptist minister, Theo M.Bamber, once said that no man was greater than his prayer life. Pray greatly, and great will be your reward.

Do you not understand that whatever goes into the man from outside cannot defile him. Mark 7:18

What Defiles a Man?

Jesus explained to His disciples that what goes in from the outside goes into the stomach and not into the heart. He therefore declared all foods clean. It is what proceeds from the heart, *out* of the mouth, that defiles a man. How we address our responsibility to another's conscience is a different issue, but the New Testament nevertheless declares all food to be clean.

Paul writes to the Romans that all things indeed are clean and states that he is convinced in the Lord Jesus that nothing is unclean of itself. When writing to the Colossians he challenges them that if they have died with Christ, why then do they submit to decrees such as do not handle, do not taste and do not touch. Although these matters have an appearance of wisdom in self-made religion, they are of no value against fleshly indulgence.

The new covenant introduces us to life in the Spirit, life from the new heart of the new creature. The kingdom of heaven is not a matter of material meat and drink. John was accused of having a demon because he abstained, while Jesus was called a glutton and a drunkard because He ate and drank.

The church has been made subject to legalistic demands that have nothing to do with the faith of Christ or faith in Christ. Whether it be the issues of circumcision, observance of days, eating and drinking, or any other outward imposition of temporal regulations, all are destined to perish with the using (Col.2:22) and are not requirements of the new covenant. What is necessary is the revelation of Jesus Christ in a man through living in the Spirit.

For you have been born again not of seed which is perishable but imperishable, that is, through the living and abiding word of God. 1 Pet.1:23

Born of Incorruptible Seed

In the splendor and wonder of creation God inaugurated a principle: vegetation and fruit trees bearing fruit after their kind with seed in them. All the different species of life reproduce after their kind. We were born naturally of corruptible seed, the fallen nature of our parents having been reproduced in us. Jesus clearly taught the need to be born again from above by the Holy Spirit.

Jesus is the true seed of God, the Word that was made flesh and dwelt among us. Peter reminds us that we have been born again of that same incorruptible seed by the word of God—not many seeds, but one seed, Jesus Christ the seed of God. Through the one Son, God has brought many sons to glory, all born of the same Father, of the same seed. That is why Jesus is not ashamed to call us brethren. He said that He was ascending to His Father and our Father.

Incorruptible means not able to be corrupted. If born-again Christians would only believe what is true of them, they would awake to righteousness and sin not. We lie against the truth when we live as those dominated by sin. We even ask, "How is it possible not to sin?"; whereas Paul asks, "How can we who are dead to sin live any longer therein?"

Being born of God, of His seed, gives us the ability to be holy as He is holy, pure as He is pure and righteous as He is righteous, enabling us to live as He lived. In John's first letter he makes it clear that we are NOW the sons of God, and therefore, as He is, so are we in THIS WORLD. We do not yet have our new bodies, but we do have our new natures that can bear fruit unto God.

Unless one is born again, he cannot see the kingdom of God. John 3:3

Born Again of the Spirit

There are two principles involved in birth. The first is that species reproduce their own kind according to the nature of the seed. Figs cannot be gathered from thistles, and cats will have kittens not pups. All mankind is descended from Adam and Eve and possesses their fallen nature. The second principle is that first comes the natural and then the spiritual. We are first born natural and corruptible, but when we are born again, we are born from above, born of God.

Jesus was born of the Holy Spirit as the Son of His Father. When we are born of the same Spirit we become partakers of Christ, partakers of the divine nature. We share His life. He is our life. We are joined to the Lord and are one spirit with Him. Our old man has been put to death in the death of Christ. We become a new creation.

As new creatures we can walk in newness of life and call God our Father, because He is. The child of God is not accounted as being in the flesh, but in the spirit, if the Spirit of God dwells within. The eternal nature of the life received from God cannot be corrupted and therefore will not perish.

We can live in truth and walk according to the Spirit, or we can live a lie and walk according to the flesh. Life lived in the flesh, that is, continuing to be what we were before we were born of God, is lost. It is wood, hay and stubble and will tried by fire, causing us the loss of all the time so spent. Life lived in the Spirit will express Jesus, please our Father and receive the reward of eternal inheritance.

Blessed are the poor in spirit, for theirs is the kingdom of heaven.
Matt. 5:3

Kingdom Living #1

It has been said that Christians are producing an alternative society, when in fact they are portraying the original society, the kingdom of God. The kingdom of darkness became the alternative to the kingdom of light, which has never ceased. When Jesus went to the cross He declared that now was the judgment of this world, and that now the prince of this world was cast out. On the cross He threw off principalities and powers, making a public display of their defeat and rendering the devil powerless.

Christians should be demonstrating that same overcoming life by executing the judgment written there. The teachings of Jesus contrast the natures of the two kingdoms. Our new birth gives us an entrance to His Kingdom as well as the nature of that kingdom.

Jesus laid the foundation for true happiness and for the acquiring of the kingdom of heaven when He said that the poor in spirit are blessed (happy), for theirs is the kingdom of heaven. This first step is integral for the ability to live kingdom life. How else could we turn the other cheek, or walk the second mile. We need to recognize our poverty of spirit and mourn it, be meek about it and hunger and thirst after righteousness. If we require God's mercy, then we are to display mercy towards others. The new, pure heart that we receive enables us to be peacemakers and to live righteously, for which we will be reviled and persecuted. But Jesus bids us to rejoice and to be exceedingly glad, for our reward in heaven is great.

Live on earth as a citizen of heaven, and you will have treasure in heaven.

You are the salt of the earth....You are the light of the world.
Matt.5:13,14

Kingdom Living #2

This passage illustrates how the two kingdoms relate. The kingdom of darkness is hostile to the kingdom of God, but it is not eternal. It displays its aggravation by persecuting, reviling and falsely accusing, but it cannot ultimately prevail because in Jesus it has already been defeated and its time has been determined.

Jesus uses two metaphors to depict the superior power of the original kingdom: salt and light. Salt is used to season what is insipid and also to preserve by restraining corruption. The warning that if the salt loses its saltiness it is good for nothing and will be thrown out and trodden under the foot of men is a terrible commentary on a Christianity that is ineffective, uninvolved and sedentary.

The second affirmation, that Christians are the light of the world, identifies them as being one with the Light of the world. Corporately, we are a city set on a hill, or individually, candles in an otherwise dark room. Light is so much more powerful than darkness. Introduce a light into a darkened area and there is no contest. The light prevails. The reverse is impossible. Darkness cannot prevail against light. The greater one who is in us makes us greater than the world and than he who is in the world.

Through Christ in you, you have the abiding power to overcome the world, the flesh and the devil. When steadfast in the faith, you can resist the devil, and he will actually flee from you. Let your light so shine before men that they may see who your Father truly is and glorify Him.

But I say unto you that everyone who looks on a woman to lust for her has committed adultery with her already in his heart. Matt.5:28

Kingdom Living #3

Jesus exposed the difference between external form and internal reform. He looked into the heart knowing that as a man thinks in his heart so is he. The Pharisees interpreted the law with carnal minds. If they did not physically kill someone, then as far as they were concerned, they had kept the commandment. If they did not tangibly lie with a woman, then in their estimation, they were not guilty of adultery.

Jesus got to the root of the problem by instructing us that anger is the cause of murder just as lust is the cause of adultery. These conditions of the heart formulate the thoughts that express themselves in physical actions. External acts are merely symptoms of the deeper offense. Jesus focuses on the heart and the necessity of internal transformation, proving the impotence of outward religion to prevent fleshly indulgence.

What we esteem as precious concerning our outward man, who is perishing, is not to be compared with the inner man and the eternal consequences of the heart. New birth gives us a new heart and a new spirit; therefore, we are not to talk and act as though the heart we have is deceitful and desperately wicked. What you were is not what you are.

Your relationship with God and your fellow men issues from a different heart. You now represent your heavenly Father to the world around you and manifest that you are citizens of His kingdom. As a child of the kingdom your values are different, as are to be your reactions. The love of God out of a pure heart is to be the controlling factor governing your life.

Beware of practicing your righteousness before men to be noticed by them. Matt. 6:1

Kingdom Living #4

A hypocrite is one who hides his true self behind what he appears to be. The hypocrites gave, prayed and fasted in order to appear good before men and to be applauded by men. The Lord Jesus taught that we should not be like them. We are not to perform our righteousness before men with the motive of being seen, but we must be men of the secret place who do things to please our heavenly Father.

Doing things in secret because of the fear of men is a snare. We are not to be ashamed of the testimony of Jesus. Our motivation is a devotion to God that is concerned with neither the praise nor the persecution of men. Jesus gave, prayed and fasted. He was constant in these disciplines both openly and in His concentrated times in secret. There must be good reason to emphasize these three exercises. These could be the three hardest things to do, yet the most rewarding—the most neglected, but the most necessary.

Giving is a way of representing the giving heart of God. Praying has to do with our fellowship with the Lord, both hearing and speaking. Fasting concerns us with God's intensity of burden and self-control. All these basic expressions of a sanctified life are to be practiced in secret.

If the things you do in secret would shame you if revealed, then it betrays your lack of the consciousness of both heaven and the presence of the Lord. The Lord sees in secret, and the day will come when He will make manifest the hidden things. Let the secret place be where you and your Lord commune and the reason for His rewarding you openly.

You cannot serve God and mammon. Matt. 6:24

Kingdom Living #5

This passage continues to contrast the kingdom of darkness and the kingdom of light, focusing on allowing either mammon or God as master. We CANNOT serve God and mammon. This is an absolute with no middle ground. A divided heart does not serve God. The Lord requires wholeheartedness and will not share our loyalty. This demand challenges us to rely upon Him alone and not upon riches.

He created the body and is to be trusted to clothe and feed it. Four times Jesus tells us not to be anxious, because our loving heavenly Father knows the things we need. Riches are deceptive and uncertain. God is faithful and trustworthy. Instead of having the same concerns as the world around us, we should rest in the assurance of having all our needs met, according to His infinite resources in Jesus.

As the world seeks after material substance we should direct our hearts to seek the kingdom of God. When we do that, all the necessary things will be added to us. "Seek first" is the directive, not that there is a second and third, but only God first. God's will is paramount—His will regarding our wives and families, His will concerning the church, His will wherever our attention is focused. Jesus came to do the will of Him who sent Him, and that is how we should live.

We have grace for today, but if we worry about tomorrow then we have no grace for our anxiety because tomorrow's grace is given tomorrow. Do not anticipate tomorrow's problems in fear, for whatever tomorrow brings is under the sovereign hand of Him who sits upon the throne of grace.

The zeal of the Lord of hosts will accomplish this. Isa.9:7

Have You Got Zeal for His House?

God is a God of zeal. His zeal will perform His purpose to increase the government and kingdom of Christ without end. Jesus had such a zeal for the house of the Lord that he made a whip and drove out of His Father's house all that was foreign to it.

Zeal is defined as energy, spirit, zest, intensity, fierceness, vehemence, readiness, urgency and sincerity. The companion word *fervent* means devout, wholehearted, responsible, eager and enthusiastic. The negative is to be apathetic, indifferent, detached, lukewarm, unconcerned, halfhearted, negligent and careless. These definitions are enlightening and challenging, because if we profess to be born again, then we are admitting to being born of the Spirit of zeal and fervor.

Paul wrote that God had purified unto Himself a people zealous for good works. Jesus told a lukewarm church to be hot and zealous, and repent. Peter tells us to love one another fervently, while Paul exhorts us to be fervent in spirit, serving the Lord.

The zeal of the Lord has not abated. He will clean house with the same zeal that he whipped out the thieves and robbers. To avoid many stripes do not neglect so great a salvation. The ineffective, unconcerned church is not what the Spirit of the Lord produces. Outstanding individuals are often recognized as being on fire for the Lord, but the whole church will be built to where her righteousness will shine forth as brightness and her salvation as a lamp that burns. Say with Jehu, "Come see my zeal for the Lord." Let the zeal for His house consume you.

How much more will the blood of Christ...cleanse your conscience from dead works to serve the living God? Heb.9:14

A Cleansed Conscience

One of the contrasts between the old and new covenants is what happens to the conscience. The gifts and sacrifices under the old covenant could not make the worshipers perfect in their consciences. The cleansing was outward, a ceremonial cleansing of the flesh, but never dealt with the internal consciousness of sin. Regeneration was ushered in by the death, burial and resurrection of Jesus. New birth made the difference in our consciences.

The ability to crucify the old man with Christ, to be buried with Him and to be raised in newness of life was the new way repentant believers were to experience a clean conscience. The liberty that born-again believers have includes not only the freedom from sin, but also a release from the consciousness of sin.

The new covenant provides a man with a new heart, a renewed mind and the new experience of a good conscience. If the blood of bulls and goats sanctified for the cleansing of the flesh, then how much more shall the blood of Christ cleanse our conscience from dead works and fit us for fellowship with God. We are washed by the water of the word, the washing of regeneration and the blood of the everlasting covenant. Even so, our new sensitivity to the will of God can be seared by disobedience.

Suppressing your conscience does not bring the true liberty that obedience does. Deception occurs when you override your conscience. To enjoy freedom of conscience, you must maintain a clear conscience. Expressing your new man will give you a conscience void of offense.

You are My war-club, My weapon of war, and with you I shatter nations, and with you I destroy kingdoms. Jer.51:20

The Kingdom: God's Battle Axe

Jesus began His ministry referring to the Kingdom. He called His gospel the gospel of the kingdom. It was the central theme of His teaching and parables. He ended His time on earth, after His resurrection, in speaking with His disciples of those things concerning the kingdom. The book of Acts starts with the theme and finishes with Paul in his own hired house preaching the kingdom of God. Understanding the prominence of the kingdom challenges the lack of it in our speaking to the unconverted and to other Christians.

The interpretation of Nebuchadnezzar's dream was that the stone, which crushed the image and grew into a mountain that filled the earth, was a kingdom. That kingdom would never be destroyed, but it would crush and put an end to all other kingdoms. Jeremiah describes how God will take up His people as a weapon of war with which to destroy nations and kingdoms, leaving no stratum of society unaffected.

Unlike Joshua and David, we are not to use carnal weapons, but rather the divinely powerful weapons of spiritual warfare. The kingdom of God is not merely the only thing left standing after the shaking of God, but it is the very instrument in the hand of God to do the shaking. "With you I will destroy," says the Lord.

Ultimately, we will destroy the God-rejecting philosophies and practices of the world by demonstrating His kingdom in our lives. As their world falls apart, they will come to the brightness of our rising and turn to the God of a people who are blessed, the joy of the earth and the light of the world.

For the Love of money is a root of all sorts of evil, and some by longing for it have wandered away from the faith, and pierced themselves with many a pang. 1 Tim 6:10

Do You Long for Money?

The subject of money is important because it has to do with heart and root, the former because where your treasure is there will your heart be also, and the latter, because the love of money is a root of all evil. Jesus said in the hearing of the Pharisees that no one could serve God and mammon. They scoffed at Him because they were lovers of money. Money is not the root of all evil, but the love of it is.

Our Lord warned us to be on our guard against every form of greed, because the life of a man does not consist in the abundance of possessions. At what cost did Jesus empty Himself? "That though He was rich, yet for your sake He became poor, that you through His poverty might become rich" (2 Cor.8:9). He did not grasp at His equality with the Father, but willingly divested Himself and took upon Him the form of a servant.

Is there left in us any vestige of trust and security in money? Our way of life is to be absolutely free from the love of money, for riches are deceitful. Our Father is trustworthy, and security in Him is well founded. He cares for us out of His great and loving heart, bidding us not to be anxious.

Our giving is often a measure of our trust. He desires us as His children to freely give first to Him from our income, cheerfully and without grudging. All that we have is His and at His disposal. He gives good measure, pressed down, shaken together and running over to those who give. You cannot outgive God. He is no man's debtor. With whatever measure you give, it will be poured back into your lap. Give your all, and God will give His all.

Not laying again a foundation of repentance from dead works and of faith toward God. Heb.6:1

The Need for True Repentance

This basic ingredient simply means to change one's mind and to turn from sin to God. Mixed with faith in the revelation of the gospel of Christ, it becomes the harbinger of the experience of the new birth. Through repentance, the power of the cross destroys the body of sin, and the exceedingly great and mighty power that raised Jesus from the dead quickens our mortal body. All that our old man was—in its disrupted personality, however mistreated and abused—is crucified.

The hurts and bruisings of the past lose their effect upon us when we see ourselves as being in desperate need of God's forgiveness. In the light of such grace extended to us, we can freely forgive others their trespasses. True repentance puts the old, offended self to death in the death of Jesus.

The need to loathe our old selves is a prerequisite to embracing our crucifixion with Christ. The preservation of any aspect of our old man undermines the power of the cross and causes an unholy mixture of doublemindedness that neutralizes the new life. Equally, the probing of what has been put to death in the cross for causes of hangups in the new life leads to confusion. It demonstrates a misunderstanding of our crucified Christ's power to crucify our old man. Shall we still live in the things that Christ through His death brought to an end? Stop picking over the bones!

True repentance is motivated not by sorrow for being caught, nor by fear of the judgment of hell. It is motivated by our sorrow that we have offended God, and by our desire for the life that was hostile to Him to come to an end.

Not laying again a foundation of repentance from dead works and of faith toward God. Heb.6:1

Faith—You Cannot Live Without It

The importance of faith is confirmed by the prominence given to it in the Scriptures. As with all foundations, it is irreplaceable. It is impossible to please God without faith; the just live by it. Faith is not something to be taken up just when the going gets tough. We are to live by the faith of the Son of God. Whatever is not of faith is sin.

There is only one true faith, the faith of God. Those born of God have received the same spirit of faith. If we were just physical, then we could live by bread alone, but we maintain our spiritual life by every word that proceeds from the mouth of God. Faith is a remarkable faculty. It comes by hearing the word of the Lord, and it enables us to live the life of Jesus in our mortal bodies. Faith is the great achiever. It is the victory that overcomes the world. It is the sustaining power that gives endurance. Jesus is the author and finisher of faith.

Faith is perfected by performance and negated by inertia. If we do not walk by faith, then faith will not be perfected. James tells us that there is a faith that is useless. It is not enough to agree with God. Not everyone who says, "Lord," shall enter the kingdom, but he who does the will of the Father.

The trial of our faith is to be expected and joyfully received. If we use our disappointments and betrayals as an excuse to go back, it only proves that it was already in our hearts to go back and all we needed was the opportunity. The life of Jesus is to be expressed in the area of the trial, making the trial of our faith more precious than that of gold.

Of instruction about washings. Heb.6:2

Washings and Baptisms

Ananias told Saul, later to become Paul, to be baptized and wash away his sins. The Jews were familiar with that concept. Jesus said that He had a baptism to be baptized with and that He was distressed, or limited, until it was accomplished. He was speaking of the baptism of His death, burial and resurrection. His baptism was foreshadowed by all the Old Testament baptisms. When we understand the significance of them, then we can appreciate what was accomplished in the baptism referred to by Jesus.

Peter refers to Noah being brought safely through the water that destroyed all sinful flesh, and correlates that to baptism which now saves us. From the baptism of Noah we learn of the first references to repentance and grace: God repented of sinful flesh, and Noah found grace in the eyes of the Lord. This is followed by the Lord destroying all sinful flesh.

Moses' baptism teaches us concerning the deliverance of God's people and the destruction of His enemies. Joshua's baptism instructs us regarding the death of the old, unbelieving generation and a new generation entering the promised land. Joshua also circumcised the new generation, an act which is equated with baptism in the Colossian letter.

All these aspects of our salvation were fulfilled in the baptism of Jesus. Jesus told His disciples that they could be baptized with His baptism and drink His cup. That is accomplished when by faith we are crucified, buried and raised with Him. Our sinful flesh is destroyed, we are delivered, and our enemies are destroyed. Our old, unbelieving man dies, and a new man enters all the promises of God in Jesus Christ. This foundational doctrine of baptisms has to be laid in our experience.

Of instruction about washings, and laying on of hands, and the resurrection of the dead, and eternal judgment. Heb.6:2

The Laying On of Hands

Who would have thought that among the great foundational doctrines of Christ—repentance, faith, baptism, resurrection and eternal judgment—the laying on of hands would have been right there in the middle of them. This neglected doctrine, and therefore unused practice, has contributed to a lack of the supernatural power of God among us. Thank the Lord that His hand is upon us. It would be unthinkable to think otherwise.

The practice is not for elders only. One of the signs that Jesus said would follow those who believe was that they would lay hands on the sick and they would recover. The other references to this practice inform us regarding the different aspects of this doctrine. The examples in the New Testament include the laying on of hands by the elders, through which God's gifts were imparted, the sending out by way of commissioning, the imparting of the Holy Spirit, and of course, healing.

These examples evidence the wonder of being used by God to convey His power. The responsibility of being an instrument of God includes the accountability to represent Him in heart and character. As we walk under the hand of God we become available to Him to convey His blessing through our hands. Our ignorance of the doctrine of the laying on of hands may cause us to deny the practice.

The knowledge of the sacred trust conferred upon believers is an added incentive to be who and what we should. It is a humbling experience to see God move in power through the laying on of our hands.

They were teaching the people and proclaiming in Jesus the resurrection from the dead. Acts 4:2

Resurrection: A Gospel Ingredient

Jesus is the resurrection and the life, and those who believe in Him are sons of the resurrection, that is, though they die yet shall they live. Paul's prayer for the church at Ephesus was that they might know the exceeding greatness of God's power towards us who believe, according to the strength of His might, which He brought about in Christ when He raised Him from the dead.

Think of the power that infused the body of Jesus, cold and stiff in death, and brought Him to life. Death was now a defeated foe, and life was now the new ruler. That same power has brought us from death to life. We who were dead in trespasses and sins have been raised up together with Christ both to be seated with Him and to walk in newness of life.

There is to be a final resurrection of the just and the unjust. Daniel tells us of the resurrection of some to everlasting life, but of others to disgrace and everlasting contempt. Moses had respect for the reward and, like others who would not accept deliverance, he wanted a better resurrection. Our reward of inheritance is directly related to the treasure we have laid up in heaven. The quality of our life's work will become evident when the fire has proved it.

Who would want to be received by the Lord with the commentary on his life, "Badly done, you no good, faithless servant"? If you do not think the Lord says such things, look again at what He said to the Laodicean church, calling them wretched and miserable and poor and blind and naked. Resurrection power is given to us so that we might live as those alive from the dead in this present world.

And as he was discussing righteousness, self-control, and the judgment to come, Felix became frightened. Acts 24:25

Eternal Judgment, Another Gospel Ingredient

God is the ultimate judge. His throne is established for judgment, and the Scriptures teach that He loves judgment. He, being the judge of the earth, will always do right. He will never, in the slightest degree, make a wrong judgment. Judgment is associated with justice and mercy; we see these come together in the cross of Christ. Those who believe, pass from judgment that awaits the ungodly, but it must be understood that we will all stand before the judgment seat of Christ to receive those things done in the body. This is sometimes referred to as the judgment of rewards.

Christians can suffer loss when time spent in disobedience is consumed as the fire tests the quality of each man's work. Those who have laid up treasure in heaven enter into their reward. If any man's work be burned up, then he shall suffer loss, even though he shall be saved yet so as by fire. Within the sovereignty of God is the principle of sowing and reaping, from which we do not pass.

If we judged ourselves then we would not be judged, but God chastens His people with weakness, sickness and even death, so that we will not be judged with the world. God will forgive us our sins, but not reward us for them. Christians receive judgment in this life because we will judge the world and angels; therefore, judgment must begin with the house of God. There is a continuing judgment that we can apply to ourselves or have the Lord apply, and a final judgment of the deeds done while in the body. Act as those who will be judged by the perfect law of liberty. We have liberty to walk as God's children, and if not, we are accountable for walking in a lie.

Therefore leaving the elementary teaching about the Christ, let us press on to maturity. Heb.6:1

Pressing on to Maturity

Going on to maturity requires God's permission. "And this we shall do, if God permits" (Heb.6:3). Maturity involves building upon foundations that must be fully completed before leaving. The Lord will not permit us to leave the elementary foundations of our faith unaccomplished. He desires our maturity and chides us for being babes when we should be teachers. We are to be in a constant state of growth, which makes change necessary and desirable.

The transformation of our character and personality is effected as our hearts are focused upon Jesus. Although we now see through a glass darkly, we can be transformed into Christ's image. The lack of such transformation can be directly attributed to our looking elsewhere.

We owe God our maturity. He has given us all things that pertain to godliness, so it is now our responsibility to be godly. If we do not have a completed foundation, then the superstructure will collapse. Repentance from dead works, faith towards God, the doctrine of baptisms, the laying on of hands, resurrection from the dead and eternal judgment are all necessary foundations. We must leave the foundations, but not leave them undone, before we go on to maturity.

Test yourself to know if the process of change is ongoing in your life, by looking for the obvious changes in your demeanor. You rob God and yourself when you stagnate. You have been given the tools for the job. Remember, it is the bride that makes herself ready. What will be your part in Zion the perfection of beauty, from which God will shine forth?

And He is the image of the invisible God, the first-born of all creation. Col.1:15

The Image of the Invisible God

Jesus represented perfection, perfectly. He is the exact representation of the nature of God, the radiance of His glory. His birth at Bethlehem was the outworking of what was first conceived in God before all things, then through Him all things were brought into being. That is what makes Him the first born. Adam was created, Jesus incarnated. Jesus was not created, for He Himself was the Creator. He was in the beginning, and His eternal life was manifested in the flesh.

He was before all things, created all things, and by Him all things consist. He upholds all things by the word of His power, and all power and authority in heaven and earth are subject to Him. He laid the foundations of the earth, and it is He who will roll up the heavens and the earth like a scroll. His divinity is evident in His creative power, as it is in His omnipresence, because He fills all things. He is to be honored as the Father and to be the object of worship. He did not regard equality with God a thing to be grasped, but He emptied Himself, taking the form of a servant. He was in the appearance of a man and proved that flesh and blood could contain divine nature.

He overcame all temptation and lived a sinless life, always pleasing His Father. He bound the strong man, the devil, in His life and destroyed him in His death. He was accepted as the sin offering and the means by which reconciliation with God could be made. He rose from the dead, ascended through the heavens and is seated at the right hand of the majesty on high. There He reigns until all His enemies are beneath His feet. He has the power and authority to build His church and bring her to perfection.

That they may all be one, even as Thou, Father, art in Me, and I in Thee, that they may also be in Us. John 17:21

Unity Was Achieved in Jesus

The unity of the Godhead is a reality and a mystery. Jesus declared, to the consternation and anger of the Pharisees, that He was one with the Father. His prayer to the Father, recorded in John 17, affirms God's intention for us to be one with Him. God wonderfully achieved this miracle, defying comprehension, in Jesus Christ.

It appears that it is easier for men to be united to God than to one another. If we have been joined to the Lord then we are one spirit with Him and with each other. The fact of our relationship with God is the basis of our relationship with one another. Unity has been achieved, and we are exhorted to maintain it.

The power of unity apart from God is demonstrated in Genesis, where God's commentary on unified men declares that now nothing would be restrained from them that they purposed to do. Such is the power of unity. Satan's strategy is to keep Christians in contention with each other to rob us of the power we have in unity, for one will put a thousand to flight and two ten thousand. Power is multiplied when we are together.

The church will ultimately be built together and come to the unity of the faith. We must start within our own hearts. "Unite my heart," said David. We cannot be at peace with our brethren if we are not at peace within ourselves. The biggest barrier lay between man and God, but God reconciled man to Himself. He also broke down every barrier between men. Whatever our race or status, He has made us one in Christ. Receive one another as God for Christ's sake has received you.

*And they were continually devoting themselves to the apostles'
teaching, and to fellowship. Acts 2:42*

Our Fellowship Is with God and with One Another

The word fellowship in this text represents a lifestyle. Fellowship was the experience of those who were made one with each other by the work of regeneration and the filling of the Holy Spirit. "They were of one heart and soul." They had been joined to the Lord as one spirit, and their union extended to His body, the church.

The outworking of their unity was evidenced by the change of attitude in their sharing. Needs in one part of the body were naturally—one might say automatically—met by the provisions of others. Sharing occurred not mechanically or dutifully, but with empathy, for other was seen as self. This newly found relationship occurred when they received common life and were baptized with the Spirit.

The self-centeredness of man, which has been intensified in our generation, wars against the Christ-centeredness of His body. Self-ambition, self-fulfillment and self-awareness are all a part of the look-out-for-number-one philosophy that saturates our society.

As members of one another in the body of Christ, our personal self is enlarged to embrace others as self. Fellowship is more than meetings. It is a *life* word: being together in everyday life sharing meals, laughter and tears, and building each other up in our faith and love. The friendship of Christians with the world has eroded the sense of brotherhood in the church. The lack of persecution has reduced our need to resort to one another for comfort and support. To think that you do not need fellowship with Jesus is the same as thinking you do not need His body.

And they were continually devoting themselves to...the breaking of bread and to prayer. Acts 2:42

Breaking Bread

The expression *breaking bread* was a common term for regular meals. It has become more specifically used to denote what is also called the Lord's supper (or table) and communion. Jesus instituted this memorial supper at the last observance of the traditional passover before the inauguration of the new covenant in His blood. He had earnestly desired to eat that particular passover with them, because the time had come to fulfill what every previous passover had foreshadowed.

Through Moses, God commanded the original passover supper to distinguish between the Israelites and the Egyptians. He told His people to apply the blood of the passover lamb to the door lintels, so that when the angel of death saw the blood he would pass over without inflicting the judgment of death. The inhabitants of the house were to cook and eat the flesh of the lamb preceding the great deliverance of Israel from Egypt and the destruction of Pharaoh and his army.

At the last supper, Jesus took bread and broke it, saying that this was His body and that they should eat it. He then took the cup and told the small group of blood-covenant Jews to drink it, saying, "This is the new covenant in My blood."

The unleavened bread represents His sinless body, while the wine represents His spotless blood shed for the remission of sin. As often (not seldom) as we do this, we proclaim the Lord's death until He comes. The bread and wine do not become the body and blood after we drink it. Jesus proclaimed it to be His body and blood before they drank it. His words are spirit and life.

'I believed, therefore I spoke,' we also believed, therefore also we speak. 2 Cor. 4:13

Evangelism

Evangelism is not only an indication of health, but an essential ingredient in spiritual warfare. A battle may be won by being defensive, but no one ever gained ground or took enemy territory by only being defensive. Evangelism is a point of attack. God is out to evangelize the world and bring all nations that He has made to worship Him. Ultimately out of every nation, tribe and tongue, that innumerable company of worshipers will come.

The early church could not STOP speaking. What a difference compared to so many Christians who cannot START speaking. The rule of their day was "We believe, therefore we speak." They believed with their heart, and confession was made with their mouth unto salvation. We absolutely must take the offensive and declare the risen savior Jesus as Lord and Christ.

When a sinner is converted, not only does the sinner die in Christ, but by new birth, a fellow soldier is added to the ranks of the church. We can deplete the ranks of Satan and swell the ranks of the redeemed through the power of the gospel. We have an effective *infectious* influence to transmit. It brings not only death, but also eternal life.

What a privilege, what an opportunity, but what a waste if we keep it to ourselves. Satan has many devices to nullify your effectiveness, but none greater than to make you silent before a lost world. God lamented that those who had His word did not speak it and turn others from their evil ways. His word worked for you, and you can see it work for others even as you speak.

By this is My Father glorified, that you bear much fruit, and so prove to be My disciples. John 15:8

Much More Fruit

God is the God of abundance. Jesus came to give us life abundantly. How abundantly or sparsely we bear fruit is the evidence of who we truly are. He is the vine, and we are the branches, so if we abide in Him we will bear fruit. We are exhorted to bear more fruit and much fruit and to abound and excel. Like trees planted by rivers of water, our source of life never fails. Even in old age we are to bear fruit. In fact, the light of our testimony should shine brighter and brighter unto the perfect day.

The life of the Spirit is so different from natural life. There is no premium on youth in the Spirit. On the contrary, maturity is the goal. Perfection is not something we reach midlife, and then comes decline as in physical form, but we press on into perfection all our lives. The fruit of the Spirit is a quality of life that should develop and abound as we get older. As in the promise to Joseph, our branches should hang over the wall, denying any imposed restriction by overcoming it. In Christ, evil has no power to overcome us, but we have the power to overcome evil with good.

Against the fruit of the Spirit there is no law, no restriction and no limitation. Whatever comes against us gives us an opportunity to express the character of Christ in us. Use your problems as fertilizer. Fruit-bearing occurs in the most repugnant circumstances. Benefit from the most obnoxious environment. If God be for you, who can be against you? Use the ground in which you have been planted to display the nature of your root. If Christ is the root then Christ is the fruit.

For the one who has entered His rest has himself also rested from his works, as God did from His. Heb. 4:10

The Sabbath and the New Covenant

God rested on the seventh day, and blessed and sanctified it. The seventh day is not mentioned again until God gives the law of sabbath observance to Moses. There is no record of Adam, Noah, Abraham, Isaac, Jacob or Joseph observing the sabbath. By the time Moses gave the law, the Israelites were unsure of what to do. Some went out to gather manna, and they had to ask the Lord concerning the man who violated the sabbath by gathering sticks.

The Scriptures tell us that sabbaths were a sign; that is, they were significant of something. The old covenant is full of significant things: things to wear, to do, to observe, to touch not and to taste not. The book of Hebrews furnishes us with the revelation of the relationship between the old and new covenants. All the significant things are fulfilled in the person and work of Jesus Christ. Sabbath "rest" is fulfilled in the finished work of Christ. When Jesus cried, "It is finished," He took our dead works into death. "For we who have believed enter that rest" (Heb. 4:3).

There is a final rest which occurs at the coming of Christ, but there is also a rest from our labors, which we can enter now in Jesus, the Lord of the Sabbath. Under the old covenant the Sabbath (seventh day) was to be observed as set apart. In the new covenant every day is to be holy. We dwell within the holy of holies and are joined to the Lord as holy ones, a status that does not change with the day. The sign of the one-day Sabbath has been fulfilled in Jesus, and the new covenant provides for holy living seven days a week.

But now we do not yet see all things subjected to him. Heb. 2:8

God-Given Dominion

God gave Adam a mandate to rule and subdue. In Psalm 8, David affirms that God has put all things under the feet of man. The Hebrew letter informs us that in subjecting all things to man, God left nothing that is not subject to him. The word *but* then occurs twice: *"But* now we do not yet see all things subject to him; *but* we do see... Jesus." The Lord Jesus has all power and authority in heaven and earth now, but the "not yet" applies to Christians still in this world.

There are obvious limitations in physical and mortal bodies, but there are areas of dominion we do have now. For instance, sin shall not have dominion over us. We can resist the devil, and he will flee from us. By the Holy Spirit we can employ the power of the name of Jesus and see miracles and works of faith with power. We can overcome, conquer, be victorious and always triumph. This body of sin can be destroyed while we yet live in it by our mortal body becoming transformed into the body of Christ.

There are two errors into which we can fall. One is to relegate to the age to come things God has given us in this age. The other is to bring into this age things that God has reserved for the age to come. The writer to the Hebrews is speaking of the world to come in verse five. We have not yet experienced the redemption of the body, where this mortal shall put on immortality and this corruptible shall put on incorruption. John tells us that it does not yet appear what we shall be. It is not yet given to us to be what we shall yet be. What is given is the provision to live in the Spirit and to manifest the life of Jesus in our mortal body in this life.

Do not harden your hearts as when they provoked Me. Heb. 3:8

The Hardening of the Heart

This condition is usually the result of a process of neglect. Hardening of the heart has to do with hearing the word of the Lord and not heeding it. Knowing what to do and not doing it is sin. The accumulative displacement of the voice of the Lord by other voices causes a searing of the conscience and a hardening of the heart. One of the promises of the new covenant is that God will take away the stony heart and give us a heart of flesh. What a tragedy, if having received a new supple and impressionable heart, we should reverse the process by disobedience and revert to a hard heart.

The centrality of Jesus in our focus and aim is the antidote to the hardening process. Having recorded an exquisite verbal picture of the Lord Jesus, the writer of Hebrews constantly directs our attention to Him as our example in every eventuality. The way of disobedience, or unbelief, will lead to deception. If we do not take pleasure in the truth, then God will send strong delusion. For instance, if we choose not to listen to the Lord concerning gathering with the saints, the next time the choice arises it will be easier to make the wrong decision.

We BECOME dull of hearing as we refuse to heed the Spirit's prompting. This process continues to where it is harder to make the right choice than the wrong one. That is the hardening of the heart. Hebrews contains grave warnings for those who do not obey, and unspeakable blessings of entering His rest for those who do obey.

I will sing to the Lord, for He is highly exalted; the horse and its rider He has hurled into the sea. Ex.15:1

Spiritual Warfare #1

In the triumph song of Moses, as Pharaoh and his army are overthrown in the Red Sea, the Lord is referred to as a warrior. He is the ultimate warrior, supreme in warfare knowledge. David said that the Lord taught his hands to war. There is no better teacher. The reason God did not drive all the heathen out of the land of promise was to teach His people to war.

This aspect of the nature of God is in us because we were created in His image. However, the fall of man and his subsequent sinful nature exert this now-marred characteristic in misdirected aggression. When we are born again by the Spirit of God, we are redirected to express valid aggression against spiritual forces. We enter a battle arena where spiritual warfare is constant. The Lord teaches us about the enemy and how to fight and conquer. Jesus as a man defeated Satan in His life and destroyed him in His death.

Daniel states that the beasts' dominion was taken away, but an extension of life was granted to them for an appointed period of time. God has allotted Satan a period of time that he knows is running out. The Lord Jesus has already written the judgment against him, and we are exhorted to execute that judgment.

Through Him who is greater and who is in us, we can resist the devil, and he WILL flee from us. The Lion of the tribe of Judah has already prevailed, and all power and authority in heaven and earth have been given to Him. Jesus disarmed and defeated Satan so that you could overwhelmingly conquer and triumph in His triumph. Be good soldiers of Jesus Christ, and fight the good fight of faith.

In the world you have tribulation, but take courage; I have overcome the world. John 16:33

Spiritual Warfare #2

God has never lost a battle. He rules by His might forever. Jesus did not come to bring dominion to God, for God never lost it, but He came to bring dominion back to man who lost it to Satan. Jesus as a man overcame sin, the world, the flesh and the devil. By a man came death, and by a man came the resurrection from the dead. Although Satan is referred to as a strong man, Jesus is called the stronger than he. In His life Jesus attacked Satan, overpowered him and took from him all his armor in which he trusted. In His death Jesus disarmed the whole army and kingdom of darkness, destroying Satan who had power over death.

Although all the powers of darkness have been defeated, they have been given a limited function for a time for the performance of God's purpose. Part of that purpose is for Christians to exercise personal victory in their Christ-centered and Spirit-empowered lives.

No one has ever gone to war as have Christians. Our enemy is already defeated, and our fight has already been won. We have the life and power of the Conqueror within, with which to put the enemy down and out. We can never be tempted above what we are able to bear; therefore, we are invincible. The overcoming life of Jesus is our life within, a resource from which we are to draw, expressing His life and victory personally in our mortal bodies. God never puts us in a no-win situation.

Two thousand years ago, the prince of this world was cast out. Today, steadfast in the faith, you can resist him, binding what Jesus has already bound, in His name.

Glorious things are spoken of you, O city of God. Ps.87:3

We Have Come to Mount Zion

Glorious things are spoken of Zion, the city of God. These glorious things are ours in Jesus Christ, because all the promises of God are yes and amen in Him. When we come to Jesus, the mediator of the new covenant, we also come to mount Zion, the heavenly Jerusalem. Zion is God's resting place forever, the habitation in which He desires to dwell.

God does not want a literal mountain, but a spiritual one, the mountain of His holiness. His people are the mountain of the Lord that will be established on the tops of the mountains in the last days, the mountain that will fill the whole earth. Ultimately, out of Zion the perfection of beauty, God will shine forth.

God is taking the church on to perfection, and will make the church a worthy bride for His Son. Our predestination takes us from being called, through being justified, on to being glorified. Today we do not yet see a glorious church, but rather a subnormal one. God's people are not yet the joy of the whole earth, but God has said that they will be.

Therefore, nations will come to the brightness of our rising, and kings will see our glory. "Her righteousness goes forth like brightness and her salvation like a torch that is burning. And the nations will see your righteousness and all kings your glory" (Isa.62:1,2).

There will be glory in the church by Christ Jesus. A glorious, effective church must be our goal. Goals discipline us toward the fulfillment of them. Jesus has made provision for the church to be glorious. Diligently apply yourself as a worker with Him, and be transformed into His image, making yourself ready.

If anyone wishes to come after Me, let him deny himself, and take up his cross daily, and follow Me. Luke 9:23, :57-63

Following Jesus

The terms on which we follow the Lord Jesus have never changed. We are not merely invited, but commanded, to follow Him. Following Jesus as the only way indicates that every other way will lead to disaster, so following Him is the best thing that can happen to us.

There is a cost. Jesus expounded the theme of counting the cost, not the cost of our redemption, for only Jesus was sufficient for that, but the cost of what we must forsake when following Him. The rich young ruler did not follow Jesus because of His terms. Every relationship, all that we possess and our very lives are to be forsaken. Taking up our cross daily is a requirement if we are to follow Jesus.

Some responded to Jesus by calling Him Lord, but they contradicted that assertion by adding "permit me first." Requesting a permit for *me first* is not compatible with seeking first the kingdom of God and His righteousness. A radical appraisal of how we are following the Lord compared with His terms is necessary if we want to be true followers of the Lamb.

The carnality exhibited among so-called Christians betrays that some have survived the cross. The old man has had a say in negotiating the terms on which they are to follow. If we begin by losing our life, then and only then can we save it.

Repentance, changing our minds and direction, is still the first requirement. Being crucified and buried with Jesus is a necessary step to being raised with Him. Take up the call afresh. Hear the Master beckon you to follow Him, and daily, deny even yourself.

*By means of the hypocrisy of liars seared in their own conscience
as with a branding iron. 1 Tim. 4:2*

The Conscience

Conscience is defined as knowledge with oneself, sometimes called the second level of awareness. This God-given indicator internally directs us to behave according to our moral values. Parental values play a major role in the development of the value system and the conscience of a child, as do also the accepted values of peers.

Although the conscience is a factor in our choosing right or wrong, it has no power to make us do what is right. Sin is the dominating power that causes us to override our conscience.

The awareness of failure affects our guilt consciousness, but man devises ways of superficially dealing with guilt. There is a philosophy that says, "If we can't keep the law, then change the law." Our generation has witnessed systematic eroding of the basis of morality in the western world. The absolutes of God have been legislated out of the law of the land. Everything is geared to steer the conscience away from guilt, especially concerning God's laws. Nevertheless, we cannot blame society or legislation for our sin.

The overriding of the conscience over a period of time produces a calloused or seared conscience. Such an evil conscience supports lies and hypocrisies which are carried out with impunity, but a seared conscience is not a clear conscience.

The conscience can be instructed for the better or for the worse. The only hope for those whose understanding is darkened is the penetrating word of God. Only God's forgiveness can bring true relief to our guilt-laden consciences. The Spirit-filled believer has both a new sensitivity to God and the ability to do His will.

You have acted foolishly; you have not kept the commandment of the Lord your God. 1 Sam. 13:13

Lessons in Obedience #1

King Saul is a valuable study in the consequences of disobedience. His compromised version of obedience lost him the kingdom. Although Saul remonstrated with Samuel and argued that he had obeyed, Samuel said that because he had rejected the word of the Lord, God had rejected him from being king. Samuel called Saul's conception of obedience rebellion.

One clear lesson we can learn from Saul's experience is that we will not reign without obedience. His impatience, compounded by the pressure of Israel's dissipation and the approaching hoards of Philistines, caused him to disobey. Instead of waiting for Samuel, he acted presumptuously and offered sacrifices himself. Shortly after that he compromised the annihilation of Amelek under the guise of sacrifice. Samuel makes quite clear what delights the Lord in his well-known observation that to obey is better than sacrifice.

Of all that motivates us to obey the Lord, the greatest is love. Jesus said that he who loves Him keeps His word and, conversely, that he who does not keep His word does not love Him. Obedience is a gauge of our love, not the dutiful adherence to legal requirements, but the expression of a loving heart.

The Lord Jesus is the supreme example of loving obedience. His love was without compromise, and therefore His obedience was total. Your reasonable response to God's love for you is surely to abandon yourself to His desires in an unrestricted demonstration of your love for Him.

He has also been undisturbed on his lees, neither has he been emptied from vessel to vessel...Therefore he retains his flavor, and his aroma has not changed. Jer.48:11

Lessons in Obedience #2

This scripture contains the analogy of wine making. Pouring from vessel to vessel increasingly purifies wine until it loses the original scent of its sediment and has an entirely new bouquet. Using the analogy of wine-making, the finished work of Christ in redemption becomes the basis upon which we can be changed. Our natural flavor, the carnal residue that remains with us, will be extracted from us by the sovereign leading of God in our lives. Different experiences and circumstances expose attitudes and responses that need to be put off.

Living according to the fact that Christ is in us and is our life displaces our old ways. The indictment of many so-called conversions is that the convert remains basically the same. The odor of carnality should give way to the aroma of Jesus. We must focus upon Jesus and hold fast to Him while trusting His sovereignty to pour us into the necessary vessels that change us into His image. The changes that occur take us from the present glory of a revelation of Christ in us, to a further degree of glory.

The apostle Paul was able to testify that wherever he went he was a sweet aroma of Christ. Have you retained your old flavor or have you developed a new aroma? If you remain faithful and obedient through the different experiences of life, then you will lose your old flavor and acquire the bouquet of Jesus Christ.

But you are a chosen race, a royal priesthood, a holy nation, a people for God's own possession, that you may proclaim the excellencies of Him who has called you out. 1 Pet.2:9

The Church: The Called Out

To be a Christian is to be a *called out* one. When Peter says that God has called us out of darkness into His marvelous light, he is reiterating what the Lord Jesus said to him: "I chose you out of the world; therefore, the world hates you." Jesus states that His disciples are not of this world even as He is not of this world. Therefore, we are not to be bound together with the world or be unequally yoked with unbelievers. If we have been called out of darkness then we should not have fellowship with darkness. As light, we should reprove the darkness. In this context Paul writes to the Corinthians what Isaiah had spoken to Israel: "Come out from their midst and be separate."

We are not of this world. We have been born from above, which is why we should not love the world. The world is hostile to God and to His children, and he who is a friend of the world is an enemy of God.

Jesus gave Himself for our sins that He might deliver us out of the present evil world. Demas, once a fellow worker with Paul, forsook him, having loved this present world. Where our treasure is there will our heart be also. Time revealed Demas' heart, and time will reveal the treasure of our heart. Our separation is not physical, but in conduct, walking as Jesus walked when He was on earth.

The lack of persecution from the world can be attributed to the lack of separation. If you have received the call from the Lord to come out of the darkness of this world, then come out, totally and cleanly, into His marvelous light.

I press on toward the goal for the prize of the upward call of God in Christ Jesus. Phil.3:14

Our High Calling

When God called us out, He also called us in—out of darkness into His marvelous light, out of the kingdom of darkness into the kingdom of His dear Son, out of death into life, out of the temporal into the eternal. We will ultimately rise out of the mortal into the immortal, out of the corruptible into the incorruptible, out of this age into the ages to come.

David graphically illustrates how God brought him out of the pit of destruction, out of the miry clay, setting his feet upon a rock, making his footsteps firm, and putting a new song of praise to God in his mouth. If that same revelation would dawn upon us concerning our depravity and lost estate, then perhaps we would appreciate the heights to which God has called us: seated with Christ in heavenly places, joint-heirs with Him who is the heir of all things.

Paul exhorts us to forget what lies behind and to press on towards the prize of the upward call of God in Christ Jesus. Glorious experiences of the Lord, more wonderful than we can imagine, are waiting for us to press in to and apprehend. At the same time demotivating factors keep us in the mire. One is the guilt of failure, but God can requalify us if we confess and forsake sin.

True repentance is always acceptable to God, and the smile of His forgiveness is absolution indeed. Ignorance of God and ignorance of our calling, plus the lack of conviction about our sinful nature, also cause stagnation. To obtain the prize of your high calling, make Jesus the consuming passion of your life.

The church of the living God, which is the pillar and support of the truth. 1 Tim.3:15

The Pillar and Support of the Truth

Among the lies, deceit and crookedness that abound in the world, God has set a pillar and support of truth. Truth came by Jesus Christ, who is the truth. There was no deceit or guile in His mouth. He was the embodiment of truth, and His life bore witness to the truth. The world was hostile to Him because He contradicted the lies and hypocrisy that existed.

Nothing diverted Him. Nothing compromised Him. At the end of His time on earth He said that Satan was coming but had nothing in Him. Jesus is the true light that comes into the world. He is the true light, the true vine, and the true bread that came from heaven. Only the Spirit of truth could bear witness of Him. That same Spirit has given birth to the church, which is His body. The true church is the testimony of Jesus, the light of the world.

To be that true light, we must be true and walk in truth. It is true worshipers that God seeks, those who worship in spirit and in truth. We can draw near to God only with a true heart. How else could we have full assurance? John says that what is true in Jesus is true in us.

Have you been created in God in righteousness and true holiness? Then lay aside all falsehood and speak the truth. James instructs Christians not to lie against the truth. The truth about you is that you are true—a true man, true husband, true father, true employee, true everything God made you to be. When you are anything other than the truth, you lie against the truth.

As the world system continues to collapse in its own corruption, Jesus continues to build a towering pillar of truth.

According to the proper working of each individual part.
Eph.4:16

A Proper Working Part

Jesus Christ is the head of His body, the church. From the head the whole body receives its direction. As individual members one of another, we are each given a function that is necessary, not only for ourselves, but also for the health and efficiency of the body. The whole body is the accumulation of the individual members. Each one must be responsible to be working properly. We can help one another, care for one another, admonish and edify one another, but we cannot live one another's lives. We cannot be the actual mechanics of victory within the hearts of each other.

The growth of the body in love and in all aspects of Christ is achieved by the proper working of each part. Each of us can hold fast to the Head, Christ. He is the life that resides in each member. The manifestation of the life of the Lord Jesus in our mortal bodies denotes that we are working properly.

Each born-again child of God is a member of Christ's body and receives of His fulness. By the Holy Spirit we are given a measure of faith, a personal gifting and an accompanying measure of grace. No one is left out; no one is less important; everyone is necessary. It is essential that each one know his identity and function properly in it. The corporate body is only as healthy as the sum of the parts.

Having such a rich deposit of Christ with His many and varied expressions in the church, our lives and gatherings should pulsate with dynamic, colorful and effective diversity. Stir up your gift, and work properly.

*Now we have received...the Spirit who is from God, that we might
know the things freely given to us by God. 1 Cor.2:12*

He Freely Gives

We have received the Spirit so that we might not remain
ignorant, but know the things freely given to us by God. Whatever our gift, it is just that, a gift. The Father gives, the Son
gives, the Spirit gives. God is the giver. He gives freely and
abundantly—pressed down, shaken together, and running over.
What we have been so generously given, God wants us to give.
To hoard or bury is to sin. To give is to be like God. "There is
one who scatters, yet increases the more, and there is one who
withholds what is justly due, but it results only in want"
(Prov.11:24). None of us have anything that was not given to us.
Freely we have received, and freely we are to give.

God's Spirit in us remains a giver; if we do not share what
we have been given we quench the Spirit. We have more seed
than the devil has "birds" of the air. Sow your seed; scatter widely;
do not hide it or hold it.

Speaking of the Spirit that was yet to be given, Jesus said
that out of the belly of him who believed would flow rivers of
living water. Let it flow, or it will stagnate. What we have received from God is not only for our personal benefit, but for the
body of Christ and for a witness to the world. Be a child of your
heavenly Father, a testimony of Jesus. Be an expression of your
new spirit in union with the Holy Spirit. Do not selfishly over-
stock all the benefits with which you have been daily loaded.

Oh, for a heart of extravagance, that pours out what is precious for the sake of Jesus. Burst the seals that the enemy has put
on the doors. Unstop the well, and as a child of your heavenly
Father give of yourself.

And they overcame him because of the blood of the Lamb and the the word of their testimony. Rev.12:11

Overcoming

The last book of the Bible, Revelation, presents to us a graphic display of Christ's total sovereignty as the final conqueror. The throne of God rules and dispenses judgment until nothing is left unjudged. Terrifying visions of the wrath of God impress our imaginations with pictures of worldwide catastrophe, the heavens themselves shaken with violent judgment. There are times of intense testing for believers, culminating in their glorious overcoming. The bride of Christ appears in all her glory, having made herself ready.

All the letters to the churches contain promises to the overcomers. A key to how we overcome is given in the statement, "They overcame him by the blood of the Lamb and the word of their testimony, and they did not love their lives even to death." There seems to be so much to overcome in this world, but the great Sovereign Architect never allows us to be tempted beyond what we are able to bear and overcome. The trials of prosperity, poverty, persecutions and the variety of pressures that constantly afflict us are all orchestrated by God to work for our good.

We have the blood of the Lamb to plead as our justification before the accuser, which is also the means of his defeat. The overcoming life of Jesus is now our life. The baptism of the Spirit enables us to be testimonies of Jesus in power, but we must speak out the word of power fearlessly. The overcomers are contrasted with the cowardly and fearful. With the fear and love of God in our hearts we can be fearless among men and resist the devil. You were created to overwhelmingly conquer.

How shall we escape if we neglect so great a salvation? Heb. 2:3

Neglect

We neglect our great salvation at our peril. Along with its close companion of procrastination, neglect has its source in the carnal nature. Negligence has a seesaw relationship with motivation, which is stimulated by vision and goals. When motivation is high, negligence is low. When motivation is low, negligence is high. Losing sight of God's goals for us will demotivate us, but the retribution for neglect should be an incentive for action.

If we remain unaffected by either vision or punishment, then we are in a critical condition. A don't-care attitude is hostile to the zealous Spirit of God who quickens us. To pay no attention to the directives of the Spirit is to slight and to grieve Him. The sad commentary on those who practice neglect is that it proves their lack of love for the Lord. Such is true of any relationship, for neglect is the antithesis of love. True love is expressed in word and deed.

The antidote for neglect is nurture. Cultivate your relationship with the Lord, and you will grow in your appreciation of Him. The immense value of what is involved in your great salvation will increasingly fill you, and your motivation will be kept high. Neglect of work, wife, children or responsibilities is neglect of your calling and of your salvation, with a recompense from which there is no escape.

Recognizing and repenting of neglect restores sensitivity to the Lord and puts weight on the motivation side of the scales. Put off dull sloth. Clothe yourself with zeal, and be fervent in spirit serving Him who will never neglect you.

*And so we see that they were not able to enter because of unbelief.
Heb. 3:19*

Missed Opportunity

When the Lord opens a door, He makes available an opportunity to increase our knowledge of Him. How long that door remains open is a matter of God's timing. It cannot be presumed to stay open indefinitely. Israel did indeed try to enter the promised land, but not until the morning after God had given them the opportunity to enter. On the day when they could have entered they instead disobeyed God. The door was then closed to that generation, even though they confessed their sin and tried to enter. A fitting epitaph over every grave in the wilderness could have been *Lost Opportunity.*

Today there is a recognition among many Christians of the need to change to a more Christ-honoring, effective Christianity. The Holy Spirit is calling the church out of worldliness into repentance and into a new phase of communion with the Lord. The question "Will I?" must be changed to the affirmative "I will," while it is still today.

The Lord never forsook Israel during their days in the wilderness, but with their granted desires came leanness of soul and the gnawing frustration that they had missed God's best. If you fail to take your opportunity, then you will miss your time. Procrastination is the thief of time. It is the enemy who robs, steals and destroys. You can become your own worst enemy if you let this time slip.

The severe warnings in the book of Hebrews concerning neglect, letting slip and rejection are not without sobering significance at this time. The solemnity of putting off obedience is that you miss something of the Lord.

For the kingdom of God does not consist in word, but in power.
1 Cor. 4:20

Power and Demonstration

Just as love, the greatest ingredient of the kingdom, is not in word only, but in deed and truth, so also the kingdom of God is not in word only, but in power and demonstration. Jesus declared His love in a powerful display of miracles and ultimately in laying down His life for us. He set a pattern and a standard that was to be maintained in His followers. He said that the works that He did and greater works would be done by those who believe in Him. Signs would follow them that believe, and out of their innermost being would flow rivers of living water, referring to the Spirit who was to be given.

Part of the reformation of the church, which is still going on, is the recovery of the demonstration of power. The Christ we preach and the gospel of the kingdom are authenticated by His power. *"You shall receive power, after the Holy Spirit has come upon you"* was the promise of the Father given by Jesus. God has asked us to give Him no rest until he establishes Jerusalem and makes it a praise in the earth. Our constant supplication should be for the Lord and His glory to be seen upon us.

There will be glory in the church that Jesus is building. Our travailing and intercession for the church should be encouraged by the declarations of promised glory, until we see them fulfilled. John saw the bride of Christ, and the messenger told John that the bride had made herself ready. The impotent, carnal church will give way to a glorious church testifying in power to Jesus, and nations will come to the brightness of YOUR rising.

And this we shall do, if God permits. Heb.6:3

God May Not Permit

Pressing on to maturity requires that the elementary teachings be left. God gives permission to leave them only if the first things have been accomplished. He does not permit us to leave neglected and undone the first principles in order to go on to perfection. The irrevocable consequences of falling away and the eternal disaster of not bearing good fruit should evoke a healthy fear. The Spirit conveys these *attention getters* to alert us to the dangers of being sluggish.

Exhortations to press on, to be diligent and to exercise faith to enter into God's rest are seen in contrast to the perils of unbelief and disobedience. The Lord invited some to follow Him, but they insisted on a permit for *me first*. "Permit me first to bury my father." "I will follow You, Lord, but..." was another response from one who wanted a *me first* permit. The Lord does not grant such permits. The "Yes, but me first" people have either never been crucified or have forgotten that they were. In any case they will not go on.

If you desire to please the Master, then you must not be the master. Salvation is much more than being born again; it is going on to maturity and perfection. Being saved is a continuous process of development that follows the crisis of conversion. To cease to grow is to lose the degree of salvation that you could have had if you had grown. If the first rungs of the ladder are not in place, then the gap is too high for you to climb. Only if you fulfill the first steps will you have the Lord's permission to go on to perfection.

Now may the God of Hope fill you with all joy and peace in believing, that you may abound in hope by the power of the Holy Spirit. Rom.15:13

Hope

God is the God of hope. He gives us expectation and a desirable future. Although the creation was made subject to vanity, it was subjected in hope. We were dead in our sins, separated from Christ, having no hope and without God in this world. We were hopeless, but Jesus has come to bring us hope. He who has the Son has not only the life but also the hope.

We have been born again to a living hope by the resurrection of Jesus Christ. Christ in us is our hope of glory. We have been called to obtain the glory of Christ. What a hope! Just as faith has its assurance hope has its full assurance. The word of God that is the basis of faith is also the basis of hope.

The promises of God are sure, and all of them are yes and amen in Jesus. Hope is likened to an anchor of the soul, both sure and steadfast, which has entered within the veil. It ever pulls us to our future, which is full of promise.

Job asked the question, "What is the hope of the hypocrite?" What indeed? Judgment, wrath, stripes and outer darkness await workers of iniquity who use the name of Jesus. The Lord wants us to abound in hope because hope powerfully affects us by anticipating joy. Jesus for the joy that was before Him endured the cross. He never lost hope even in His death.

You too can be carried through the various trials of life with an anticipation of glorious things to come. You can rejoice in tribulation knowing what it is working for you. Your labor is not in vain in the Lord. You shall receive the reward of your treasure in heaven and be like Him. Glorious Hope!

Come to Me, all who are weary and heavy-ladden, and I will give you rest. Matt.11:28

Come to Jesus

There is no substitute for the direct encounter and relationship that the Lord Himself affords to every believer. Jesus says that we should come to **Him** and **He** will give to us. One of the doctrines unearthed in the reformation was the priesthood of all believers. No longer is the individual believer relegated to an indirect relationship. We need no human agency to mediate our personal access to and union with the Father through the Son. When the Lord gives the invitation to come, it is for a direct meeting with Him, out of which **He** gives. It is to Him we come and from Him we receive.

The children of Israel had a consciousness of sin; therefore, they feared an encounter with God. They asked Moses to speak with the Lord and to convey to them what the Lord said. Under the old covenant the Levites were a tribe of priests who officiated and mediated for the people. Under the new covenant Jesus is our Great High Priest to whom we are joined by being born again of the same Father. His sheep hear His voice, and all, from the least to the greatest, know Him and are taught by Him. As a kingdom of priests we mediate the gospel in our mortal bodies, showing Christ to a world that does not know Him.

Every born-again child of God is a priest unto God. We all can offer acceptable sacrifices to God, sacrifices of praise and thanksgiving. The Christian is to present his own body as a living sacrifice. God no longer has a holy tribe, but a holy nation, a kingdom of priests. Come directly to Jesus, and mediate to a lost world what you receive from Him.

Rather it was sin, in order that it might be shown to be sin by effecting my death through that which is good, that through the commandment sin might become utterly sinful. Rom.7:13

Sin

Although the consequences of sin are eternal, sin itself is a temporal insertion and shall one day be no more. It will not occur a second time. The true nature of sin is widely misunderstood. Generally Christians treat sin too lightly and undermine its seriousness. Our false evaluation comes from our ignorance of God. God is more holy than we have imagined, and our sin separates us from Him.

Sin is neither ethereal nor abstract, but it is an insidious power. Sin deceives, degenerates, dominates and kills. The sinner is driven by sin in blind impotence; knowing it is wrong, he has no power to avert the action. The whole dilemma of human tragedy, in all its suffering and ultimate death, is the result of a single sin. The worst thing anyone can do is sin. Sin hides its consequences. It promises the opposite of what it delivers.

The ability to sin is not the essence of freedom, but on the contrary, it is a manifestation of bondage. The wonder of the gospel is that God has supplied Jesus Christ as the complete and comprehensive answer to deal with every aspect of sin. The Lord has laid on Him the iniquity of us all. He who never sinned was made sin for us, that we might be made the righteousness of God in Him. He overcame sin in all its seducing power and brought deliverance to a world in bondage.

Jesus proved the superior power of righteousness in flesh and blood, and He wills to prove Himself in your mortal body as your life and strength. Having been freed from sin and born again of God, you have the inherent power of an indissoluble union with God enabling you not to sin.

Let us run with endurance the race that is set before us. Heb.12:1

Endurance

The illustrious list of men and women acting out stories of courage, valor and patience offers a strong incentive for us also to endure. Having arrayed before us those who through the ages have conducted themselves in such faith, the writer now puts the capstone upon all examples by pointing us to Jesus. If you ever feel like quitting, if you feel weary and hard done by, think of the Lord Jesus.

Sin is something to strive against. Jesus did, even to the shedding of His blood. If those under the old covenant, without the indwelling Christ and the promise of the Holy Spirit, had such a bold testimony, then why cannot we who have received the promise endure?

The goal of God behind all that we have to endure is that we become partakers of His holiness. That fact should incite us to lift up the hands that hang down and strengthen our feeble knees. Exercise begets exercise. Once the effort has been made to get going, the going gets easier. The heart set on Jesus will make a straight path for its feet, which is easier than a crooked path. The key to endurance lies in the relationship between us and the Lord.

We must look to Him, consider Him, set our minds and affections on Him and be taken up with Him as our aim. Pleasing Him and the prospect of receiving His commendation when we are rewarded for those things done in the body are incentives to endure.

He is able to keep you from falling. You will never be tempted beyond what you are able to bear. If you would only register the facts, you would know that you are invincible through Him who loves you.

What will be the outcome for those who do not obey the gospel of God? 1 Pet.4:17

The Good News and the Bad News

The good news of full salvation is for all who believe, receive and obey the gospel. The bad news is for all who will not believe and obey the gospel of God. The good news comes to those who are under the judgment of the bad news, in order to let them know that there is a way out. If the good news is not accepted, then there is no other good news further down the line. The foolishness of rejecting God's great love and forgiveness is that there is no other good news.

When a nation falls to the invading power of an enemy, it becomes occupied and dominated. Such a captivity continues until a greater force comes to liberate the nation. In World War II, when the allied forces overcame the enemy, the captives were liberated. People rejoiced and danced in the streets, greeting the liberating armies with hugs and kisses because the burden of the oppressor had been broken. They had been set free. This is a picture of what the gospel does for us.

In Adam, man had fallen to the cruel bondage of the oppressor, Satan, and the rule of the kingdom of darkness. But an ally, one who loved us and saw our plight, intervened for us. Jesus attacked the enemy, overpowered him and took from him all his armor in which he trusted.

Jesus came to set the captives free. Now we can shout and sing songs of deliverance, and we can kiss the Son who has made us free indeed. This news is the best that has ever been told. It would have been better never to have known than to know and turn from it. Do not let the good news become bad news for you.

I have fought the good fight, I have finished the course, I have kept the faith. 2 Tim.4:7

An Achiever

Jesus is the only man who ever achieved what He was given to achieve, with no failures. Before He went to the cross He told His Father that He had finished the work that He had been given to do. On the cross He uttered those final words, "It is finished."

As born-again children of God, we have not been consigned to live lives of failure. We are destined for purposeful living. Paul said that he had not been disobedient to the heavenly vision. He was always reaching forward to apprehend that for which he had been apprehended. At the end of his life he was able to testify that he had fought a good fight and finished the course. What he had begun he had finished.

Many men, lack that ingredient of *stickability*. How many things do we start, but leave unfinished, unachieved? Must regrets be the commentary on our lives of unreached goals? The knowledge of unfulfilled goals and unfinished business is an unnecessary burden of guilt. God gives us attainable goals that are to be achieved with joy. We have been called to satisfaction, not frustration. Achievement qualifies us for a crown.

To be proven is to be qualified; to be unproven is to be unqualified; to be a failure is to be disqualified. A man does not have to remain a failure. It has been said that he is not a failure who picks himself up one more time than he falls. The grace of God enables us to turn failure into a stepping stone to higher ground. John Mark is an example of one who failed, yet became a necessary minister.

For all who are being led by the Spirit of God, these are the sons of God. Rom.8:14

Led by the Spirit

Those who are led by the Spirit are the sons of God. Obviously, those born of the Spirit are sons of God, but not everyone who is born of the Spirit walks in the Spirit. As our Shepherd and guide, the Lord desires us to walk with Him and be led by His Spirit. Hearing His voice and being taught by His Spirit should be our normal experience.

We are comprised of spirit, soul and body, but the most sensitive part of our being is our spirit. It is in our spirit that we commune with God. The one who is joined to the Lord is one spirit with Him. We can see the invisible, hear the inaudible and touch the intangible. We can detect the heart of God, whether grief or pleasure, by His Spirit witnessing with our spirit.

Our walk in the Spirit is a positive experience. He will lead us. Sin is knowing what to do and not doing it. We can override the promptings of the Spirit and rationalize away the leading of the Spirit. Walking in the Spirit is not automatic. We must contend with carnality, with Satan and his cohorts who deceive, with ignorance and bias. These all militate against the voice of the Spirit.

The obedience of faith expresses our new man and keeps our old man under the power of the cross. Sin will not have dominion over us when we walk in the Spirit. We can put on Christ and make no provision for the flesh to obey its lusts. Although the flesh lusts against the Spirit, the Spirit also lusts against the flesh and is more powerful than the flesh. The power of Christ in you is your strength to overcome. If you boast that you have been made alive by the Spirit, then walk in the Spirit.

He must be one who manages his own household well.
1 Tim. 3:4

Managing Well

Should we fall, there are many consoling scriptures that encourage us, but God has not consigned us to failure. He has provided for us, in the Lord Jesus, to rule and to reign. What He has given us to be is accompanied by the corresponding grace to rule in that capacity. If we are men, we have the grace to be men. If we are married, we have the grace to be a husband; if we have children, then we have the grace to be the fathers He wants us to be.

Being what we have been given the grace to be is to rule in that sphere. Christ who is our strength has given us all necessary ability and authority to overcome. If we are never tempted beyond what we are able to bear, then we are only tempted within the capacity we have to conquer, and that makes us invincible.

Faith is the victory that overcomes the world, and faith comes by hearing from God. To hear and obey is to rule well. The impulsive man anticipates God with his own conclusion and timing. The indecisive man vacillates, and like the procrastinator, puts off following through with the decision. These are examples of not ruling well. There is no need to be intimidated by any demand God puts upon us. All requirements are meant to increase our faith and cause growth.

The time will come when "as soon as they hear, they shall obey" (Ps. 18:44). To walk in the Spirit is to rule well, because we promptly comply with the voice of Him who rules. You can reign with Christ if you have been seated with Him. You can receive the "Well done" if you have done well in ruling.

You will know them by their fruits. Matt. 7:16

What Is Your Fruit Like?

Jesus made a simple statement that declared the obvious, but it was profound because of its implications. "By their fruits you shall know them." A tree bears its own fruit in type and quality. The type defines the particular tree, and the quality describes the condition of the tree. A good tree bears good fruit, while an evil tree bears evil fruit. Jesus said that we must be either good or evil. A mixture is an abomination to God. Be either cold or hot, for the lukewarm mixture makes Jesus vomit! He declares that He will spew the lukewarm out of His mouth. We should be clearing ourselves of every vestige of mixture.

God is at work in us to bring to fruition our new life, and we are to work out what He is working in. Even a natural fountain produces only bitter or sweet water. To produce blessing and cursing from the same mouth is a contradiction. Our Adamic life was cut off when we were crucified with Christ. Our new root is Christ. If the root is holy, then so are the branches. Remember, we do not support the root, but the root supports us.

If we are rooted in Christ, then we should bear holy fruit, the fruit of the Spirit. If we want to glorify God in our lives, then we should bear not only good fruit, but much fruit. The spirit now working in the children of disobedience is obviously producing disobedience. Our union with Christ exists so that we might bear fruit unto God.

If you have been born of the Spirit and now live by the Spirit, then walk in the Spirit and mortify the deeds of the flesh. The truth about you will be obvious, for you will be known by your fruit.

As many as received Him, to them He gave the right to become children of God. John 1:12

The Results of Receiving the Gospel

The gospel, in a word, is **Jesus**. God sent His Son to be received, and to as many as received Him, to them He gave power to become the children of God. When we receive Jesus in God's way and on His terms, then we are numbered among the many sons He brings to glory. The Father of Jesus is the Father of all His brethren, and Jesus is not ashamed to call us such.

Death no longer holds terror, for the grave is merely a portal to immortality. Jesus is the resurrection and the life; therefore, he who has the Son has the life. Through Jesus forgiveness of sins is preached. Our guilty conscience, laden with the conviction of our rebellion against God and the burden of knowing our uncleaness, is absolved. His shed blood cleanses and justified us and frees us from condemnation.

Jesus came to preach deliverance to the captives and to set prisoners free. He came to heal the brokenhearted and set at liberty those who are bruised. Broken, battered and bruised humanity can be restored through receiving the redemption that is in Jesus Christ. Receiving Jesus must include accepting Him as the baptizer with the Holy Spirit, just as He promised. That also is part of the gospel.

God provided a crucified Savior so that our old self could be put to death in Him. The power of the cross is death to every other power that had dominion over us. Being reconciled to God, baptized by His Spirit, knowing Him increasingly, partaking of His nature and becoming what we were created to be is the ecstatic experience of those who receive all that Jesus is and thereby become His disciples.

Let us draw near with a sincere heart in full assurance of faith.
Heb.10:22

Assurance

The old hymn *Blessed Assurance* illustrates the change that occurs when we receive Jesus as Lord and Savior. When Adam sinned, he lost his assurance. Ever since, men and women have been born alienated from God, and therefore without assurance. Dread, terror, despair, anxiety, fear of the future, and death itself have dominated the minds of men. When we receive God's provision of redemption in the person of Jesus Christ, then God also gives blessed assurance.

The revelation of the gospel comes with full conviction and much confidence. Repentance reaps assurance—not some assurance, but much assurance, even full assurance, the full assurance of faith.

A wealth of assurance awaits those who believe what God has done out of His great love for us. The lack of assurance causes the insecurity that tears at our hearts and torments our minds. Insurance companies flourish because they offer a degree of assurance for future catastrophe, but they cannot offer the ultimate assurance that a sinner needs when facing an angry God. The judgments of God cannot be avoided by monthly payments, but Jesus can be relied upon and trusted with full confidence for what He has done and what He will do.

God exhorts us to show diligence until the end in order to realize the full assurance of hope. Faith and hope are both sources of assurance because they are founded upon the word of God. Tranquility and serenity of assurance come when we have peace with God, and when we trust His sovereignty.

I stand at the door and knock; if anyone hears My voice and opens the door, I will come into him, and will dine with him, and he with Me. Rev. 3:20

Does God Seem Distant?

We might not question the theology of God's omnipresence, but we can at times lose our awareness or appreciation of His presence. There are reasons why the Lord seems to withdraw from our awareness of Him. He wants to draw us more fully into a depth of searching that will culminate in a more profound fellowship with Him. Often the sin of not giving the Lord enough time is the problem.

If we neglect our personal times of shutting the door and praying in secret, then it becomes easier to neglect Him while going about our everyday activities. God is not short of time. He created time in order to fulfill His purposes. If we do not have enough time, then we are spending time doing unnecessary things. This generation refuses to wait or to sit and think as we fill all silence with sound and entertainment. Amuse means to not think. The media are geared to think for us.

The call to spend our time pursuing materialism and pleasure is like the siren's voice drawing us into illicit activities. A day can go by without waiting upon God, and days can become weeks before we notice. Such neglect will cause our minds to become insensitive to His presence. The church at Laodicea had somehow shut Jesus outside the door. Imagine putting Christ out and closing the door on Him!

What then is the antidote? Those who seek Him shall find Him when they seek with a whole heart. If as the prodigal, you walk back to your Father, He will come running to you and embrace you, and you will know Him.

By your endurance you will gain your lives. Luke 21:19

Possessing Your Soul

Jesus said that in our patience we will possess our souls. The word possess can also be translated gain. Through the tribulation of life, God works patience in us. Patience in turn works the controlling of our souls. In effect, we gain control in areas that were out of control and therefore controlled us.

God wants people who are in control, not who are irrational, rash, irritable, short-tempered reactionists. He does not want us to be led like powerless, impotent wimps, swayed by every whim and driven by exterior pressures. Jesus was always in control, even when it appeared that others were dictating the events. He was led as a lamb to the slaughter, but He knew what He was doing and could have called legions of angels to assist Him. He gives us the power of His Spirit when we are joined to Him and become one spirit with Him.

By His Spirit we can gain control of our souls as well as our thoughts, emotions, actions and reactions, and even that most unruly member, our tongue. The exercise of patience in our frustrating circumstances is the exercising of control and possession of our souls. Meet a self-controlled person and you meet a fulfilled person. Meet an uncontrolled soul and you encounter a frustrated fool.

Maturity comes through exercising patience and thereby gaining one's soul. Gaining control of our disrupted personality is a process, but God is at work in us. The tribulation that Jesus foretold we would have in this world works for us. Tribulation works patience, patience works proven character, and proven character works hope. Do not lose ground. Possess it, and increase your hope.

I recognize Jesus, and I know about Paul, but who are you?
Acts 19:15

For What Are You Known?

When Jesus cursed the fig tree, He was instructing us that to give the appearance of fruit and yet be without it is unacceptable. Professing to be a Christian and going to church may give a false reading if in fact the fruit of Christ is not evident in our lives. How are we impacting the world around us? Both the visible and invisible realms should know about us. Our effect is to be felt in the heavenlies and in the society in which we live.

Jesus impacted the world, and the early church turned the world upside down. The power of the Holy Spirit was the dynamism which demonstrated the kingdom of God on the earth.

There are magnificent and wonderful promises for the church in our generation. Isaiah prophesies that nations will see our light, and kings our glory. They will come to the brightness of our rising. The glorious light of Christ in the church will shine into and overwhelm the gross darkness, and her righteousness will go forth as brightness, and her salvation as a lamp that burns. There will be glory in the church through Jesus Christ, and of the increase of His government and kingdom there shall be no end. God's zeal will see to that.

If the scale were one to ten for effective witness, where would you rate? We know the effects of the powers of darkness, but are those powers fearfully conscious of your superior power? "Jesus I know, and Paul I know, but who are you?" retorted the evil spirit as he set about to thrash the sons of Sceva. Are you an insignificant statistic, or are you known as a testimony of Jesus in power?

Therefore, since we receive a kingdom which cannot be shaken, let us show gratitude. Heb.12:28

A Kingdom Which Cannot Be Shaken

To be born again of incorruptible seed by the word of God is to be introduced into a Kingdom unlike anything we have known before. We come to God Himself, who is no longer hidden, and to the awesome realm of the Spirit listed in our text. Even while we still have mortal bodies, we experience life in ultimate reality, untouched by corruption, eternal and unshakable. The earthen vessels of our humanity contain the excellent treasure of the seed and life of Christ. Our bodies are meant not to conceal but to reveal this treasure as we manifest the life of the Lord Jesus.

The life we enjoy in the Spirit is not limited to the tangible or physical. Partaking of the divine nature transfers us from a kingdom that can be shaken to an environment transcending contamination and corruption. Although we cannot fully experience our eternal inheritance while we have mortal bodies, we can partake to the extent that we are recognizable as God's children. Now we see through a glass darkly, but then (when we leave this body) we shall see face to face and know as we are known.

All that can be shaken will be removed. Therefore, *we should* live incorruptibly, that is, by the Spirit, and by faith. All that is not of faith is sin, but we can lay up eternal treasure in heaven if we live as displaying the treasure of Christ's eternal life. Since you have already come to God and His kingdom, set your affections there. Become better acquainted with the unshakable than with the shakable.

For to me, to live is Christ, and to die is gain. Phil.1:21

For Me to Live Is Christ

Jesus came not only to sacrifice His life for us, but to make us partakers of His life. To the degree that we are crucified with Him and buried with Him in baptism, we can enjoy life from the dead with Him. In exchange for an existence that is dead in trespasses and sins, we may receive eternal and abundant life. This being true, why is it that so many Christians lack the vitality and power of Christ as their lives? Much of the answer lies in the limited degree of conviction that they experienced when they initially received the word. The degree of conviction determined the measure of repentance, which shaped their experience of conversion.

The lack of total commitment often results from a deficient conviction that has not cut to the heart to bring deep-seated repentance. Repentance that holds nothing back from the cross results in unqualified abandonment to the Lord Jesus Christ. Total crucifixion of totally depraved nature is the doorway to total freedom and to the uninhibited flow of the life of Jesus.

A maximalist is one who holds out for the maximum and rejects compromise. A minimalist is one who accepts the least amount attainable. The minimalist will suffer loss. He teeters in the precarious position of losing what he thinks he has. "Whoever does not have, even what he has shall be taken away from him" (Matt.13:12). Minimal conviction, minimal repentance, minimal expression of Christ, minimal commitment, minimal fruit—these will result in minimal reward and inheritance, if any. Be a maximalist, and give maximum expression to Christ as your life.

You did not choose Me, but I chose you, and appointed you, that you should go and bear fruit. John 15:16

God's Choice

The words *predestination*, *election* and *chosen* first occur not in the writings of church fathers, but in the Scriptures inspired by the Holy Spirit. The anger generated in opposition to these words betrays how much man wants to be responsible for his own salvation. Man still wants man to be the initiator and God the responder. These words however, do not permit man to have the initiative. They lay the initiative squarely and rightly at God's door. While many would agree that we are not saved by works, when we make God the responder to our choice we trust in a subtle form of works.

It is not true that our work of choosing God results in God then choosing us. Jesus said that we did not choose Him, but He chose us. God does not need to look into the future, for that would suggest that He needs telling what will happen. God produced the future. He PREdetermines, FOREordains, PREdestines and chooses, then works it out in history.

He appoints the times and seasons, and the boundaries and habitations of nations. As many as have been **appointed** to eternal life believe. His counsel shall stand, and He will work all things after the counsel of His own will. This clear, biblical teaching is resisted vehemently. Some people would like to eliminate all references to God's sovereignty in predestining, foreordaining, electing and choosing, but when all the ranting and raving is finished God's word will abide. God will carry out, in this present age and in the ages to come, what He counseled in Himself before the world existed.

But I have this against you, that you have left your first love.
Rev. 2:4

First Love

Jesus told the Ephesian church that they had left their first love, the love which Paul had previously commended in his letter to them. They had worked out this love in a practical way toward the body of Christ. Their faith in the Lord Jesus was accompanied by a corresponding love that was talked about until it reached the ears of Paul. Then their faith changed in its character, for it ceased working by love. They still labored and exercised patience; they knew the difference between good and evil; they put false brethren to the test, and endured without growing weary; but with all they had going for them, Jesus had something against them. They had left their first love, which meant that they had fallen.

In working out their repentance they needed to return to their first works. Jesus warned them that if they did not repent and do the first works He would personally come and put their light out.

Our first love for the Lord comes in response to being loved by God and being full of gratitude. We express this thankfulness in how we treat other saints and the world around us. If the works of love cease, then no matter how doctrinally correct we are or how much we endure because we are Christians, we betray that we have fallen from our first love.

First love must be added to, not left. Jesus demonstrates the preeminence of love in giving the Ephesian church such a severe warning despite all their other achievements. Do not neglect the love that God has so abundantly poured into our hearts.

To whom God willed to make known...this mystery...Christ in you, the hope of glory. Col.1:27

Christ in You

There was once a mystery waiting to be revealed that no one would have ever guessed. In past generations it remained unknown, but God has now revealed it. The mystery is Christ **in** believers. At His incarnation Jesus' eternal life was in His physical body, but now a further unfolding of the mystery reveals Jesus Christ in His body, the church. The multi-membered body of Christ is now indwelt by Jesus, who is our life. With Christ as the head, both Jew and Gentile become one new man as fellow heirs.

The Word that was in the beginning with God, and was God, became flesh and dwelt among us as the man, Christ Jesus. He overcame sin in the flesh, being tried to the full in every respect. He was accepted as our sin offering and raised from the dead. He was glorified, and now He not only lives forever to make intercession for the church, but He lives **in** His body, the church.

Those who have been crucified and buried with Him have also been raised with Him to walk in newness of life. Who could have conceived such a thing: Christians as the light of the world, the very manifestation of Him who is the light of the world?

Our union with Christ seats us with Him in heavenly places and joins Him with us on the earth as our life. Christ now indwells our hearts, and His Spirit joined to our spirit makes us one Spirit with Him.

God has willed to make known this mystery. Now you are to be a revelation of this mystery to the world around you. Jesus accomplished all the will of His Father, and will enable you to do the same.

He has taken it out of the way, having nailed it to the cross.
Col.2:14

He Has Taken It Out of the Way

The it spoken of here is the certificate of debt that consisted of decrees against us. God has charged all men under sin. The debt we owed by way of transgression we could never repay. The certificate of debt is full of decrees that are hostile to the offenders of the law. Should we have had to face the ultimate tribunal of the great white throne on our own merits, we would have been utterly condemned. However, God in his great love and mercy has taken away the whole certificate of debt, including the contrary decrees.

How were we relieved of such deserved condemnation? Jesus paid the price. He stood condemned in our place, and the judgment was executed upon Him. He bore our sins in His body upon the cross and shed His blood for the remission of our sins.

When we confess and forsake our sin and sinful self and receive Jesus as our sin-bearer and Lord, God justifies us. Unlike the blood of the old covenant which only covered sins, Jesus' blood takes away our sin. God in Christ reconciled us to Himself, imputing our trespasses not to us but to Christ. God made us alive together with Jesus, even when we were dead in our sins. He commended His love to us while we were still sinners, because in His Son before the world existed He had taken away and nailed to the cross all that condemned us.

If we realized how far our sins have been removed from us, how pristinely clean we are legally and literally, how forgiven and holy we are, then we would not so easily contaminate ourselves.

But God, being rich in mercy, because of His great love with which He loved us. Eph. 2:4

But God!

Thank God for the *but Gods* that occur in Scripture. We were altogether lost, *but God* in His great mercy and love retrieved us. We were sinners, *but God* commended His love to us while we were sinners. God did not leave us to ourselves or to the fate we deserved. In His exceeding great love, He intercepted the disastrous consequences that would have otherwise befallen us, and in their place He mercifully changed both us and our situation.

In brief, we can say from this scripture that we were dead and God made us alive. We walked according to the course of this world, but God created us new in Christ Jesus, having prepared good works beforehand that we might walk in them. We were all in the dunghill of degradation, but God seated us together with Christ in heavenly places. We were by nature children of wrath, but God made us by nature His children. Satan accused us, but God justified us through the shed blood of His dear Son. Instead of a lost eternity, He gave us an inheritance that is incorruptible and reserved in heaven.

Our works could have never achieved what His grace performed and provided. Paul contrasts how we ought now to be in comparison with what we used to be. We are not to be deceived; for neither fornicators, nor idolaters, nor adulterers, nor effeminate, nor homosexuals shall inherit the kingdom of God. God washed and sanctified us. He justified us in the name of our Lord Jesus Christ and in the Spirit of our God. We were among the lost, but God sought and saved us. Thank you, Lord!

For the Lord has chosen Zion; He has desired it for His habitation. "This is my resting place forever; here I will dwell, for I have desired it." Ps.132:13,14.

Here I Will Dwell

In our flesh dwells no good thing, for we were utterly fallen. However, we are no longer in the flesh, but in the Spirit, if indeed the Spirit of God dwells within us. In place of indwelling sin and every evil intention is the indwelling Christ.

The body of sin, given over to all manner of greed and lust, has undergone a transformation. Our old man was crucified with Jesus so that the body of sin might be rendered powerless. We have been cleansed by His blood. We have been washed with the water of the word. We have received the washing of regeneration and the renewal of the Holy Spirit. This is house cleaning *par excellence*. Such sanctification fits us to be God's desired resting place.

With our new nature comes our new heart which is pure, and our new spirit joined to His Spirit. Our bodies become temples of the Holy Spirit, and a mystery is now revealed: God makes His abode in us.

From within our hearts come new desires for the knowledge of our Lord and the awareness of His presence. Our faith embraces goals that were unattainable in our flesh. We hear His voice, see with the eyes of spiritual understanding, and can know Him increasingly.

Spiritual life must become our dominant awareness, and a living reality. Instead of being led by diverse lusts, we are led by His Spirit. He has totally gutted the inside and rebuilt it as it pleases Him. God has desired His people to be His resting place forever. Some house-cleaning He leaves to you. Cleanse yourself from all filthiness of the flesh and spirit, and keep yourself pure.

The manifold wisdom of God might now be made known by the church to the rulers...in heavenly places. Eph. 3:10

The Manifold Wisdom of God

The church was destined to make known the manifold wisdom of God. There will be glory in the church because Jesus, the Lord of glory, is Head of the church. We have all received of His fulness, and together we make up His fulness. Only in the context of all saints can we comprehend what is the length, breadth, depth and height of the immense, manifold Christ. The measure of faith, gifting and grace afforded to each individual will give a glorious collective expression of Christ.

Manifold means variegated, multifaceted or of many kinds. Each member of the body has a particular function, but ultimately it is the whole body that gives the various functions their context. A severed limb or disjointed member is not seen as the miraculous functional part of the body that it is when it is joined and in place. The church will not finish up dismembered or decapitated, but as a perfect man, with Christ the Head of His body. The church displays the rich wisdom of God, not only to the world around us, but to principalities and powers in heavenly places.

God's purpose in redemption; the great love and grace that He continually exercises towards us; the poor, the weak and the foolish that He has chosen to save; the babes to whom He is pleased to reveal Himself—these speak of His unsearchable wisdom and understanding. Whatever we were naturally, however inept and unsuitable, God has taken us up and transformed us with the life of His Son. No one can justly criticize God or blame or accuse Him. The church will demonstrate His wisdom to all.

Thanks be to God for His indescribable gift. 2 Cor.9:15

God's Indescribable Gift

God is a giver. Unless He gave we would be without. Life is a gift. The ability to breathe air as well as air itself is a gift. He causes His rain and sunshine to come upon the just and the unjust. None of us have anything that we were not given, which is why no one can boast. An old hymn tells us that out of His infinite riches in Jesus, God gives and gives and gives again. David said that daily He loads us with benefits. The variety of gifts is vast, but when God gave His Son, the Lord Jesus, He gave the most He could give.

Jesus, the indescribable gift, was despised and rejected of men, but to those who receive Him, He gives the power to become sons of God. Jesus held nothing back. He gave His all. He took upon Himself the form of a servant, becoming poor that we through His poverty might be made rich. He humbled Himself, that we might be exalted. He suffered and died, that we might live.

The worth of the gift of Jesus with the accompanying blessings is indescribable, and man proves his insanity by refusing to receive Him. Although we cannot add to God, by His grace we can give to Him. We can give thanks, praise and worship, and present ourselves to God as His servants—spirit, soul and body.

Through new birth you now have the nature of the Giver. Having freely received so much, you must now freely give, generously and continually. God loves a cheerful giver. When you give to the least of His brethren you give to Him.

I bow my knees before the Father. Eph. 3:14

I Bow the Knees

We express ourselves to God in various ways, from weeping to rejoicing, from quietness to exuberance, but bowing our knees before our Maker and Master must be a regular feature of our lifestyle. Bowing before Him should be a consistent attitude of heart in whatever circumstance we find ourselves. Worship is a posture of the heart, and our whole life is to be a living sacrifice. However, that does not exclude the necessity of physically bending the knees. Pagan people bow themselves before their gods, who are demons. The call to worship cries out over all Islam, and with shoes removed, thousands bow before their false god.

With all the wonder of God's grace that has fitted us for union with Himself, it is still fitting that along with our love we adopt an attitude of humility and godly fear. Never become so over-familiar with God that you lose the sense of His awesome majesty. When John saw the glorified Jesus, as close as he had been to Him on earth, he still fell at His feet as if dead. Bow the knees before Him daily. That act will enhance the necessary perspective of who God is and who we are.

In heaven they fall down before Him in their worship. Have you ever fallen prostrate before Him, declaring your worship and adoration? Do it more often. The alternative to "I bow my knees" is "I do not bow my knees," and that is unthinkable. Worship the Lord in the beauty of holiness. Bow down before Him and proclaim the glory of your Redeemer.

If earthly majesties and false gods receive homage and the bended knee daily, how much more the true and living Lord God almighty.

So that you may walk in a manner worthy of the Lord. Col.1:10

Walk Worthily of the Lord

One of the wonders of our salvation is that we can walk worthily of God. Although our calling could not be any higher, we can attain to a walk that is worthy of our calling. The essential ingredients and necessary characteristics for a worthy walk are humility and gentleness. Being poor of spirit is a prerequisite for the meekness that Christians should display. How else could we ever turn the other cheek, walk the extra mile and esteem others better than ourselves.

The love that preserves unity will be tested and will demand of us patience and forbearance. Diligent, constant watchfulness and expressed love are ever-present needs if we are to walk worthily of the Lord and remain in fellowship with others.

There is only one body of Christ; however, the fragmentation of the church cries out for repentance and the unity that is in Christ. The antithesis of humility is pride. The sin of pride includes thinking more highly of ourselves than we ought and disdaining others, believing ourselves to be superior. Not recognizing our dependence upon others is a form of pride. Promotion of self and lack of a servant's heart are not worthy of God.

Jesus, as always, is the supreme example. He was not humbled, but rather He humbled Himself and took upon Himself the form of a servant. He came, not to be served, but to serve, even to the point of laying down of His life. This same Jesus is your life, and when through love you serve His body, then you walk worthily of your Head and provide the basis for true unity.

He has sent Me to proclaim liberty to the captives. Luke 4:18

Liberty for the Captives

Jesus is the Liberator, and there are many scriptures referencing the variety of things from which man has been liberated. The word used in this text for liberty means simply to "send away" as when a captive is released.

The term deliverance is used today in connection with exorcism, or the casting out of demons. Both Jesus and the apostles cast out demons. Demon possession is certainly no less prevalent today. Regrettably, the gospel preached today is often dispossessed of the casting out of demons. This accounts for the deficient experiences of some "converts" who find themselves constantly plagued by defeat and sin.

Demon possession is a condition singled out in Scripture like many other conditions, but not every convert needed to have deliverance ministry. When the casting out of demons is necessary, then it should occur as exemplified in the New Testament, that is, in the name of the Lord Jesus. Further, nowhere in the New Testament is deliverance ministry offered to believers who have already been freed.

If Christians who are walking in newness of life without demonic possession become entangled with demonic oppression, then the responsibility for their release rests upon themselves as individuals. Repentance removes the ground upon which Satan stands; therefore, the Christian can deliver himself.

The power of the human heart to be desperately wicked is not accredited to demons, and we have no mandate or ability to cast out someone else's flesh. When James calls Christians sinners, he does not attribute the responsibility of their sin to Satan. Their deliverance comes through their repentance.

And that you be renewed in the spirit of your mind. Eph. 4:23

Renewed in the Spirit of Your Mind

Having started this chapter by telling us how to walk worthy of our calling, Paul continues to explain why we ought not to walk like the unconverted world. They walk in the futility of their mind, being darkened in their understanding, alienated from the life of God. We all lived in ignorance once, calloused and given over to sensuality and the practice of every kind of impurity with greediness. By contrast, Paul cites the life of Christ, from which we now learn.

We have received the invitation from Jesus to learn of Him, and in doing so we are taught totally different behavior. A transformation takes place beyond the mind. It renews the spirit of our minds. Our thoughts are formulated by our spirits. When we were dead in our sins, we walked according to the spirit that now works in the children of disobedience. When we were born again, we received a new heart and a new spirit, His Spirit, by which we can now walk.

The new heart has different motives, appetites, wisdom and objectives. Therefore, as part of the renewal that we are undergoing, we must put off our old man and mind and former behavior, and put on the new man with a renewed mind, created in true righteousness and holiness. We can guard our minds by setting them on eternal things where Christ is seated.

Satan was at work in us, but at this moment God is at work in us to will and to do His good pleasure. Work out what God is working in you, and show the change Jesus brings. Please the Spirit and grieve Satan by resisting him.

But we all, with unveiled face beholding as in a mirror the glory of the Lord, are being transformed into the same image from glory to glory. 2 Cor.3:18

We Are Being Changed

Our new birth brought a radical change of spirit, heart and mind. Our citizenship changed, for we were translated from the kingdom of darkness into the kingdom of light. Our nature, name, function, direction and purpose were changed. The change that began must be continued until the transformation is complete. As we walk in obedience to what we know of the Lord, then the inner change becomes outwardly evident.

The glory of God is revealed in the face of Jesus, and we can look into His face through the eyes of our understanding and be changed into His image. Being changed from glory to glory is not a mere platitude, but a vital experience for every true believer. Another word for change is growth. We must grow up into Christ in all aspects of our personality, growing out of what character-ized us naturally and into what characterizes Jesus.

How and what we eat and drink determines our natural growth. The same principle applies to our spiritual growth. Jesus invites us to partake of Him, to eat His flesh and drink His blood, for in so doing we change into His image. Taste and see that the Lord is really good.

This process of sanctification is to continue until the day when He who is coming will come. At that time there will be another dramatic change, when in the twinkling of an eye our mortal shall put on immortality.

If the incorruptible seed is already growing within you, then give full attention to the implications of Christ in you, and be changed into His likeness.

Being diligent to preserve the unity of the Spirit in the bond of peace. Eph. 4:3

Fellowship Should Be Functional

Armchair and fringe Christians who belong to the T.V. church never experience what the Lord wants them to through fellowship and relationships. The proper working of each individual occurs only in the context of the body. Being members one of another indicates how necessary we are to each other. No one can say to any part of the body, "I have no need of you." All the rigors, stresses and strains of functioning with one another are essential ingredients for growth. "Who needs the aggravation?" may be used as an excuse for not gathering with other Christians, but it will not hold up before the Lord.

He gave His life for the church and still loves her. He is at work building His church, and anyone who is not gathering with Him is scattering. If we are not building up His body, then we must take heed that we are not siding with the destroyer. Satan laughs up his sleeve at the way many Christians do his job for him. What we do to the least of Christ's brothers we do to Christ. What we fail to do we fail to do to Him.

We were designed by God to grow **together** with others in His body. Beyond the deficiencies that Christians have is the life of Jesus that is to be shared. We need His body, as His body needs us.

Millions of Christians daily experience love and edification from their fellow believers. The alternative to being bound to each other is to be loosed, and that takes us back to armchair Christianity. Fulfillment, maturity and identity are found only in His body. The church is His body, the fulness of Him who fills all things.

Therefore be imitators of God, as beloved children. Eph.5:1

Imitators of God

Those fathered by God can imitate Him as His children because they have been created in righteousness and true holiness. Imitating does not mean putting on an act, for that is unnecessary if we now bear His likeness. Sharing the life of the Lord Jesus and partaking of the divine nature enable us to think, speak and live like God. Jesus revealed that the life of God was possible in flesh and blood. His Father is now our Father, and He is not ashamed to call us brethren.

Jesus exhorts us to manifest the evidence that we are God's children in our attitude toward each other. He also exhorts us to be children of our heavenly Father in our responses to our enemies who persecute us. In both instances we testify to our Father by expressing His love.

God is love, and if we are His children, we display His likeness most evidently when we love. We are to walk in love and to love as He loved. Being imitators does not mean producing an imitation, indicating an inferior quality of life. Christ is our life, and as the Holy Spirit teaches us concerning our Lord, then we are to know that what is true in Him is also true in us.

Putting off the old man and putting on the new man is done from within. The mystery that was hidden has now been revealed, Christ in us. Imitating God as His children means expressing Him from within. The reason Paul was a savor of Christ is the same reason we can be like that.

Learn not to see yourself apart from God in a way that denies the provisions of the new covenant for your unity with Him. Imitating is being.

Making the most of your time, because the days are evil. Eph.5:16

Make the Most of Your Time

Time was created by God for the fulfilling of His purposes. Jesus came in the fulness of time. While here on earth, He was conscious of His timing, saying at one time, "My hour has not yet come." He fulfilled His time to the last hour. Satan and demons know that their time is short and that they will be destroyed at the time appointed for them. Even Jerusalem, the center of God's people, did not know the time of her visitation.

Paul exhorts us to make the most of the opportunities that time permits. There is time to do all that God wants us to accomplish. God is not short of time. Jesus was never short of time, and at the end of His life He said to His Father that He had finished the work He had been given to do. Paul also testified that he had finished the course and the time of his departure had come. King Saul's sad commentary on his own life was that he had erred exceedingly and played the fool.

We have all the time in the world to do what God wants. If we lack time to do what we should do, we betray that we are doing what we should not do. We may need to adjust our priorities.

There is much to lure us into wasting our time. The vain pleasures of sin appear in manifold varieties, geared by Satan to distract, to deceive and to destroy. The exhortation to use time purposefully is surrounded by charges to be wise and not foolish. The television has become the biggest time-waster of our time. Do not let it be the household idol. To waste time is to miss God's timing in your life. Redeem what is left.

Always giving thanks for all things in the name of our Lord Jesus Christ to God, even the Father. Eph.5:20

Giving Thanks FOR All Things

A continually thankful frame of mind requires a total acceptance of God's sovereignty in one's life. If our life is hid with Christ in God, then everything that comes to us must come through God. If God is for us, who or what can be against us? If we love God and are called according to His purpose, then all things do work together for our good; therefore, we can give thanks for all things. Even God's discipline is for our good, that we might partake of His holiness.

If Satan stands against us, it is by God's permission, and it will work for our benefit, even to teach us to fight the good fight. Whether it is tribulation, affliction, persecution or suffering, we can count it all joy because it teaches us endurance with patience. What appears to be against us is in fact for us because all things are for us.

Satan has never been a free agent. He is a defeated foe and can only act within the bounds that God sets. He knows that God has appointed his end, and there is nothing he can do about that. Satan cannot do what he pleases when he pleases. God sees to it that we cannot be tempted beyond what we are able to endure. Satan was rendered powerless at Calvary. We can now resist him by being steadfast in the faith, causing him to flee from us.

Paul reminds us that all things are ours, whether Paul, Apollos, or Peter, or the world or life or death or things present or things to come. Therefore, you can genuinely receive with thanks all that comes your way, for it all comes under the sovereign hand of God upon your life.

And he will restore the hearts of the fathers to their children, and the hearts of the children to their fathers. Mal. 4:6

Fathers and Children

With the eroding of God's word as the basis for law, and the acceptance of humanistic philosophy, the breakdown of family life has been inevitable. The lack of moral consciousness produces dishonesty, covenant-breaking and the loss of self-control. When the role models in the home are self-centered and irresponsible, how can integrity and responsibility be expected from the children?

Children have been taught by parents who blame and punish them for imitating them. How many fathers have abdicated their responsibilities and deserted both wife and children? Even the tragedy of abortion must fall squarely on the shoulders of those who fathered the victims to mutilation and death. The hearts of such fathers are against their children. Little wonder that the children are in turn against their fathers.

As with all human dilemmas, the answer is in Jesus Christ. One of the signs preceding His return is that the hearts of the fathers will be turned to the children and the hearts of the children to the fathers. Family relationships cry out for this to happen. (Lord please turn the hearts.) The first responsibility belongs to the parent. Then the responsibility for the right response belongs to the child.

The generation gap sadly deprives parents and children of expressed mutual love. God's ways produce successful relationships, but His ways must be learned and obeyed. Inestimable blessings of deep joy through shared love are God's design for the family. He can reverse what has been shattered and build it again if we heed His word.

Put on the full armor of God. Eph.6:11

The Full Armor of God

God is a God of war. He fights, but never loses. His armor is impenetrable and His weapons unconquerable. Jesus embodied the eternal attributes in flesh and blood. He overcame the world, the flesh and the devil with a defeat that was absolute. The armor we are to put on is not ours, but God's. It now fits us because Jesus proved it as a man. We can now triumph in His triumph and conquer because He conquered.

Having now the same spirit of faith, we can overcome the world, the flesh and the devil. Our weapons are mighty through God, and our strength is in the Lord and the power of His might. When we put on all God's armor and wield the sword of the Spirit, we are invincible. We must be reminded that we do not wrestle against flesh and blood and that the weapons of our warfare are not carnal. The war is a spiritual war, and the focus is upon principalities and powers, upon the rulers of darkness and spiritual wickedness in high places. The fight is not against man, but against the spirit of disobedience.

We are exhorted to resist the devil and he will flee from us because He that is in us is greater than he that is in the world. Jesus wrote the judgment of this world and cast Satan out nearly two thousand years ago, so all we have to do is execute the judgment written. That honor is given to all who work out their great salvation, who walk by faith in truth and righteousness, who have the word of God in their hearts and are always ready to speak it and who give time and attention to prayer. That is also how to put on the armor of God.

Stand firm therefore, having girded your loins with truth.
Eph. 6:14

Girded with Truth

Truth is referred to here allegorically as the girding of our loins. Peter tells us to gird up the loins of our mind. To put it bluntly, if we are going to fight, it does not matter how good our weapons are if while we are fighting our trousers fall down!

Truth is foundational to being fit and ready to fight. It is sure and certain ground, as opposed to the uncertain ground of lies. Jesus is the truth. All that He was and did was in truth. He never had a conflict within His conscience as He engaged in the fight. Truth in the inward parts is required of us. A clear conscience girds us up for battle, while condemnation makes us unfit for warfare. The battle is already lost when we bring guilt upon ourselves because of our lack of truth and integrity. Any crookedness loosens our girding, and we cannot fight while trying to hold up our pants.

The devil is a liar from the beginning, and there is no truth in him. Falling to lies causes us to yield to the devil. The warfare then rages within. How many Christians never get to the place where they engage the enemy out there because they are defeated by the enemy within? Only those whose loins are girded with truth can fight in the heavenlies.

All lies will ultimately fall to the truth—all lies about God, all lies about creation and all lies about us. Liars shall not inherit the kingdom of God. Therefore, we are to walk in truth, speak the truth and rejoice in the truth, even when exposed by it. David said that he had chosen the way of truth. Do not hide from the truth, but choose the truth and abide in Him.

Paul, an apostle of Christ Jesus...to the saints who are at Ephesus, and faithful in Christ Jesus. Eph.1:1

Paul's Letter to the Ephesians

This letter was sent by a converted Jew to converted Gentiles nearly two thousand years ago. As with all Scripture, it is timeless in revelation and relevance. In the first ten verses it covers such gigantic themes as predestination, adoption, the mystery of His will, redemption and the summing up of all things in Christ. The sheer weight of revelation, couched in words that are pregnant with life, is a constant source of amazement and disclosure for the ardent student. At the very center of this revelation, the apostle, moved by the Holy Spirit, focuses our attention on the aim of God for Christians.

His first prayer is that God would give us a spirit of wisdom and revelation in the knowledge of Him, the eyes of our heart being enlightened so that we might know the three great *what's* of that prayer.

In his second prayer, the focal point of this letter, he prays three great *that's*: "That Christ may dwell in your hearts by faith; that you, being rooted and grounded in love; and that you may be filled up to all the fulness of God."

From revelation he turns to the application of God's purposes and how they will be achieved through His body, the church. The practical outworking of relationships is the setting for the fulfillment of God's goals. Finally, we are instructed in both the fact and the art of spiritual warfare and in the necessity of persevering in prayer. In less than thirty minutes one can read this letter and enjoy fellowship with its profound mysteries.

It was for freedom that Christ set us free, therefore keep standing firm and do not be subject again to a yoke of slavery. Gal.5:1

Stand in Your Freedom

There are many forms and degrees of bondage, oppression and slavery that man experiences. The greatest, common to all, is the bondage to corruption and the fear of death because of sin. Man is enslaved to sin in its variety of facets. The lusts of deceit move unregenerate man with impulses that drive like a hard taskmaster, and from which there is no natural escape. Overriding of the conscience brings the bondage of condemnation. The willful searing of the conscience is a vain attempt to relieve the weight of guilt.

All humanity is held captive, and all his lifetime man is subject to bondage. Jesus came to set us free and bring liberty to the captives. He is the promised deliverer who bound the strong one who held us in bondage. Jesus was never bound by sin, and as a man He overcame the world, the flesh and the devil.

Whoever the Son sets free is free indeed—free from sin, free from guilt, free from the fear of death and ultimately free from corruption. In Jesus we now have liberty to enter the holiest place of all and to stand confidently in the presence of almighty God, in all the awesome purity of His holiness. The liberty we can enjoy in Jesus is called the glorious liberty of the sons of God.

If you are conscious of bondage and slavery to the dominion of sin, then cry out by reason of your bondage to Him who is able to save. He did not come just to try and save, but to actually save all who call upon Him. Jesus accomplished the bringing in of a law higher than that of sin and death; it is the law of the spirit of life that sets absolutely free.

But we all, with unveiled face beholding as in a mirror the glory of the Lord, are being transformed into the same image from glory to glory. 2 Cor.3:18

Transformation

To transform means to change form or appearance, not just a little, but radically, as when a caterpillar is transformed into a butterfly. New birth is a crisis experience that transforms the heart and spirit of the believer and makes him a new creature. At whatever age a convert is born of the Spirit, he starts off as a babe. The initial transformation of the inner man develops to where the whole personality matures and the life of Jesus is manifested in the mortal body.

It is God who has shone in our hearts to give the light of the glory of God in the face of Jesus Christ. We now have the veil taken away, and we can look to Jesus and be transformed into the same image, from glory to glory.

The key to being changed is to keep our focus upon the Lord Jesus and our new habitation, the kingdom of heaven. As our hearts are set on Him and His righteousness, with our affections directed towards His pleasure and will, the Holy Spirit involves us in a glorious transformation. Instead of being conformed to this world we are transformed by the renewing of our minds.

Stagnation and retardation are the result of letting our minds be caught up in the cares of this world and the deceitfulness of riches. What sort of transformation occurred at your new birth? In what way has the transformation developed since then? These are relevant questions which require needed self-examination. Most of the seven churches of Asia were quite out of touch with the Lord's appraisal of them. How much we are like the Lord betrays the amount of time we have spent with Him.

For those whom the Lord loves He disciplines, and He scourges every son whom He receives. Heb.12:6

Discipline Is for Disciples

Being a disciple involves being a follower and a learner of Christ, with all the necessary disciplines. The Lord Jesus learned obedience by the things He suffered, leaving us an example to follow. There are different forms of discipline. Goals discipline us. If our goal is to win a race, then that desire becomes the motivation for the rigors of training: eating and drinking the right things, denying the wrong things, getting enough sleep, working hard and pushing ourselves for maximum performance.

If our goal is to be like Jesus, we have the motivation to discipline ourselves to that end. We can test the level of our desire to be like Him by how disciplined we are in reaching forward and pressing in to apprehend our aim.

Fear of punishment is a discipline. It curbs sin. How often have you braked when seeing a police car? If all threat of retribution were removed and there were no accountability, there would be wholesale carnage and unbridled wickedness.

Then there is punishment itself as a discipline. The Lord chastens those whom He loves and scourges **every** child He receives. It is for our good, even though at the time it may be grievous to us, because by punishment the faculties are trained to respond the right way. The soul that is exposed to discipline takes steps forward in the development of Christlike character.

Do not despise the discipline of the Lord, for through it you become a partaker of His holiness. Judging and disciplining yourself is a mark of maturity and makes you a wise son.

And the angel said to them, "I bring you good news of a great joy which shall be for all the people." Luke 2:10

Good News

Good news is the missing element in the general run of news items. Tragedies, cruelty, violence in its many ugly forms and unnumbered fearful prospects are all graphically transmitted daily. Little wonder there is so much despair, with suicide at one end of the spectrum and living for the pleasure of the moment at the other.

Mankind lives under the dominating influence of the prospect of death. Into this environment God sends us with the news of His love and deliverance. As the disastrous history of mankind unfolded, God was there giving progressive revelation through His servants, the prophets, concerning the One who was to bring hope and eternal life.

The good news came in the person of Jesus Christ, God's Son. He came and preached deliverance to the captives and peace with God. Through forgiveness and reconciliation He removed the curse. Even death itself was to be conquered and abolished as eternal life and union with God were established. The terms bondage and slavery are used in conjunction with sin, death and corruption, proving that we were not created for them. Jesus is the one who alone can free us from this wretched body of death, and there is no one outside of His reach.

We cannot purchase or earn our justification before God, but it will cost us everything, including our own life. The good news is that God has provided for the death of our old, evil selves in the death of His Son, Jesus, and when He rose from the dead, He raised us up together with Him.

If you have received Jesus as your Savior, tell others the good news about Him.

Not by might nor by power, but by My Spirit, says the Lord.
Zech. 4:6

By the Spirit of the Lord

When this word of the Lord came to Zerubbabel, it was to contrast the might and the power of man with what God does by His Spirit. God alone builds eternal things, but we can be workers together with Him by His Spirit. To enter His kingdom we must be born of His Spirit. We can mortifying the deeds of the body, and achieve the will and work of God by His Spirit alone.

The natural forces of carnality are no substitute for the work of the Spirit. Jesus told His disciples that they were to receive power after the Holy Spirit had come upon them, and then they would be His witnesses. That is still the only way that we can be His witnesses. The Holy Spirit is the author of what is to be done, and He is the power to perform it. If we have been made alive by the Spirit, then let us also walk in the Spirit, and not fulfill the lusts of the flesh.

The Holy Spirit is the comforter, the teacher and guide who leads the sons of God. Our gifts are from Him, and He gives individually as He wills. Jesus was born of the Spirit, anointed and filled with the Spirit and led by the Spirit. He did everything that He did by the Spirit, even to offering Himself up. The Spirit raised Jesus from the dead, and Jesus is the one who baptizes us with the Holy Spirit.

The scourge of the church is uncrucified flesh. Natural abilities and strengths are no substitute for divine power. It is in our weakness that His strength is made perfect. He calls the poor, the weak and the foolish to demonstrate His riches, strength and wisdom. He gives the Spirit to those who ask, and who obey Him.

When Jesus had received the sour wine, He said, "It is finished!"
And He bowed His head and gave up His spirit. John 19:30

It Is Finished

What vast boundaries are contained within the little pronoun *it*. What, in fact, was finished? At the time when Jesus said it, His life was expiring on the cross, and with His death so much was finished. The rule of sin and the dominion of Satan were finished. Man was no longer limited by or in bondage to fallen human nature.

Jesus had condemned sin in the flesh by living a sinless life as a man. Having died to sin once for all, He was raised from the dead, bringing to an end the fear of death and providing hope of the resurrection. Death itself was dealt the death blow. The law of the spirit of life in Christ Jesus now sets us free from the law of sin and death.

All the ordinances that were written against us in heaven, everything that was hostile to us, He took away, nailing them to His cross. Jesus finished in His death much more than we can imagine. Before Jesus went to the cross He said that He had accomplished the work that the Father had given Him to do. He had conclusively proved that divine nature could inhabit flesh and blood. Then on the cross the next phase of the plan of redemption was completed. "It is finished," was the cry of confidence that rang out across every realm of creation in heaven and earth.

All that the prophets had foretold, all the types and figures were fulfilled, and God's purpose for the purchase of man's salvation was finished. Believe His finished work for your redemption. Believe that the dominion of your old man is finished by your death in His death, and enjoy freedom from sin and a new beginning.

Break up your fallow ground, and do not sow among thorns.
Jer. 4:3

How to Prepare the Ground

Preparing the way of the Lord is a task that involves us all. There are individual and corporate aspects of preparation. Individual responsibility is a priority and leads us into the corporate. The fallow ground we are to break up is the hardened and uncultivated areas that are unfruitful for God in our lives. The weeds of carnality grow there, but not the fruit of the Spirit.

Self-examination and prayerful consideration are necessary under the Spirit's illumination to reveal waste ground. Breaking it up means working on the ground by turning it over, and that takes effort. Such application makes rooting out, destroying, plucking up and pulling down former behavior easier. If the Jesus that overcame sin and all temptation is now the strength and source of our life, then we can do it all through Him. The work of preparation must be thorough, drastic and radical. It may mean just what Jesus indicated, the figurative plucking out of the right eye or the cutting off of the right hand, but such violent purging from all filthiness of the flesh and spirit is required.

This is not a feather-duster job. It is at least a sharp-knife job, and beyond that it may take a bulldozer, but in Christ we have the ability, by faith, to say to this mountain, "Be removed," and it shall be done.

What is the failing in your life that looms as large as a mountain in its intimidation of you and seduces you more than anything else? That is the ground to be broken up in order for the incorruptible seed to bear fruit. You can break up the fallow ground. You can do all that is necessary through Christ who strengthens you.

Although He was a Son, He learned obedience from the things He suffered. Heb 5:8

The Necessity of Suffering

Suffering is included in the "all things" that work together for good to those who love God. Jesus learned obedience by the things He suffered and was made perfect through them. His suffering was not on account of any wrong He had done; nevertheless, He suffered.

There are three main causes for suffering, which call for differing responses. Firstly, we can suffer for wrong we have done. Sin is a common cause of suffering. Even after the Lord forgives us, there may be consequences, for reaping what we have sown is an ongoing principle. Suffering for sins committed can be the very instrument in the hand of God to humble us and bring about repentance.

Secondly, suffering at the hands of an adversary in the context of spiritual warfare does not call for repentance, but a fight. The fight is not against flesh and blood, but against spiritual forces. God teaches our hands how to war, and instead of enduring the problem, He teaches us how to overcome in the strength and the name of Jesus.

Thirdly, suffering can be a necessity to learn patience and endurance. Job is held out as an example of patience through suffering. Jesus Himself is the supreme example, and we must learn of Him. A revelation of God's perspective on suffering would enable us to appreciate it to the point that we could glory even in tribulation. Tribulation works patience for us, and we must let patience have its perfect work. How else can we count it all joy when we enter into various trials?

Whatever the cause, the Lord wants us to respond the right way and become partakers of His holiness.

Consider it all joy, my brethren, when you encounter various trials. James 1:2

The Desirability of Trials

If it is desirable to know the genuineness of natural gold—how much impurity it contains or whether it is merely fool's gold—then how much more desirable should be the trial of our faith, proving what sort it is. The fiery trial manifests the dross of mixture and reveals fool's faith.

Many people have fool's faith, the useless faith to which James refers. Jesus said that **many** will say to Him, "Lord, we preached in Your name, prophesied in Your name, cast out demons in Your name and performed miracles in Your name." His response will be that He knew their iniquitous works but never knew them.

Genuine faith grows through trials, while fool's faith fails. A consciousness of eternal possessions gives a perspective that enables us to receive joyfully the loss of our temporal possessions. Jesus said that we should rejoice and be exceeding glad when being persecuted for the sake of righteousness, for great is our reward in heaven. We can endure the outward man perishing, even though we might groan a little, if we have the assurance that our inner man is being renewed daily.

Unjust suffering is the great violator of the old man. The Spirit of God and of glory rests upon those who suffer unjustly for Him. Peter goes on to say that it is sometimes necessary and according to the will of God that we suffer. God desires to do us good in the end. Making ourselves ready for our presentation in the perfection of beauty will one day prove to have been worthwhile. The sufferings of this life are truly not worthy to be compared with the glory that shall be revealed in us.

Gird your minds for action, keep sober. 1 Pet.1:13

Gird Your Minds for Action

Peter puts a perspective before persecuted Christians that is designed to lift their spirits. It is the revelation of Jesus Christ and the grace that is to be theirs at His appearing. He reminds them of the larger scene and greater purpose so that they will not grow weary under the present pressure. He incites them to gird up their minds, to think soberly, and to be alert and psychologically prepared for action; that is, action that is commensurate with the destruction of this present world and with the encounter we shall all have with Christ at His coming.

Act according to what you are as a child of God. Listen to Him, obey Him, love Him and walk with Him. Do not be conformed to the former lusts which were yours in your ignorance, when you were unmindful of your accountability to God. Having now been enlightened, our behavior should display our newly created state of holiness.

Actions are the outworking of thoughts, which in turn are formulated by the spirit of a man. We gird up the loins of our mind by being fervent in spirit, not by being neglectful. His appearing is the incentive to purify ourselves in order to appear with Him. Our life here on earth is a necessary step to equip us for our eternal calling.

We endure as seeing Him who is invisible until we see Him face to face. Is that your hope? The more you live conscious of the presence of the Lord, the more you will live accordingly. The enemy wants to rob you of your life with Jesus as well as your reward. Actively resist him steadfast in the faith.

But the word of the Lord abides forever. 1 Pet.1:25

The Word of the Lord

When God spoke the worlds into being, His thoughts materialized. We understand that the universe came into being and is upheld by the word of His power. It is like a hammer, like a fire, living and powerful, enduring forever. It is the incorruptible seed by which we are born again. The Word that was in the beginning with God and was God became flesh and dwelt among us. Jesus Christ is Emmanuel, God with us. All who receive Him are born again of His seed and have the seed within themselves and can sow that seed to others.

His word is powerful like light dispelling the darkness. It brings us from death to life. We who have been made alive by this word are now to live by His word, not by bread alone. His word is to abide in us richly so that we can admonish and edify each other. We are commended to the word of His grace, which is able to build us up and give us an inheritance among those who are sanctified.

His word is written upon our hearts, and by it our minds are renewed. We express the word that is in our hearts by obeying. Being doers of the word is the only valid response to the word. Faith comes by hearing the word of God, and all things are possible to him who has faith.

To merely agree with the word is not sufficient. To store the word just for information has no merits. Transformation takes place only when the word is heeded. Although much obedience is required of those who receive much, much is accomplished in those who obey. Through obedience all the power of the word is released within you to conform you to Christ.

You also, as living stones, are being built up as a spiritual house for a holy priesthood. 1 Pet.2:5

We Are a Spiritual House

Both Peter and Paul teach that Christians are a spiritual house. We are being built together into a dwelling place of God in the Spirit. We are living stones, built upon Jesus, the foundation and corner stone. His life is in all the stones and gives the house its identity as a dwelling of God.

The fulness of the Godhead dwelt in Jesus bodily. As those joined to the Lord, we are to discard all things that do not correspond to a holy environment, all that is not congenial to His holy habitation. We are to divest ourselves of all malice, guile, hypocrisy, envy and slander. In contrast, we are to offer spiritual sacrifices and bear the fruit of the Spirit.

As a holy nation and a spiritual priesthood, we are to present our bodies a living sacrifice unto God. Taking up our cross daily and dying daily are other ways of saying that we are putting off the old man that was crucified with Jesus.

The financial support that the Philippian church gave to Paul was a fragrant aroma and an acceptable sacrifice, well pleasing to God. As a royal priesthood we can offer sacrifices of praise to God, that is the fruit of our lips, in thanksgiving to His name. Part of the spiritual activity in this spiritual house is to not neglect doing good and sharing, for these things are acceptable to God and please Him.

This house is not a cold, stone edifice, but a living habitation of the living God. Your mortal body is a temple of the Holy Spirit who indwells you. Make the Lord comfortable. Make Him feel at home in His temple.

But you are a chosen race, a royal priesthood, a holy nation, a people for God's own possession. 1 Pet.2:9

God's Special Treasure

If ever there was an antidote to poor self-image, it is the declaration that we are a chosen generation, a royal priesthood, a holy nation, a people for God's own possession. Peter is obviously alluding to Exodus 19:5-6, which says, "you shall be My special treasure among all the peoples....you shall be to Me a kingdom of priests and a holy nation." Paul writes the same thought in Titus 2:14: "Who gave Himself for us, that He might redeem us...and purify for Himself a people for His own possession."

What costly stones were skillfully shaped and placed to build the temple. How much more noble is the material used for God's permanent dwelling.

Jesus will build His church of living stones, and nothing can withstand that. The church is His special treasure, precious, purchased and purified to Himself. As Christians we are embraced by everlasting arms into the divine bosom and held close to the heart that has desired us greatly and loves us unceasingly. He wields His anger towards our enemies, and He taunts them with the threat that they who touch us touch the apple of His eye.

We are to God the pearl of great price. He gave all He could to purchase us. Of all creation, we are His special treasure. He has entrusted to us His very life to share in an indissoluble union with Him for all eternity.

He has chosen us to be heirs of salvation, joint heirs with Christ whom He has appointed heir of all things. How privileged we are to be partakers of Him and His glory. Show your gratitude with extravagant love and praise.

Beloved, I urge you as aliens and strangers to abstain from fleshly lusts, which wage war against the soul. 1 Pet.2:11

Aliens, Strangers and Pilgrims

The definitions of these terms are most instructive for the Christian. Alien means not one's own, under foreign allegiance, differing in nature, repugnant, belonging to another. A stranger is a person in a country or company to which he does not belong, where he is unknown. A pilgrim is one who journeys to a sacred place as an act of religious devotion, journeying to a future life.

Peter reminds us that we are aliens and strangers, or what is sometimes translated pilgrims, in this present world. We have an allegiance to another which makes us repugnant to the world. We are in the world but not of it. Jesus said that we are not of this world as He is not of this world. He and we were born from above by the Holy Spirit.

The world and its system will pass away with its lusts and corruption. That is why we have no continuing city here, but seek one to come. While we are in the world we are the light of the world. We are not to have fellowship with the unfruitful works of darkness, but rather reprove them.

Because the things of the world will be dissolved, we are to abstain from fleshly lusts that war against the soul. Denying ungodliness and worldly lusts we are to live righteously and soberly in this present world.

As citizens of another kingdom we are to testify to that kingdom, and to our Lord who called us out of the kingdom of darkness to shine as sons of light.

Mammon, materialism, the pleasures of sin for a season, and all the cares of this life, barrage the mind in their attempt to divert the Christian from his allegiance to Christ. The truly repentant sinner sees them all as the mire from which he was saved.

*Submit yourselves for the Lord's sake to every human institution,
whether to the king as the one in authority, or to governors...for
such is the will of God. 1 Pet.2:13-15*

Submitting to the Law

Peter instructs us to submit to every human ordinance for
the Lord's sake, or because of the Lord. Whether to kings, mag-
istrates or authorities, God desires that we submit to them and
keep the law. Paul states that there is no authority except from
God; therefore, he who resists authority opposes God's ordinance.
Those authorities that exist are established by God. Peter's argument continues to demonstrate the just condemnation and wrath
of God upon those who will not submit.

These clear commands were written under the rule and dominion of the Roman Empire where Caesar himself as emperor
was upheld as a god and received the Jews' taxes. Neither Jesus
nor the apostles advocated protests or rebellion. Even in the face
of the injustice of the law, they loved not their lives unto death.

Their defiance of the law came only when they were commanded to deny their faith, or to stop preaching Jesus. Their
reply was limited to what they were commanded, and that is very
important: "Whether it is right in the sight of God to give heed to
you rather than God, you judge."

If the law demands that we offend God, then we do what is
right in the sight of God. If the law allows sin but does not demand it, we have no mandate to physically impose our conscience
on the heathen. Moses' parents defied the law when they were
commanded to kill their baby, but we have no such demand upon
us in this nation yet.

Do not lose sight of the overall teaching of the Bible that
officers of the law are to be viewed as ministers of God and obeyed.

Servants be submissive to your masters with all respect, not only to those who are good. 1 Pet. 2:18

Submission and Respect

This admonition is couched between the declaration of our privileges as a chosen people and the example we have in the Lord Jesus. Our behavior towards civil authority and our attitude as employees is addressed. We may grumble and gripe at unfair treatment, but quite remarkably we are told that we were called for this purpose.

We are reminded of how Jesus was treated and how He responded. His example is plainly there for us to follow. We once pursued many vain things as we strayed, being driven by various lusts and passions—not just some of the time, but continually. But now we have returned to the Shepherd and Guardian of our souls. Now our sins have been borne away in Christ's crucified body so that we might die to sin and live righteously.

We will suffer for righteous living, but that is to be expected because we were ordained to express the life of our Lord through suffering. The responses of Jesus to unjust suffering are to be our responses. He was reviled but He did not revile in return. While He suffered He uttered no threats, but He entrusted Himself to Him who judges righteously. This response comes from knowing and trusting the sovereignty of God over our temporal circumstances.

Vengeance belongs to God. No one will get away with anything, but God will bring justice to light and judge even the hidden things. If you do what is right and suffer for it, you find favor with God. If for the sake of conscience you bear up under sorrows when suffering, the Spirit of God and glory rests upon you.

You husbands likewise, live with your wives in an understanding way, as with a weaker vessel. 1 Pet. 3:7

Men of Understanding

Every wife desires an understanding husband. He should be considerate and thoughtful, always cognizant that the woman is the weaker vessel. There are many and varied pressures that come upon a woman both from external circumstances and internal physical adjustments. As the head, the husband should absorb pressures and shield the woman from added stress. In practical terms, this will involve the man helping out in areas normally attributed to the wife and mother, such as taking the children off her hands to give her time for herself and the Lord.

Husbands have been given the grace to be a security for their families. Simply stated, they are to be to their wives as Christ is to the church. A man can do nothing greater to give his wife a sense of security than to be secure in his submission to his head, Christ.

The husband must honor his wife, for they are heirs together of the grace of life. She may be the weaker vessel, but she is not inferior. The price of the woman's salvation was the same as the man's. The woman has a differing role in which to function, but her role is still an expression of God.

Christ is in the woman as her life as well as in the man; therefore, the husband is to show due respect and esteem while exercising his role as head of the woman. Christ loved the church and gave Himself for her, and so also ought a man to love His wife. Jesus served us without fear that He was abdicating His headship, and He is our example.

But sanctify Christ as Lord in your hearts. 1 Pet. 3:15

Christ, the Only Lord in Your Heart

To separate Jesus as Lord in our hearts involves the removal of all other controlling factors. Jesus is not to share His place of authority with anyone or anything. No man can serve two masters. Jesus must be the only master. Confessing with the mouth that Jesus is Lord is only part of what produces salvation. Believing in our hearts that He is Lord is the priority and is key to experiencing His lordship.

Having an intellectual grasp that He is Lord does not necessarily constitute it as fact in our experience. We must resolve it in our hearts if it is to be effectual. Mere words and outward observances were the practice of the Pharisees, whom Jesus so scathingly rebuked. Jesus always referred them to the heart and thereby invalidated their outward performance.

When we consciously sanctify Jesus as Lord in our hearts, we are submitting to His rule alone. His voice is the one to follow, and His word the one by which to live. We can always test whether or not we have truly sanctified Jesus as Lord in our hearts by our obedience to Him. "Do you not know that when you present yourselves to someone as slaves for obedience, you are slaves of the one whom you obey, either of sin resulting in death, or of obedience resulting in righteousness?" (Rom. 6:16).

Paul commends the Roman Christians for obeying from the heart and calls them slaves to righteousness. Jesus dwells in your heart by faith. His pleasures and griefs will be known in your heart as you live by faith. What is the alternative to Him being the only Lord? The outcome of a union with Him should be to know Him, to love Him and to serve Him alone as Lord.

Keeping faith and a good conscience, which some have rejected and suffered shipwreck... 1 Tim.1:19

Keep a Good Conscience

The radical nature of the new birth furnishes us with a good conscience. Our consciences were defiled and evil, but the blood of Jesus has cleansed them from dead works. Paul testified that he did his utmost to maintain a conscience void of offense towards God and man. That is a helpful definition of a good conscience. A bad conscience is a violated conscience, aware of offenses committed. The consciousness of sin, a violation of our conscience, comes when we serve another lord. If we obey sin, then we bow as servants to sin, making it the master.

The born-again believer receives freedom from sin and its power by reason of a new heart in which Christ dwells. You now possess a superior power that enables you not to sin. "Sin shall not be master over you" (Rom.6:14). Living with more than one lord is an unacceptable mixture which produces a double mind. A divided heart never has a clear conscience, and it makes a man unstable in all his ways.

A bad conscience neutralizes the Christian. It is a major cause of the lack of evangelism, for who wants to share the good news if it is not true about himself? A guilty conscience robs us of joy and peace. The Holy Spirit is grieved when we resist and quench Him, and He lets us know that.

To violate our new conscience is to lie against the truth, the truth about us as God's children. If we constantly overrule our conscience we will gradually desensitize it until it is seared. We will become dull of hearing if we do not obey our conscience.

You formerly could not live above condemnation, but now you can maintain a good conscience.

*In the days of Noah...eight persons were brought safely through
the water. And corresponding to that, baptism now saves you.
1 Pet. 3:20, 21*

Baptism Now Saves You

This does not propose that a mere act of being submerged in water itself will save us. It has to do with being baptized with the baptism of Jesus, which is referred to in the Gospels. Jesus said that He had a baptism to be baptized with and that He was distressed until it was accomplished. He was speaking of His death, burial and resurrection, that was to be followed by His ascension and the outpouring of the Holy Spirit. It is our identification with Christ in His death, burial, resurrection and the baptism of the Holy Spirit that saves us.

Noah's baptism is referred to as a type of the baptism that Jesus was to bring. God destroyed all flesh except those in the ark when He baptized the earth with water. It was the destruction of sinful flesh, which pointed to what Jesus was to accomplish through the baptism of His death, where the destruction of our body of sin occurred.

Baptism has two elements, water and fire. The earth was baptized in water when it was submerged during the flood, and Peter tells us that it is now reserved for its final baptism with fire. Even Israel was baptized in to Moses in the cloud of the fiery pillar, and the sea.

John the Baptist declared that Jesus was the Lamb of God who takes away the sin of the world, and that Jesus would baptize with the Holy Spirit and fire. The baptism that now saves us does not nullify either of these aspects of the one baptism. The sacrifice of Jesus and the shedding of His blood for the remission of our sins was not a separate message from the good news of the outpouring of the Holy Spirit, in the early church, and should not be now.

You wives, be obedient to your own husbands. 1 Pet.3:1

Wives Be Submissive

The clear instruction for wives to be obedient to their husbands is diametrically opposed to feminist philosophy. Feminism is not only broadly accepted in the world, but rife in the church. The importance of rejecting feminism cannot be over-emphasized. Three times this same commandment appears in the New Testament. It is an indisputable doctrine given by the Holy Spirit for our instruction. Paul said that what he wrote was to be recognized as the Lord's commandment (1 Cor.14:37).

Submission to civil government is necessary to maintain order and avoid anarchy. Submission to employers is necessary, covering the economic structure. The domestic scene is particularly highlighted so as to be a testimony of Christ and the church, and God's beautiful order.

To submit means just that. The definition is to commit to the discretion or decision of another, to yield, to surrender. The order of Christ and the church is so beautifully portrayed in the relationship between a man and a woman. The behavior of the woman is to be respectful, with the imperishable qualities of a gentle and quiet spirit which is precious in the sight of God.

What reaction do you have to the following statement? "Let a woman quietly receive instruction with entire submissiveness" (1 Tim.2:11). You will know how much you have been affected by feminism by how much you disagree with it.

Sarah is held up as an example for women, calling her husband "lord." Such language denotes an attitude that is totally foreign to our generation, yet if the kingdom of God is to come, we are to embrace the God-pleasing expressions of life rather than the men- (women)-pleasing. We do not have the option to take it or leave it when it is clearly taught as part of the expression of the new covenant.

Be of sound judgment and sober spirit for the purpose of prayer.
1 Pet.4:7

A Mind for Prayer

Men should pray always, be devoted to prayer, and keep watchful not to neglect prayer. Peter exhorts us to be of a sober spirit for the purpose of prayer. This frame of mind does not contradict the joy of the Lord which brings a rejoicing heart, but addresses vain frivolity which does not consider the seriousness of the moment.

Thank the Lord for fun and laughter. Both are in Him and from Him, but for the purpose of prayer we are instructed to be of a sober spirit. We are more inclined to pray when we consider the seriousness of prevailing conditions. As we contemplate the plight of the lost, or even the reproach that the church is to Christ in all that goes on in His name, we realize the need for prayer.

Our generation more than any other has the means to be amused. Amuse means to not think. The amusement craze is designed to stop us thinking for ourselves. It gives no incentive to pray. "It is better to go into the house of mourning than the house of feasting, because that is the end of every man, and the living take it to heart. The mind of the wise is in the house of mourning, while the mind of the fool is in the house of pleasure" (Eccles.7:4).

We must devote ourselves to prayer. There are a multitude of vain pursuits that can engage our minds and distract us from prayer. The whole world of fantasy involves our minds in unreality and is an aspect of deception. The mind is dulled to the truth when constantly submerged in figments of fantasy.

The truth is sobering and cries out for the intervention of God. Prayer brings a supply of the Spirit. Stop and think of situations or of people that need such a supply, and pray.

Above all, keep fervent in your love for one another, because love covers a multitude of sins. 1 Pet.4:7

Keep Fervent Love

The phrase "above all" denotes the importance of maintaining a fervor in our love. Love can grow cold. When love begins to wane, we become less accommodating. Instead of a love that covers, a critical attitude takes over, and it becomes easier to uncover. Where the loss of love occurs there follows a loss of fellowship. We then spend less time with each other, and invitations to share decrease. We begin to practice hospitality only grudgingly, until it is no longer exercised. We even cease to use the gifts we have received to build up one another.

Those who were once inseparable separate with little or no concern. At that point the body divides, individuals are weakened by negative attitudes, and Satan laughs up his sleeve. What God had joined for mutual edification becomes dissipated and isolated by broken fellowship.

Perhaps we can understand why Peter puts so much emphasis on keeping fervent love for one another. The body builds itself up with love, so love must be carefully maintained. It requires diligent application. Jesus informed the Ephesian Church that they had left their first love. He told them to remember from where they had fallen and to repent and return to their first works.

Love can be rekindled. Love can become fervent again. If you have fervent love, then be careful to maintain it. If you have lost what you had, you must repent and work at restoring it. Laugh up your sleeve at the impotence of divisive spirits as they hit against the greatest bond of unity, your love.

The earth is also polluted by its inhabitants, for they transgressed laws, violated statutes...and those who live in it are held guilty. Isa.24:5,6

Polluted by Its Inhabitants

How many times have we made mistakes because we failed to read the manufacturer's instructions? The humorous adage "When all else fails read the instructions" has never been more relevant than in today's world. God is the sole Creator, and having made us it is He who knows how best we function. He has given us detailed instructions for every area of life. From personal, through family and community relationships, to economic, political, recreational and all other human conditions, He has provided the manufacturer's instructions. "All else" has failed and will continue to fail.

Mankind has built without reference to the instructions and is suffering the consequences. God has written an instruction manual, the Bible. It is the only true written record of God Himself, creation, God's dealings with man, the redemption He has provided because of His great love, and the future. The horrifying mess that man has made of life on earth is a direct result of rejecting the Creator and His instructions.

God has instituted physical laws such as gravity, which we ignore at our peril. He has also provided the guidance of moral laws which when rejected have equally disastrous effects. Venereal disease and aids are evidences of doing what is contrary to God's declared instructions. Death itself is a constant reminder of the result of violating the word of the Lord.

All happiness is derived from our experience of God through His instructions and His provision for us in Jesus. We were created for God, to live in fellowship with Him. That is ultimate fulfillment.

Your heavenly Father knows that you need all these things.
Matt. 6:32

Your Heavenly Father Knows

These words, spoken by our Lord Jesus, are comforting and reassuring. They come in the context of repeated instructions on why we should not be anxious. When we were without Christ, we were without hope and separated from the life of God, with every reason to be anxious. Fear is the first recorded emotion of Adam after the fall. Anxiety has become the constant plague of mankind, but Jesus consoles us with His assurance that we have a loving heavenly Father.

God has no limitations and can meet our deepest needs from His inexhaustible resources in Christ Jesus. His heart towards us never wavers, and His love never wanes. His capacity to forgive and exercise mercy was demonstrated in the gift of His Son for us. While we were His enemies He reconciled us to Himself; so how much more, now that we have been reconciled, will He take care of us. If He can be trusted for our redemption, He can be trusted for everything else.

Do not be mistaken about His loving concern for you personally. When circumstances are perplexing, He can still be trusted for the resolution. To be disappointed with God betrays both ignorance of His character and a lack of trust. He withholds no good thing from those who love Him. Our timing and appreciation of what is good is not necessarily in alignment with His.

His will is good, acceptable and perfect. It works all things together for our good, and that is why we can give thanks, not only in all things, but for all things. Remember, if God is for you, who can be against you?

As each one has received a special gift, employ it in serving one another. 1 Pet.4:10

Employ Your Gift

It is Paul who reminds us that we have nothing that we were not given. What we have received, we have been freely given. We neither earned nor determined the gift we would be given. The Holy Spirit gives individually as He wills. We have received freely so that we should serve one another freely with our gifting.

Many Christians show an open disregard for the body of Christ, the church. What rich resources have been deposited in the body, but what neglect and poverty because of the lack of function. Many churches function on the gifts of the preacher, administrator and music director.

Peter's reminder is a timely one: "employ your gift." The body is retarded because of nonfunctioning members. The body builds itself up when love is expressed through the proper working of each individual part. Are you an unemployed Christian? Are you around just for the handouts?

Jesus lamented that the laborers were few; they are still few. When you use your gift, it is Jesus who is at work in you, and that will result in God being glorified. Bearing much fruit glorifies the Father. Jesus makes an interesting connection when describing the result of bearing fruit: "that your joy may be made full." The lack of joy in so many Christians can be directly attributed to being *use-less*.

The dynamics of the Kingdom of God are entirely different from those of the world. Whatever you give away and expend in the service of others increases in you. Look at the "helps wanted," and get to work!

Beloved, do not be surprised at the fiery ordeal among you...as though some strange thing were happening. 1 Pet.4:12

Do Not Be Surprised

It should not be a surprise that we have to encounter trials at every level of life. Peter calls them fiery ordeals. He consoles us by adding that we share in the sufferings of Christ. We can therefore keep on rejoicing. There will be a final unveiling at the revelation of the Lord Jesus Christ, and if we rejoice in our tribulations now, we will rejoice with exultation then. Our attitude towards our trials determines our condition at Christ's coming.

James says that we should count it all joy when we encounter various trials, because God has designed them for our good. Patient endurance with a joyful heart will bring us to maturity.

We learn to trust God and His sovereignty in our lives through suffering. Suffering is an opportunity to put off the old man with his grumbling and complaining, and to express Christ. Our faith will grow through trials, and our trust through perplexities. This process continues until we can present to God with a declaration of confidence in Him what would previously have been a disappointment. However hard things may appear, we have grace to adequately cope with each situation and press on into Christ. We can overwhelmingly conquer through the strength of Christ. All our trials are designed to put meat on our bones and make us good fighters and testimonies of Jesus.

Christ, who loves you, strengthens you to conquer. You are to expect tribulation, persecution and fiery trials, but the will of God is good, and the fight is good. Do not be surprised.

*I exhort the elders...shepherd the flock of God among you.
1 Pet.5:1-4*

Shepherding the Flock of God

The use of the term *shepherd* as a designation for rulers was not unfamiliar to the early church. Such a tradition had existed for centuries. David called the Lord his Shepherd, and he himself was called a shepherd of Israel. Through Ezekiel God pronounced His judgment upon shepherds of Israel who had neglected and manipulated the flock for their own profit and gain. Then God promised that He would shepherd them. He further promised through Jeremiah that He would give them shepherds after His own heart.

Jesus, the Chief Shepherd, contrasts good shepherds with hirelings who see the wolf coming and flee to save their own necks. The term *flock of God* denotes whose sheep we are. We all belong to God, but in His infinite wisdom He has designated certain sheep to also be shepherds. God allots to these shepherds certain sheep for whom they are accountable to God. These men are the rulers and overseers of the flock of God. They qualify when they represent the heart of the Chief Shepherd and serve as examples to the flock.

Despite abuses by some shepherds, God still gives shepherds to His flock. They are to rule without lording it over God's heritage, and they are to give direction without taking dominion over the faith of others. They are to teach, admonish, encourage, rebuke (sometimes sharply) and even deliver over to Satan as they represent Christ to His flock.

True spiritual authority serves sacrificially, pouring itself out in order to bring to maturity those it serves. The aim of a shepherd is to bring the sheep into a place of maturity where they clearly hear the voice of the Chief Shepherd for themselves.

*For it is time for judgment to begin with the household of God.
1 Pet. 4:17*

It Is Time for Judgment

God showed Amos the prophet the means of judging His people, for he saw God contending with fire, consuming fire. Amos interceded with God to stop because Jacob would have been totally consumed. Paul speaks of judgment by fire that will test the quality of each man's work. Peter speaks of a final, fiery judgment, as well as the fiery trials that test and refine us in our daily walk. It is time for judgment to begin with the house of God.

The Lord will purify the sons of Levi and thoroughly purge His floor. The church will be built, and there will be glory in the church through Christ Jesus.

Both Amos and Isaiah talk of the plumb line that God sets over what we are building. Isaiah defines the plumb line as righteousness. There are various responses we can have to a plumb line standing against what we are doing. We can confess our faults and repent, adjusting to the plumb line; we can move away from the plumb line; or we can say that the plumb line is crooked.

Just as Jesus cleansed the physical temple in Jerusalem, He will cleanse the spiritual temple of His habitation. Part of the completion of the church will be the casting out of all that is foreign to its perfection. If we were to judge ourselves, then we would not be judged of God, but the Lord disciplines us in order that we may not be condemned with the world. God's house will be judged before the world because those who comprise God's house will judge both the world and angels.

Judge yourself and cleanse yourself from all filthiness of the flesh and spirit.

For he who eats and drinks, eats and drinks judgment to himself,
if he does not judge the body rightly. 1 Cor.11:29

Judge the Body Rightly

The church is the body of Christ, and one way or another it will be judged. One way is that the Lord will judge us, and another way is that we will judge ourselves. The forbearance of God gives us time to repent, but judgment will surely come, and it is time to begin with the house of God.

Paul instructs us to examine and rightly judge ourselves as members of the body of Christ. If we despise the church by selfishly indulging ourselves while letting our brothers go hungry, then we do not judge the body rightly. Where this state of affairs exists, God's judgment in the form of discipline results in some being weak, some being sick and some even dying.

When Jesus gave His verdict to the seven churches, it appears that most of them had an entirely different assessment of themselves than He did. It proves how important it is to be current with the Lord's estimation of us.

One of the functions of elders is to judge. Their rule and oversight necessitates their reproving, rebuking, correcting and disciplining. Paul dealt with a situation which the church at Corinth was tolerating. "For I, on my part, though absent in body but present in spirit, have already judged him who has committed this"(1 Cor.5:3). He then pronounced his judgment, commanding that the church deliver the guilty one to Satan for the destruction of the flesh, that his spirit may be saved in the day of our Lord Jesus.

When individuals will not repent of their sins, the elders must judge in order to maintain purity of doctrine and practice in the church.

Present your bodies a living and holy sacrifice, acceptable to God...your spiritual service of worship. Rom.12:1

What Is Worship?

Worship has become so departmentalized that it has lost much of its comprehensive meaning. Like prayer, it must not only be exercised behind closed doors, but it must also be a constant practice. Prayer is but one expression of worship, for all that we do should be worship. All that we do we are to do heartily, as to the Lord and to His glory. All that life entails is to be a series of offerings and acts of worship.

Worship is a mind set. It is a basic attitude motivating and giving sanctity to every thought and action. Life is a sweet aroma to God when lived from a heart of worship. The caliber of life is upgraded when we see life as a continual act of worship.

Half-heartedness and neglect are unacceptable to us when we live life consciously to God as an act of worship. Private life, church life and public life would merge into one if lived as an offering of worship out of a loving heart.

The new covenant takes us from the limitations of rites, places and certain times of worship. Those who are born again by the Spirit are no longer in the flesh but in the Spirit, and can now worship in Spirit and in truth. Being joined to the Lord and made one Spirit with Him enables us to live by that same Spirit and not fulfill the lusts of the flesh. No longer is any of life humdrum or monotonously dull. All life is holy and acceptable when Christ is our life.

The way you think, speak and act, how you treat your wife and children, your boss and your neighbors—all is to be worship, everywhere and all the time. Your heavenly Father seeks such worshipers.

Clothe yourselves with humility toward one another. 1 Pet.5:5

Humility

This godly quality is graciously manifested by God in His dealings with men. Christ manifested humility both as God and as man. Pride is the contrasting characteristic. Satan fell due to pride, for he had lifted himself up. Humility is the making low of oneself. Jesus said that He was meek and lowly of heart. Humility and pride are always matters of heart. Natural birth produces fallen nature, and pride is as natural to us as humility is foreign.

God in His mercy gives us a new heart and a new spirit and brings us low in repentance. Without true humility there can be no exaltation by God. God's terrifying response to pride is resistance. He opposes the proud and destroys their house.

Pride is arrogant insubordination at its worst. It wants God and His will to become subordinate to man's whims. Pride is the basis of rebellion and of what we know as humanism. The haughty spirit is an abomination to God, and He will tolerate no vestige of pride.

Repentance expresses poverty of spirit. "Blessed are the poor in spirit, for theirs is the kingdom of heaven" (Matt.5:3). Clothing oneself with humility is nothing less than expressing Christ who humbled Himself and came as a servant. If He is our life then we can in honor prefer others, esteem others as better than ourselves and wash each other's feet.

What else could motivate you to turn the other cheek or walk the extra mile and lay down your life? Emulate the Lord Jesus, our supreme example, and humble yourself under the mighty hand of God.

*Casting all your anxiety upon Him, because He cares for you.
1 Pet.5:7*

Cast All Your Anxiety upon Him

Reassurance, comfort and relief can be found in this declaration of God's care. Life is full of problems, for man is born to trouble as the sparks fly upward. All the rigors of sorrows, distresses, and afflictions that torment and cause fear are included in the "all" of this verse.

Jesus said that we would have tribulation in the world. That involves persecution, irritating misunderstandings, the heartbreak of broken relationships and unjust suffering. The tragedy of losses which can never be replaced, of everything that causes anxiety—this is what we are invited to cast upon Him. Jesus expressed the same sentiment when He said that all who labored and were heavy laden should come to Him and He would give them rest.

He who bore our sins in His body and took our infirmities upon Himself is able to accommodate all that plagues the human breast. He is our peace. Come to Jesus, and take His yoke because His yoke is easy and His burden light, and you will find rest for your soul.

When you come, you come to a fervent and generous love which knows no limitations and will not run out. His arms are already extended, for He longs to embrace you and absorb your anxiety. He cares for you. Literally, this reads, "it matters to Him concerning you." What a wonderful thought: you actually matter to God. What an incentive to come!

Man does the offending and is the debtor, while God pays the debt and does the forgiving. Come, cast your anxieties upon Him and leave them there. Know the buoyancy of everlasting arms under you lifting you beyond your cares.

Grace and peace be multiplied to you in the knowledge of God and of Jesus our Lord. 2 Pet.1:2

Grace and Peace

How necessary these blessings are in order for us to be sustained in life. Not only can they be ours, but they can be multiplied to us through the knowledge of God our Savior. Such knowledge is the true knowledge referred to in the next verse. There is knowledge that is merely information and that puffs up. True knowledge embraces the experience of Him who calls us; it is knowing Him and His power.

God is the God of grace, of peace and of abundance. Only the true knowledge of Him will cause His grace and peace to abound towards us. Jesus said that this is eternal life: that they might know Thee the only true God and Jesus Christ whom Thou hast sent. Peter concludes his letter as he began it with the exhortation to grow in grace and in the knowledge of our Lord and Savior Jesus Christ, which is the formula for a life that is characterized by grace and peace.

Such growth in the knowledge of the Lord is the basis for our becoming more godly, and it is the antidote for the backsliding and deception that he mentions.

If we have tasted of the Lord, then we know how good He is, and that should whet our appetite for more of Him. Our pursuit of God will unveil more of His nature and of the promises that enable us to be partakers of that divine nature.

Are you in need of more grace? Is your peace intact, or could you do with more? Grace and peace will be multiplied to you as you seek the Lord to know Him. Count everything as loss in order to gain Christ who is our peace. Nothing excels the knowledge of Him who is full of grace and who is the Prince of peace.

As you practice these things, you will never stumble. 2 Pet.1:10

As You Practice These Things

As we practice these godly qualities they increase and abound in us, and we never stumble. This is not an exaggeration or an unobtainable standard. God is able to keep us from falling, and as we do what we know to be right, we grow and do not fall. On our part we are to exercise diligence to be found in Him blameless and unspotted by the world. He is able to sanctify us entirely and preserve completely our spirit, soul and body until the coming of our Lord Jesus Christ.

Paul encourages us by saying that faithful is He who has called us, who also will do it. The salvation that God in His wisdom accomplished through Jesus Christ does not fail. He does not fail, and when we practice what we have learned of Him, we will not fail. If He has brought to life those who were dead, how much more can He keep them from falling!

Those go on to maturity who by reason of use have their senses trained to discern good and evil. Those avoid deception who practice righteousness by walking according to the Spirit.

Pressure to compromise comes from inside the church as well as outside. Those who do not practice righteousness will be deceived, and their discernment will become faulty. Disobedience and faulty discernment will keep them deficient in their knowledge.

This vicious circle ensnares the unsuspecting. If you lack divine qualities, it is because you have forgotten your purification from your former sins, and have lost sight of the indwelling Christ. Be all the more diligent to make your calling and election sure.

For if these qualities are yours and are increasing, they render you neither useless nor unfruitful in the true knowledge of our Lord Jesus Christ. 2 Pet.1:8

Neither Useless nor Unfruitful

It is possible to be useless and unfruitful in the true knowledge of the Lord Jesus. The language is strong, but it emphasizes the importance of having divine qualities and increasing in them. If we add to our faith, moral excellence, knowledge, self-control, perseverance, godliness, brotherly kindness and love, and continue doing so, we will be neither useless nor unfruitful in the true knowledge of Jesus. We either add to our faith or lack these qualities.

James says that faith without works is useless and that by itself it is dead. If the light in us is darkness, how great is that darkness. If the faith in us is by itself, without expression, it is dead, or at the very least not perfected. God's divine power has granted to us precious and magnificent promises by which we become partakers of His nature. Put off the old man with its lusts, and put on the new man which is an expression of Christ.

God has laid a glorious foundation in Jesus, and He supplies exquisite building material to apply to the foundation. If we neglect to add to our faith, then we reject the gold, silver and precious stones of Christ's nature, and we build instead with the wood, hay and stubble of our old man.

How shall we escape if we neglect so great a salvation and deny ourselves the opportunity to grow in grace and in the knowledge of our Lord and Savior, Jesus Christ. All the treasures of wisdom and knowledge that are hidden in Him are unavailable to those made impotent through the pursuit of carnality.

For he who lacks these qualities is blind or short sighted, having forgotten his purification from his former sins. 2 Pet.1:9

Becoming Forgetful

Being forgetful is a subject for the humorist, especially when directed at those "getting on a bit." There are things that we should forget and leave behind, but there are things that we must also remember. Peter stirs up our minds to remember by giving us reminders. At the time of our conversion, it may have seemed impossible to ever forget how relieved we felt, how clean and free from the burden and conviction of sin. We were deeply moved and grateful for the peace we now enjoyed with God through the redeeming work of Jesus—an unforgettable experience indeed. But Peter says that if we are not adding to our faith, then we have become blind or shortsighted, having forgotten our purification from our former sins.

Walking in the flesh is the alternative to walking in the Spirit. Just as we can become dull of hearing when we fail to practice righteousness, so we become shortsighted, blind and forgetful if we do not add divine qualities to our faith. A seared conscience is the outcome of neglect and disobedience. Spiritual senility and forgetfulness will set in.

Being denied the ability to bathe would result in our being conscious of our filth and stench. How wonderful the feeling of cleanliness when at last we bathe. If at the point of being squeaky clean we were stood into a dung pile, we would certainly know it. Sin intrudes upon our lives more subtly, but with a similar result. How unobtrusively it can cause our defilement until we stand in the filth of our old way of life, having forgotten our former purification.

This is My beloved Son with whom I am well-pleased. 2 Pet.1:17

How Pleased Is God with Us?

This acclamation broke into the audible arena of our world when God the Father was owning, with honor, His Son in whom He was well pleased. Jesus had lived for thirty years in obscurity, growing up into manhood. He had not done a work of power, for His first miracle was yet to occur at the wedding in Cana. He had been subject to Mary and Joseph as a boy, even though at the age of twelve He knew that He was to be about His Father's business. For thirty years He had lived in sinless devotion to His Father, completing His first phase of ministry as a man.

God the Father anointed Jesus with the Holy Spirit and power launching Him into the second, much shorter, phase of His ministry. The second time God audibly witnessed His pleasure in His Son was on the Mount of Transfiguration after Jesus had accomplished the work His Father had given Him before the cross. Moses and Elijah, the law and the prophets who had testified of Him, were speaking of His coming decease. He was now poised to give His life as a ransom for all men. Jesus fulfilled His Father's pleasure before He went to the cross. Two phases of His life were completed with His Father's commendation from heaven.

The third phase of offering Himself was met with Father's approval when He raised Him from the dead and seated Him at His right hand. Jesus demonstrated that divine nature could inhabit flesh and blood and that God's armor could now fit a man. Because of this you can now demonstrate the life of Jesus in your mortal body. You can put on God's armor and live to please your heavenly Father.

For speaking out arrogant words of vanity they entice with fleshly desires, by sensuality, those who barely escape from the ones who live in error. 2 Pet.2:18

Sensual Verses Spiritual

This and the surrounding verses contrast false teachers with those who were moved by the Holy Spirit. If we are not moved by the Spirit, then our fallen nature will exercise itself in some form of self-indulgence. Being led by the Spirit is the positive direction that keeps us from devolving back into fleshly gratification. Fulfilling the lusts of the flesh is a substitute for the satisfaction that we experience through our union with God in the Spirit.

Whenever we lack fulfillment in the Spirit we tend to seek satisfaction through physical senses and fleshly indulgence. We must not to denigrate our God-given physical and mental faculties or obscure the dignity of our humanity. Indeed the life we enjoy with God in our spirit should be manifested in our physical body. Aesthetic satisfaction, creativity and physical fulfillment are at their best when exercised by one who is current with God in spirit.

Abundant life and ultimate pleasure are found in sharing the life of God. If a man were alone in solitary confinement, he could still enjoy unhindered fellowship in spirit and truth with the Father, Son and Holy Spirit. Eternal life does not depend upon the five natural senses in order to be experienced.

Tragically, much of the church is riddled with materialism and sensuality. John instructs us not to love the world—the lust of the eyes, the lust of the flesh and the boastful pride of life—because it is not of the Father. If you have been born of the Spirit your fulness and completion are a continual spiritual experience, not a sensual one.

Now we have received...the Spirit who is from God, that we might know the things freely given to us by God. 1 Cor.2:12

Personal Communion

No cymbal clangs more emptily than a man who preaches God beyond where he knows Him and exhorts others to walk in a way that he does not. The scribes and Pharisees quoted the Scriptures, but they did not know God. Many Christians never really enjoy the Lord. The small amount of time given to seeking Him and having conscious fellowship with Him betrays a lack of enjoyment of Him.

God longs to be known and has made Himself known in many and varied ways. He supremely declared Himself known in the Lord Jesus. God was in Christ reconciling us to Him. We should investigate the full knowledge and nature of that reconciliation with the zeal of those on a quest for treasure. Ours to have is not the fading treasure of this world, but the lasting treasure of God Himself.

His love and goodness should incite us to draw near in deep personal communion, where a vital relationship replaces the dead letter and old ruts give way to new revelations of the pearl of greatest price.

The ever-increasing realization of our union with Him will be characterized by the abandoning of ourselves in extravagant devotion to the lover of our souls. He invites us to come. Come whatever the cost; leave all and come; fight and travail, but come. The Lord is not elusive, but wants us to seek for Him in greater depths of revelation.

The Spirit searches the deep things of God, and deep calls unto deep. Break free from a superficial relationship with God by diligently seeking Him with all your heart. Those who so seek will find Him, and enlarge their conscious capacity of Him.

Where is the promise of His coming? 2 Pet.3:4

The Promise of His Coming

Among Christians there is no subject upon which such divergent views are expressed as the coming of the Lord. In this chapter the promise of His coming, the day of judgment, the day of the lord, and the coming of the day of God are synonymous. All that is recorded in the Scriptures concerning mankind and the gross darkness that will cover the earth, the emerging of the church with the glory of the Lord upon her, and the final harvest of the nations will be fulfilled before Jesus returns.

When He comes, He will bring judgment and the destruction of the ungodly with the brightness of His coming. Paul paints the same picture, stating that the Lord shall be revealed from heaven with His mighty angels in flaming fire, bringing retribution upon those who do not obey the gospel, whose penalty will be eternal destruction.

Peter uses the destruction of the earth and its works as an incentive to live holy and godly and to be found by Him in peace, spotless. John conveys the same sentiments, telling us to abide in Him so that when He appears we may have confidence and not shrink away in shame. These arguments are one and the same: because the world and its ways will be dissolved, do not be worldly.

The Bible states that the tares are taken **first**. The wicked are severed from the just. The angels take out of His kingdom all stumbling blocks and those who commit lawlessness, just as the flood took away Noah's generation. The elements shall melt with fervent heat, but he who does the will of God abides forever.

You are looking for Jesus the Nazarene, who has been crucified. He has risen, He is not here. Mark 16:6

Jesus Is Risen From the Dead

If ever an apparent failure was turned into glorious victory, it was at the resurrection. The disciples, having witnessed the ignominy of Christ's death, were disillusioned and despondent. While they were commiserating with each other on their dejection, the dead body of Jesus was being energized with Spirit and life. The corpse that had lain cold in the dark of the tomb stood up, and the angel rolled the stone away from the entrance.

God had achieved the reconciliation, for an acceptable sacrifice had been made, and sins were to be forgiven on the basis of His shed, acceptable blood. Jesus put Satan and the powers of darkness to open shame and defeated death itself. Jesus was alive again, and He declared that His brethren should be told that He was ascending to His Father and their Father.

He appeared to His disciples, who could not believe for joy as they marveled. Their incredulity soon warmed into a full realization of the truth, and their depression evaporated with a surge of elation. Jesus had foretold that their sorrow would be turned to joy, and that He would see them again.

Paul prayed that the Ephesian church might know the surpassing greatness of God's power towards those who believe, in accordance with the strength of His might which He brought about in Christ when He raised Him from the dead. Only those who are crucified with Christ know the power of His death over their old man. Only those crucified with Him know the power of His resurrection and can walk in newness of life.

Be on the alert, stand firm in the faith, act like men, be strong.
1 Cor.16:13

Be on the Alert

Both our Lord Jesus and the apostles exhort us to be watchful. Being on our guard and alert must become a constant state of mind. Looking out for intrusions of sinful flesh and Satan with his wiles is of necessity a continual exercise. Jesus told His disciples to watch and pray so that they would not enter into temptation. Sin is always crouching at the door, but we must master it. Our alertness can keep the door shut. If we drop our guard, we can be sure sin will pounce.

Watching is often linked with praying, and prayer is a great stimulant to spiritual sensitivity. How often a victim of an attack relates that he was caught off guard, that the attacker crept up unawares. The term *watch* as in "the fourth watch" refers to those who were put on guard. They were responsible to watch while others slept. With eyes and ears scanning the surroundings, they kept alert under threat of severe penalty should they fail to keep awake. Peter tells us to be sober and vigilant because our adversary, the devil, prowls like a roaring lion seeking whom he may devour.

To become dull and insensitive can be costly, for you could be devoured. The enemy does not sleep, but he is relentless in his desire to ensnare you; therefore, your vigil must be constant. Christians, who are children of the day, should not act like those who sleep.

If you walk in the light, darkness will not overtake you. When you are humble before God and steadfast in the faith you can resist the devil, and he will flee.

Be on the alert, stand firm in the faith, act like men, be strong. Let all...be done in love.   1 Cor.16:13,14

Stand Firm in the Faith

The faith is not the same as faith. Faith comes by hearing the Word of God, while *the faith* is the sum of God's Word. Jude commands us to contend earnestly for the faith once delivered to the saints. The key to our ability to resist Satan is our steadfastness in the faith. We cannot be in the faith without exercising faith, but the faith is the sound doctrinal entity for which we can contend.

The faith aligns perfectly with the truth of the gospel as opposed to any other so-called gospel. There are deficient versions of the gospel that detract from the full truth of the gospel. Systems of theology can lack parts of the whole counsel of God. If there are scriptures that are an embarrassment to a particular system, then that system is not the faith.

In order to stand firm in the faith and contend for the faith, we must be taught the faith. The unity of the faith is not an unobtainable goal, but it is where God is taking the church. The diversity of systems of theology will bow the knee to the Spirit's interpretations, and our unity of the Spirit will produce the unity of the faith.

God is not looking for small-minded bigots, but for men mighty in the Scriptures who can be shown the way of God more perfectly, men who will overthrow godless philosophies with sound doctrine.

The doctrine on any subject is the compilation of all the scriptures on that given subject. Apostles, prophets, evangelists, pastors and teachers are given to the church **until** we come to the unity of the faith and of the knowledge of the Son of God. The church will get there.

All Scripture is inspired by God. 2 Tim.3:16

Why Should I Read the Bible?

The Bible is a phenomenon that defies cynics and remains intact after centuries of attack by antagonists. It represents itself as the word of God, stating that fact over two thousand times in the Old Testament alone. Nothing is more important than knowing what God has to say. The Bible is the unique vehicle that communicates God's word to us.

Jesus, who is called the Word, is the embodiment of the word. He said that the Scriptures testified of Him. He began at Moses and the prophets and explained to His disciples the things concerning Himself in all the Scriptures.

It has been said that a book is the embodiment of thought. God's book is the embodiment of divine thought. J. Sidlow Baxter quotes Bonar, a saint and scholar of a past generation, who wrote, "If it be true that bad men could not have written so holy a book, and that good men could not have written a forged book, the Bible must be what it claims to be, the word of the living God" (Explore the book).

Men of God wrote as they were moved by the Holy Spirit. Forty very different men with equally dissimilar perspectives and styles, over the course of sixteen hundred years, contributed to the collection of sixty-six books and letters that make up the Bible. The fact that all the writings have a common focus and fulfillment in one man, the Lord Jesus, is beyond any coincidence.

God has written a book! Neglect this book, and you will remain in the ignorance and poverty of failed human philosophy. Read it, believe and obey it, and you will find abundant life.

He was telling them a parable to show that at all times they ought to pray and not to lose heart. Luke 18:1

Do I Need to Pray Every Day?

This question can be answered with the question, do you need to breathe every day? Equating prayer with breathing is not the overstatement that it might appear to be. Jesus instructed us to pray without ceasing. Thousands of decisions must be made daily, and prayer is the key to making them wisely. Being led by the Spirit means hearing His voice and making choices according to His will. Jesus taught us to pray also by entering our closet and shutting the door and praying in secret to the Father.

The neglected art of listening can be cultivated in the secret place. We to often bring our presumptuous demands before God and then quickly depart, but the full value of communion must incorporate listening.

The Lord has much to say to us, so we must give time to listen. Isaiah 51 records that three times God told Israel to listen before finally pleading, "Please hear this!" Can you ever imagine the Lord crying to you, "Please hear this"? Hear what? Listen, and you will find out. Concentrated times of prayer are essential, as exemplified by the Lord Jesus.

Undistracted worship and adoration are necessary for the intimacy God desires with us. The intimacy we experience in secret enhances our constant awareness of Him, enabling us daily to live out our love and worship. The petition "Give us **this** day our daily bread" emphasizes the daily practice of prayer.

Prayer is a gift for the privileged to enjoy. It is not only for crisis, but for life. Get involved in the mystery of His will and the fulfillment of His purposes through prayer.

In the last days, the mountain of the Lord will be established as the chief of the mountains. Isa.2:2

The Last Days

The Bible is the only source of truth concerning the end of the age and Christ's return. Both the New and the Old Testament furnish us with information about the prevailing condition of the world in the last days. The book of Isaiah contains much unfulfilled prophecy that focuses upon the same time, particularly from chapter sixty.

From the wide spectrum of end-time prophecies there have emerged many conflicting projections of the sequence of events, causing confusion and division in the church. Most charts will have to be discarded as unfolding events prove the various systems of eschatology false.

Paul directs Timothy away from false teachers to his own teaching and the Scriptures. What we cannot yet put together will become increasingly clear as the events unfold, and there is yet much to unfold. The Scriptures cannot be broken, and all that is prophesied will come to pass.

Christ's return is not in question, but the present contradicting variations of the timing of the rapture need to be questioned. Pre-tribulation, mid-tribulation and post-tribulation, plus the nature of the rapture and the tribulation, will have to be thoroughly overhauled in the light of scriptures that forbid present interpretations. Amillenial, premillenial and postmillenial teachings are not compatible, yet each is represented by huge sections of the church.

The unconverted nations will yet be affected by the church, and come to the brightness of her rising before the wicked or the righteous are taken. The church will be built, and her righteousness and praise will spring up before the nations. Make yourself ready!

Let us cleanse ourselves from all defilement of the flesh and spirit, perfecting holiness in the fear of God. 2 Cor. 7:1

Perfecting Holiness

This charge is given with the added direction of doing it in the fear of God. Perfecting involves change and growth. It is not automatic. Exhortations to work, fight, watch, labor, strive, wrestle, put off, put on, and be diligent place the responsibility squarely on our shoulders to apply ourselves to change.

We must become different. If we have been given a new heart and a new spirit, then we are to think, speak, act and live differently. God is at work in us, but we must work out what He is working in (with fear and trembling).

The new creature by new birth now has new appetites and desires. It is normal for those born of the Holy Spirit to be holy. The process of development takes us from one degree of glory to another. It leaves no part of our personality untouched.

Regeneration is a renovation that totally clears out the old interior and creates a new inner man. Even the mortal body which is perishing conveys the new life. The countenance that betrayed darkness within now radiates the light of life within.

Perfecting holiness means applying your will by faith to what the Holy Spirit is directing you to change. What is the Holy Spirit teaching you at this time? Upon which area of life are you aware of Him putting His finger? You are no longer under obligation to sin. Instead you are obliged to express Christ, with the strength He supplies. If you follow the positive leading of the Spirit, you will find that sheer neglect of old habits mortifies them.

For the kingdom of God does not consist in words, but in power.
1 Cor. 4:20

The Kingdom of God Is in Power

Luke relates how the Lord Jesus returned from His Jordan baptism full of the Holy Spirit. After defeating Satan in the wilderness, He returned to Galilee in the power of the Spirit. He displayed His authority and command of demons powerfully with many signs. He contradicted the Pharisees' assessment of what was occurring by saying that if He through the finger of God cast out demons, then the kingdom of God had come upon them. Jesus openly showed that another rule had come among men. The kingdom of darkness no longer dominated the earth.

Jesus gave His authority to the seventy He sent out, and they rejoiced that the demons were subject to them. Among the promises He gave to those who believe in Him was that they would cast out demons and heal the sick. The promise of the Father was the outpouring of the Spirit of power. Jesus in referring to the coming baptism of the Spirit said that they would receive power when the Holy Spirit came upon them. The kingdom manifested in Jesus was now to be demonstrated in His body, the church.

It is unthinkable that Christ in us no longer rules and that we who are seated with Christ cannot exercise certain authority. By virtue of our union with Christ we can resist the devil, and He will flee from us. If the life of the Lord Jesus is to be manifested in our mortal bodies, how can some say that the kingdom of God is not yet among us? Daniel informed Nebuchadnezzar that the stone that destroyed the image and grew into a mountain filling the earth was a kingdom. Have you received that kingdom of power? Beware of those who deny the power.

A man after My heart, who will do all My will. Acts 13:22

A Man After God's Heart

The great, loving shepherd's heart of God was manifested in Jesus, the Chief, Great and Good Shepherd. God had promised His people shepherds after His own heart. David was such a man. What higher commendation could any man hope for than to be called a man after God's own heart, who would do all His will?

The terms of the new covenant make it possible for all those who are God's children through faith in Jesus to be men after His heart. Not just leaders hear the Lord. Not just one tribe of His people are priests holy unto the Lord. All Christians should express His heart because Jesus is their life.

Jesus was not austere, with a harsh quality that made Him unapproachable. He was inviting, with a welcoming manner. He was not hard or unfeeling towards the plight of people, but was empathetic, showing genuine concern. He had a listening ear, and gave people a sense of worth by giving time to all who came.

Jesus was not an opportunist who used people and dropped them when they had outlived their usefulness. He absorbed the weaknesses of His followers and was the great encourager of those who were failures. He was unlike a manager who directs yet does not communicate himself in depth.

Jesus led through example, opening His heart to the point of vulnerability. He did not justify Himself at the expense of others, nor did He try to survive at all costs. He laid down His life sacrificially at ultimate cost to Himself, bearing wrong rather than uncovering the faults of others. Be such a man after God's own heart!

Knowing, brethren beloved of God, His choice of you. 1 Thess.1:4

Knowing God's Choice of You

When a man knows that he is called of God, his life becomes purposeful. A sense of destiny will inspire him to seek the Lord for clarity concerning the outworking of God's purpose in his life. Even as a child Jesus knew that He should be about His Father's business. He was confident in what His Father had destined for Him. As He faced the spectacle of the cross He said that to this end He had been born and to this end He had come into the world.

To miss God's purpose is a fearful prospect. A wasted life is a lost life. The Lord would have us be men with a vision from Him rather than those motivated by selfish ambition. People without a vision dwell carelessly because they have no direction. Visualization is merely the projection of self unless our vision is God-given.

We were born to be achievers, to finish what we were given to accomplish by God. Jesus promised that the Holy Spirit would lead us into all truth and teach us all things. As we are led by the Spirit we can apprehend what the Lord opens up before us. We can reach out for what lies ahead and press into our high calling in Christ Jesus.

A man once prophesied over another, "Thus saith the Lord," then after a pause continued, "I forgettest thy name." Obviously God had not really said anything, for God forgets neither our names nor what He has purposed for our lives.

Paul finished the course and kept the faith, while king Saul confessed that he had erred exceedingly and had played the fool. Do not fool around with your high calling.

He who separates himself seeks his own desire. Prov.18:1

Fellowship and Independence

Fellowship is defined as participation, sharing, intercourse or association. Independence is unwillingness to be under obligation to others. There is a tension of truth concerning both fellowship and independence. The priority in all relationships is the dependent relationship a man has with God. When fellowship with others becomes a substitute for a relationship with God, then God in His wisdom will displace that prop. On the other hand, if a man maintains that he is serving God while isolating himself from the body of Christ, he is deceived. Christ is not decapitated from His body.

We cannot boast in a relationship with Christ and have no function with His body. The proverb reminds us that he who separates himself seeks his own desire. The independent man is independent also from God. He is self-willed and remains uninvolved because he is threatened by the involvement of others in his decision-making.

The man of fellowship may be isolated by God for a season in order to achieve a bonding of his heart to God, but only for a season. When we were baptized, it was into one body. We are closer than kin, for we are members one of another. We are made for each other and can realize our identity and gifting only in the context of the body.

Our differences make us necessary for each other. We were created to share the life we have received with each other in the context of God's order in the church. If your independence will not permit you to submit to those whom the Lord has given as overseers or function in the gathering of believers, then it is God, not man, that you are rejecting.

Seek first His kingdom and His righteousness; and all these things shall be added to you. Matt. 6:33

Seek First the Kingdom of God

God has invited us to seek Him and has promised that we will find Him, if we seek Him with all our hearts. The purpose of finding Him is to know Him and to become more like Him. That is how we shine as lights in this crooked and perverse generation.

Seeking the Lord is a mind set and a priority beyond all other considerations. "Seek first" denotes the priority. "All these things" refers to the concerns of life that can distract us from our focus on the Lord and His kingdom.

New birth translates us from the kingdom of darkness into the kingdom of His dear Son. As men of God's original kingdom we serve as testimonies to the alternative kingdom of darkness. We bring the Kingdom of Christ on earth when we express what we discover of Him. We actually become the light of the world when we have kingdom morality, kingdom marriages, and kingdom families and values. The bankrupt kingdom of darkness collapses before the demonstration of power that is in righteousness.

Have you shelved your quest for the Lord to give time and attention to other pressures? The name of the Lord is hallowed, and His kingdom comes when we do His will. It is of no value to pray for these things to come upon the earth if we refuse to apply them personally.

Babylon, the great world system, is already judged and awaits its inevitable fall. The Kingdom of God has come and will continue to come. Put your efforts into what will abide, by passionately seeking God's kingdom and His righteousness and shining brighter and brighter until the perfect day.

For their sakes I sanctify Myself, that they themselves also may be sanctified in truth. John 17:19

Sanctifying Yourself for the Sake of Others

Jesus desires His disciples to be sanctified. He knew that the truth sanctified, and as the Truth, He was called to sanctify Himself so that we might be sanctified. Jesus fulfilled His responsibility as our head and Lord. Men must exercise God-given headship towards their families. Although only God can ultimately sanctify, if men desire their wives and children to be sanctified, then they must first sanctify themselves.

Jesus did not please Himself, and although He was rich, for our sakes He became poor, that we through His poverty might be made rich. He knew that our sanctification rested in His sanctification; therefore, He kept Himself holy and free from sin. We cannot sanctify anyone as Jesus sanctified the church, but there is a principle here that is important. Headship is significant and must be exercised responsibly because of its implications for those who submit to it.

We must adopt the attitude of Jesus towards those under our headship. For their sakes we must sanctify ourselves. We must not please ourselves at their expense. Many families break up because of the irresponsibility of the fathers. Fathers who act in ways conducive to holiness please God, benefit their families and keep the enemy at bay.

When a man walks in the truth, his family has the same opportunity. God requires truth from the heart. What sort of head is a hypocrite? The scepter of wickedness shall not rest on the lot of the righteous.

He still holds fast his integrity, although you incited Me against him, to ruin him without cause. Job 2:3

Holding Fast to Integrity

God said to Satan that Job had held fast his integrity. Job had no idea what had transpired between God and Satan. He trusted the sovereignty of God implicitly, even to the point of being slain by Him. God boasted of Job's righteousness to Satan, but Satan complained that Job was hedged about by God. Satan accused Job before God, saying that if the hedge was taken away, then Job would curse God. God gave permission for Satan to touch Job's substance and family, but not Job. Job faced the devastating loss of his children and all that he owned by worshiping God.

Subsequently he felt the touch of Satan upon his own body. God had given Satan further permission to do that, but not to take his life. Still Job maintained his integrity, proving Satan's forecast to be false. Even when Satan used Job's wife to tempt Job to curse God and die, Job's reply honored God: "Shall we indeed accept good from God and not accept adversity?" The Scriptures tell us to be happy in the day of prosperity, but in the day of adversity we are to consider that God made the one as well as the other.

Can you be trusted with such adversity, trusted not to accuse God or blame Him as though He had made a mistake with your circumstances? Paul said that he was instructed both to abound and to be abased. He had learned to be content in whatever circumstances he found himself. That is a statement of trust in God. Job did not sin with his lips, because it was not in his heart to blame God.

To become a disciple of the Lord Jesus you must learn of Him, forsaking every relationship, every benefit and even your own life. To learn of Christ you must entrust yourself to His keeping and hold fast to your integrity.

Sin is crouching at the door, and its desire is for you, but you must master it. Gen.4:7

Sin Is Crouching at the Door

Sin crouches at the door. It desires to come in and overtake us. The judge also stands at the door to assess our response to the temptations of sin. We can resist by putting on Christ at the very point of temptation. If we succumb, the judge is there to bring chastening that makes us aware of our failure and brings us to repentance. If we judged ourselves then, we would not be judged, but we are chastened by the Lord so that we will not be condemned with the world.

The analogy of the door emphasizes the nearness of both sin and the judge. Both are within reach, close at hand. Jesus told His church that He was standing at the door knocking, waiting for someone to open that He might come in and eat with them. We must fellowship not with the unfruitful works of darkness, but with the Father, the Son and the Holy Spirit. Our union with the Lord enables us to resist the devil and reprove the deeds of darkness.

Be wary of entertaining sin in any shape or form. It comes in different guises to deceive us into thinking that it is harmless. Be on your guard, and always consult with the Lord. That can be done in a split second by rehearsing it in your heart before the Lord. The Judge will make known His judgment on every issue, as well as His pleasure or His grief.

Satan can be resisted, but so can the Holy Spirit. The Spirit is grieved when we open the door to sin. Close the door to your old manner of life that tempts you. Bring grief to Satan by choosing to please your only Lord and Master.

I am writing a new commandment to you, which is true in Him and in you. 1 John 2:8

True in Christ and in You

Jesus commands us to love one another as He has loved us. This commandment is true in Him, and John tells us that it is also true in us. Under the terms of the new covenant God has written His law on our hearts. The death of our old man in Christ involved circumcising our hearts. God promised to take away our stony hearts and give us new hearts. The new creature in Christ has a new heart in which the love of God is shed abroad by the Holy Spirit who was given to us.

The truth about our new heart is that it is not our old heart. It has been purified by faith and is a pure heart. We can now love one another fervently out of a pure heart. We can even love our enemies.

The commandment is true in Christ and in us. The old heart was deceitful above all things and desperately wicked; it was an evil heart of unbelief. That heart was taken away when we were circumcised with the circumcision of Christ. God promised through Ezekiel to remove the old heart and give a new heart and a new spirit and to put His Spirit within us.

When we act other than our new hearts motivate us, then we lie against the truth. James warns us that these things ought not to be so. A fountain does not send forth sweet and bitter water, yet from the same mouth proceed blessing and cursing. This sort of duplicity and double-mindedness will always cause instability. Jesus said that we were to let the tree be either good or evil, one or the other, but not an unholy mixture.

When you act according to what God has done in you in Christ, then you will be true to what is true of you.

He will speak out against the Most High and wear down the saints. Dan. 7:25

Wearing Down or Enduring

One of Satan's strategies is to wear down the saints. Jesus made known the conditions existing at the end of the age, saying the love of many would grow cold because of the iniquity that abounds. Paul teaches that in the last days perilous times will come, including persecution for all who live godly in Christ Jesus. Enduring hardship is nothing less than the tribulation that Jesus foretold.

What then is the antidote to wearing out or growing cold? There is always a way in God in which we can overcome. Conquering, triumphing and being victorious are all terms that express the superiority of the power that works in us.

God is able to do exceeding abundantly beyond all that we can ask or think, according to the power that works within us. It is God who is at work in us both to will and to do of His good pleasure. Christ in us will enable us to endure because He has already endured and overcome.

The writer to the Hebrews gives clues as to how we can be found spotless and blameless in these last days. Like Moses, we have to endure by seeing Him who is invisible. Looking to Jesus and considering how He endured will help us not to grow weary.

Paul's testimony was that He did not lose heart because he compared what he was enduring with the weight of glory it was producing for him. He was looking not at the things which could be seen, but at the unseen, eternal things where Christ is seated. Your ability to endure is directly related to your awareness of the throne of God and of your being seated there with Christ now.

Through perseverance and the encouragement of the Scriptures
we might have hope. Now may the God who gives perseverance
and encouragement.... Rom.15:4,5

Keys to Endurance

When God makes us alive to Him, we can see the invisible, hear the inaudible and touch the intangible. Our spirit is the most sensitive part of our being. God communicates with us in our spirit. We are in two places at once: in the world, with all its darkness and the knowledge that it is passing away; and seated with Christ in heavenly places, in a realm that will not pass away.

Our mind is to be set on things above, where Christ is. As we wait upon the Lord in an attitude of faith, we will renew our strength, mount up with wings as eagles, run and not grow weary, walk and not faint.

One way God gives perseverance, encouragement and hope is through the Scriptures. Giving time to fellowship with the Lord in the Scriptures is a vital ingredient for endurance. A prime cause for growing cold and wearing out is the lack of hope. Both hope and comfort are to be found and experienced through the Scriptures. Food for living is not found in bread alone, but in every word that proceeds out of the mouth of God. His word washes and refreshes us, illumines our path and stops us sinning.

With all the sources the world has for communicating its word to us, we neglect the Scriptures at our peril. We can counteract the effects of the seducing world around us by filling our minds with God's thoughts.

Knowing God, as well as who we are in Christ, is revealed to us through the Scriptures. If you are feeling weary, then pick up the Bible and feed your languishing soul on the bread of life, and find how refreshed you become and how sweet He is to the taste.

According to the proper working of each individual part, causes the growth of the body for the building up of itself in love. Eph. 4:17

Pulling Down or Building Up

The choice is one of either losing what we have or adding to it. We lose what we have by hiding it or not practicing it. We add to what we have by obeying what we know. Neglect or disobedience means that we are walking in the flesh, which is Satan's playground, and that will weaken us. Individually we can build ourselves up in our most holy faith by praying in the Spirit and keeping ourselves in the love of God.

We are also individually members one of another in the body of Christ. The body builds itself up in love. The supply of every joint holds us together according to the proper working of each individual part. The weakness of the body can be attributed to the lack of working order in many and to the divisions that exist. Each one has been designed to function as a particular member within the many-membered body of Christ.

To disregard our place in the body will open us up to being worn down by the enemy. Neglecting the gathering of ourselves together robs us of the edifying effects of the body, and robs the body of what we were ordained to contribute to it.

Isolation is not a normal experience, but it denotes an unhealthy condition. There may be a season of isolation that God for His own purposes in us may take us through, but generally we are called to function alongside other members. A maverick is one who is an unbridled calf, a masterless person, a rover. That definition could be applied to many Christians today. A willingness to go anywhere in serving the Lord is to be seen in contrast with an unwillingness to be planted somewhere.

For there are many rebellious men, empty talkers and deceivers.
Titus 1:10

Deluded and Diluted

The men spoken of in these verses are detestable and disobedient because they profess to know God but by their deeds they deny Him. They are rebellious, empty talkers and deceivers. They are Christians who are deluded in thinking that as long as they profess to know God they are acceptable. Paul directs that they be severely reproved in order that they may be sound in the faith.

How many Christians could take a severe rebuke? How many elders give severe rebukes? Many empty talkers leave their congregations when they are silenced. Their conduct is at best diluted Christianity, and that sort of mixture is an abomination to God. Their actions reveal a wrong heart attitude. Their rebellion proves them to be unruly.

The Holy Spirit is not mistaken when He commands us to obey those who have the rule over us. To be unruly is to refuse to be ruled! Occasions of abuse and lording it over God's flock are no excuse for rebellion. Rebellion is as witchcraft.

This passage in Titus poses questions: Am I deluded? Is my Christianity diluted? What are my motives? Am I in a condition to receive a severe rebuke? If your behavior denies the Lord then your profession of Him is of no profit.

The caliber of these rebels is seen in contrast to the elders in the previous verses, men above reproach, having their own homes in good order, God's stewards, not self-willed, not quick-tempered, not given to wine and certainly not quarrelsome or given to fighting. When character represents God then profession is acceptable.

How can a young man keep his way pure. Ps.119:9

How Can You Keep Your Way Pure?

This question is followed by the answer—by keeping it according to God's word. The psalm starts by acknowledging the blessedness of those who walk in the law of the Lord. Under the new covenant we are no longer under the law, but that does not mean that there is something wrong with the law. The law could not save us, because we could not keep the law. The law is holy, righteous, good and spiritual, but it is weak to save us only because of the inability of the flesh to keep it.

The righteousness of the law is fulfilled in those who walk according to the Spirit, because God has written His law in their hearts. We are justified by the blood of Jesus, but we show our new heart of love to Him by keeping His commandments. He that loves fulfills the law, and we can now love because God has shed His love abroad in our new hearts.

David records the blessing attending those who OBSERVE God's testimonies and seek Him with their whole heart. Jesus commissioned His disciples to teach everyone to OBSERVE what He had commanded. If we have a heart for God, then we can obey Him from the heart. The key is to have an appetite for God. God fills all who hunger and thirst for righteousness.

His commandments are not grievous, but they are life to those in whose heart is His law. Taking heed to His word is not foreign to those born of God; rather, it is the natural expression of Christ in them. You miss the zenith of all experiences when you deny your new nature by pursuing impurity. Intimacy with the Lord transcends all sensual pleasure and will keep your way pure.

By this we know that we have come to know Him, if we keep His commandments. *1 John 2:3*

Knowing Him and Knowing We Are in Him

John's letter was written to counteract the error which says that God cannot be known. Over twenty times throughout the letter he emphasizes that we can know, and in one instance he states that we know that we have come to know. Although this letter contains truths that jolt the senses with the revelation of doctrines that are meat indeed, it also gives very practical evidence by which we can test whether we do in fact know.

We may say that we know Him, but if our lives betray evidence to the contrary, then John says that we lie. One repeated test asks if we keep His commandments. If anyone says that he knows Him and does not keep His commandments, he is a liar, and the truth is not in him. These instructions are full of warnings for those who are deceived in thinking that they know God when by their behavior they deny Him.

The ultimate test for the one who says he abides in Him is to walk as Jesus walked. Having religious moments, or behaving differently for the duration of a service, does not necessarily indicate true knowledge of God. These tests prove the condition of the heart in every mundane chore and in every decision that is made.

Paul addresses the same thing when he talks about the life of the Lord Jesus being made manifest in our mortal bodies. He extensively uses the term *manifest*, denoting our manner of life. There is a focus on love as being the aim and the proof of walking in the truth. He who does not love does not know God, for God is love. When you love, God is revealed through you and to you, and you become more aware of being in Him.

Beloved, I am not writing a new commandment to you, but an old commandment which you have had from the beginning. 1 John 2:7

The New Commandment

God is love; therefore, whoever is born of God has love as a basic character trait. God sheds His love into our hearts by the Holy Spirit who was given to us. This experience is the basis for the new commandment being fulfilled in us. To be a Christian is to have a new, pure heart of love. It could be said, "Love because you have a heart to love."

Loving is not difficult for someone who has a heart of love. If we profess to be partakers of the divine nature, having been Fathered by God, but we hate our brother, then we are in darkness. There are things that we should hate. For example God hates divorce, so we should hate it. However, our attitude toward our brother should express what Christ's heart is toward him.

How can we love our enemies if we cannot first love our brothers? To respond in a way that overrules love is to deny the truth of our new heart. Paul testified that the love of God controlled him. When love is our source and our aim, then we can walk in love.

Love is evidence to the world that we are disciples of Jesus. Loving our neighbor as ourselves is like loving God. Jesus said that the second commandment is like the first.

A profession of love for God is exposed as spurious if it is not worked out towards our neighbor. Our hearts have been purified by faith; therefore, we can love one another fervently with all propriety, from pure hearts. The new covenant furnishes you with a new heart from which you can keep the new commandment to love as He loves.

The world is passing away, and also its lusts; but the one who does the will of God abides forever. 1 John 2:17

The World Is Passing Away

The sands of time are running out for this world. When Paul says, "then comes the end," he means the end of this age as we know it. There are ages to come in which God will show the surpassing riches of His grace in kindness towards us in Christ Jesus, but this world and its lusts are to pass away.

Jesus said that we are not of this world even as He is not of this world. We are of course in the world, but we are not of it, for we are of God. Therefore we are not to love the world or the things that are in the world. All that is in the world is not from the Father, but we are born of our heavenly Father.

The life that we are to display is eternal and is to be seen in contrast to that which will pass away. We are children of the light who are to so shine in the darkness around us that people may see our good works and glorify our heavenly Father. Peter conveys the same sentiments when he reminds us that all things pertaining to the world shall be dissolved; therefore, our conduct should be holy and godly.

We ought to be looking for a new heaven and a new earth wherein dwells righteousness, being diligent to be found in Him spotless and blameless. James says that friendship with the world is hostility towards God. Whoever wishes to be a friend of the world makes himself an enemy of God. The logic of the argument is that we should not waste our time and affections on what is to pass away. We are to labor for the meat that endures unto eternal life and lay up treasure in heaven.

Live as one who has been called out of that which will perish into an imperishable kingdom.

Pay close attention to yourself and to your teaching. 1 Tim. 4:16

Does Doctrine Matter?

The simple answer to this question is yes. The importance of doctrine cannot be overstated. If we are taught unsound doctrine, we will believe wrong things. Another gospel will give us another Jesus. There are many different Jesus's but only one true Jesus, who is known by the true gospel. Doctrine is not a certain verse that proves a point. Sound doctrine is the sum total of all scriptures on any given subject.

"All Scripture...is profitable for doctrine, for reproof, for correction and training in righteousness, that the man of God may be adequate, equipped for every good work" (2 Tim. 3:16). If we want to be men of God, then it will not happen without doctrine.

We are without the knowledge of God and the redemption that is in His Son, Jesus, unless we are taught. The word of God is the basis of our faith. One of the indictments against the church in our generation is that it has a shallow appreciation of the teachings of Scripture. These are the days of doctrines of demons, and many are led astray because they hear a preacher quote a scripture. The devil quoted Scripture to Jesus, but Jesus refuted the misapplication of Scripture by quoting other Scripture. The inability to say, "Thus says Scripture also," will open you up to deception.

If our system of theology is embarrassed by certain scriptures, then as with all such systems, it is not completely sound. Doctrine instructs us how to relate to God and man and teaches us concerning all matters of time and eternity. Take heed to your doctrine by giving sufficient time to learn of Him who is your life.

He has sent Me to proclaim liberty to the captives. Luke 4:18

Having a Dependency Problem?

One feature of the fall was the loss of control, even self-control. Habits began to form that were contrary to good health and morality. Beneficial habits need to be enforced by diligent application and discipline. Harmful habits need no such effort to maintain. Wrong tendencies that develop into habitual practice, finally dominating and enslaving, prove the inability of the natural man to be in control.

We tend to limit the term addiction to substance abuse, but all men are addicted to sin. Some *enthusiasts* are really addicts, and fanatics (fan for short) can be found in every stratum of society. The religious as well as the irreligious experience bondage. Anything that a man has no power to resist is an enslaving, addicting force. A man is called an alcoholic if after a period of abstinence he is given a taste and has no power to stop but indulges until inebriated. If this scenario can be paralleled in any area of experience, then there is addiction in that area.

Jesus came to set the prisoners free, bringing deliverance to the captives. Whoever the Son sets free will be really and truly free. Only Jesus can liberate from every bondage known to mankind. It will require a confession of total inadequacy, plus a desire to forsake addiction even though powerless to do so.

Charles Wesley wrote of the Lord Jesus, "He breaks the power of canceled sin and sets the prisoner free." His own testimony was "My chains fell off; my heart was free; I rose, went forth and followed Thee." Enjoy the glorious liberty of the sons of God.

Do not be anxious then...for your heavenly Father knows that you need all these things. Matt.6:31,32

Fear and Anxiety

It is natural to be anxious and fearful, because the natural man is in a state of separation from God. The first recorded statement concerning Adam after the fall was that he was afraid. He had never known fear, for he used to walk with the Lord, but now he tried to hide. Fear ravaged his mind as alienation from the life of God brought awareness of death and judgment. Corruption entered his body. Mentally and emotionally he lost his moorings. Adam was adrift from God, facing impending doom and destruction. He was at enmity with God and under the dominion of Satan, sin, darkness and death.

To face time and eternity without being reconciled to God is a fearful prospect. Anxiety drags at the heart as things we were created to rule and subdue are now out of our control and, in fact, control us. We were all as Adam, lost souls, victims of our own folly, without God, without hope in this world. But Jesus came to seek and to save that which was lost. He gives hope as an anchor of the soul with His message of forgiveness and reconciliation to God. He came to introduce us to our loving heavenly Father, who knows all our needs and gives abundantly out of His riches in glory.

Jesus repeatedly tells His disciples not to fear or be anxious. He points to the birds of the air and the flowers of the field, encouraging us that we are of much greater worth and that God will take care of us. Fear and anxiety are the result of a severed relationship with God. If in repentance we forsake our sin and receive all the provisions of God in Jesus, we shall lack nothing.

I say to every man among you not to think more highly of himself than he ought to think. Rom.12:3

Pride and Self-Promotion

Pride was first expressed by Lucifer, his beauty being the cause of his corruption. The shining one became the prince of darkness. It appears that his own view of his splendor took him beyond his measure to where he wanted to be like the Most High. Paul gives us a caution, that none of us let our minds run ahead of the measure which we have received from the Lord. The one who sees the effect of what he has and forgets that it is a gift from God is in danger of thinking more highly of himself than he ought.

Humility originates in God and was clearly displayed in Jesus. He denied Himself, made Himself of no reputation and humbled Himself even to death on the cross. He did not exalt Himself, but His Father exalted Him. He never became a free agent to bring about His own promotion by doing His own will. Promotion comes from the Lord, for whom He wills He sets up and whom He wills he sets down.

Trusting in God's sovereignty over our lives and in the fact that our times are in His hands should prevent us from striving and should bring us contentment. If we promote ourselves or are promoted by man, then it will not be long before God brings us down. Equally, if we are passed over by man and God wants us promoted, then despite man, God will promote us.

At the final reckoning, there will be many surprises. Men who have not been in the limelight, but who have served the Lord in obscurity, will be exalted by Him. Take the lowest seat, for it is better to be asked to step up, than to be asked to step down. Remember, He who humbles himself shall be exalted.

A double-minded man, unstable in all his ways. James 1:8

Inconsistency

To be steadfast, unmovable, always abounding in the work of the Lord, is not the condition of babes and children. Babes are often carnal, and children can be tossed to and fro, being easily influenced by different pressures. A lack of consistency betrays immaturity.

There is an old saying in London that people give in response to the question "How are you?" The answer is "Up and down like Tower Bridge." This condition is prevalent among many Christians. It is difficult to determine how some Christians are doing on any given occasion because of the extreme highs and lows that they experience. The stopping and starting of old habits and the starting and stopping of new ones—both are all too common among Christians who should know better.

Much of this attitude can be traced to a lack of motivation caused by a deficiency of conviction. When we override the voice of the Spirit, a vicious circle starts. The gradual searing of the conscience makes it easier and easier to sin. Inconsistency is a manifestation of double-mindedness and mixture.

Jesus set his face like a flint and did His Father's will without wavering. The inconsistent Christian has no lasting joy because he is not at home in sin, and he knows that he is grieving the Spirit. Jesus delighted in the fear of God and the will of God. Are you delighted in the will of God? Have you both the beginning of wisdom, which is the fear of God, and the end of the commandment, which is love for God?

The antidote to inconsistency is the awareness of the Lord moment by moment. Pleasing Him should be the motivation that produces consistency.

You too be patient, strengthen your hearts, for the coming of the Lord is at hand. James 5:8

Short-Tempered or Patient?

Patience, like all true fruit of the Spirit, is foreign to the sinful nature. Irritability is part of the nature we were born with. When separation from the life of God occurred, fear of death and of accountability to God became the dominant feature of life. Insecurity is the result of sin. Gossip is common, because fallen nature has a twisted sense of how to get relief from its own guilt: project condemnation upon another.

A short temper is mainly the result of an offended conscience and the accompanying feeling of condemnation. It takes surprisingly little to arouse aggression in someone who feels condemned in his conscience. Ironically, this carnal trait can be detected in many Christians. The remedy for a short temper is peace with God.

Reconciliation with God recovers our security. Those who are secure in God, who walk with a conscience void of offense toward God or man, are not intimidated by criticism. They are more patient with others because they are at peace with God in their own hearts. Initially, the revelation of the forgiveness of God removes guilt, and subsequent continuance in the grace of God keeps from condemnation.

The blood of Jesus Christ cleanses from all sin and cleanses the conscience. Through justification, God can now be enjoyed. Obedience increases the awareness of His presence, which brings peace. The peace and joy that we experience can now be extended to others in our responses to them. Instead of practicing the aggression that comes from insecurity, you can be numbered with the peacemakers.

There is none righteous, not even one. Rom. 3:10

All Have Sinned: No One Is Righteous

We were all born with a fallen nature. Doing and saying wrong things does not need to be taught to children, for being naughty is natural. Our genes and our environment compound each other to disrupt our personalities. Thanks be to God that Jesus did not come to save the righteous, but to bring sinners to repentance. He came not to save the respectable, but lost sinners. Whoever needs to be saved needs to be saved totally, because sinners are totally lost. There are none who are a little bit alive, but all are very dead in trespasses and sins.

All mankind needs to be saved, to be brought to life. No one needs salvation less than anyone else. Jesus came that we might have life and have it abundantly. His arm is not too short to save. He saves to the uttermost; that is, there is none outside of the measure of His love and provision for salvation. There is no personality that does not need transforming, and there is no personality so bad that it cannot be changed into His likeness.

The awful tragedy about many Christians is that, having been brought to life, they remain unchanged in their basic personality. There must be a recognition of the need to change in every area of personality. We cannot bring any saved aspect from our old selves, for we have none. We wrongly think that certain aspects of our old man were Christian enough not to be crucified.

God does not patch up the old man, but He puts him to death. The new creature, the result of new birth by the Spirit of God, is all new. Uncrucified flesh cannot be joined to resurrection life.

And not holding fast to the Head, from whom the entire body ...
grows with a growth that is from God. Col.2:19

Holding Fast to the Head

Every member of the body of Christ has a direct relationship with the Head, the Lord Jesus. There are no indirect connections. No one is born-again with a disadvantage regarding access
to the Head. There is no need for another mediator because Jesus
said that His sheep would hear His voice. We may become dull of
hearing, and even sear our consciences, but these conditions must
be addressed personally.

If hindrances arise in our communion with the Lord, then it
is of paramount importance that time is spent before the Lord to
search our own souls to find what could have grieved the Spirit.
True repentance always resensitizes us to the leading of the Lord.

The purpose of a time of leanness in our walk with the Lord
can be to drive us deeper and more earnestly into Him. The Lord
desires more intimacy with us than we appreciate. Even when we
put Him out, He knocks at the door, wanting to come in and have
a meal with us. He jealously desires us.

It is true that we experience His life through others, but we
must never let go of the Head. There are things that the Lord does
not delegate. When He says that we are to come to Him, then to
Him we must come. When He says that He will give rest to us,
then we must receive His rest from Him.

Some Christians live through a vicarious relationship of others, with little or no relationship with the Lord themselves. This
is a travesty of what the Lord desires. The son of God who loves
you, and gave himself for you, called you personally, by name.
All true Christians have the capacity to hold fast to the head, and
as sons of God, to be led by the Spirit.

For sin shall not be master over you. Rom.6:14

Can We Stop Lusting?

Adam was created in God's image. God has desires, and Adam had those God-given desires in all their purity. When the fall occurred and sin entered, those godly qualities were perverted into the lusts of the flesh. The image of the divine nature was marred to a grotesque degree. What had been a magnificent specimen of created glory was reduced into the ugliness of sin-ridden, death-dominated, fallen man.

No longer did Adam and Eve view anything from the vantage point of purity and innocence. Unblemished desires turned into lusts, and their own nakedness became a shame to them. That nature was transmitted to all men through natural birth. Jesus, however, was not conceived through natural procreation. He was conceived of the Holy Spirit as the Son of God. He came with the good news of another birth, which was not of the flesh, but of the Spirit. He lived a life free from the lusts of the flesh, proving that divine nature could be expressed in flesh and blood.

Those who turn from their sin and receive Him by faith receive a new heart and a new spirit, becoming new creatures. Sin no longer has dominion over the born-again man. He can stop sinning, something he had no power to do before.

The power of the new life, which is Christ in you, is greater than the power of sin. Would God have gone to the extreme length of putting His Son to shame in agony and travail when in death He became sin for us if it were not going to work? Can you stop lusting? The answer is emphatically yes, for when Christ is your life He will lead you in triumph, even in your thoughts.

But when He, the Spirit of truth, comes, He will guide you into all the truth. John 16:13

How Can a Marriage Be Saved?

If failure is recognized and confessed, then God who forgives can also restore. When a man's ways please God He makes even his enemies to be at peace with him—how much more his wife. Getting right with God should not be motivated by an underlying bargaining mentality that uses reconciliation with God as a means for marital peace. Being right with the Lord is a paramount necessity, whether or not the marriage is to be saved.

Jesus said that the Holy Spirit would lead us into all truth and teach us all things. He will teach men how to be godly men, husbands and fathers. He will teach how to be reconciled and how to restore. The key is to be teachable, with a heart submitted to the Lord.

The Lord desires a relationship with each individual that does not include any other relationship or thing. "If anyone comes to Me and does not hate his own father and mother and wife and children... even his own life, he cannot be My disciple" (Luke 14:26). These are the Lord's terms in coming to Him. How does this affect the saving of your marriage? Only when we have a right relationship with God can we experience His pleasure towards us.

When a man's ways please Him, then God makes extraordinary things happen. Love can be rekindled if you do the things that were done when love was hot; cooling love can warm up again. Woo her again, knowing that if you are a king she is to be honored as a queen. Jesus laid down His life for His bride, so also a man ought to love his wife. Reconciliation with God came through the sacrifice of our Bridegroom. That principle still works.

Then I will make up to you for the years that the swarming locust has eaten. Joel 2:25

When Children Are Out of Control

Raising children to know the Lord is a challenge that can be met adequately by the grace of God. The Christian has advantages that those who do not know the Lord do not have. God's promises are to us and our children. We can pray and speak the word of God, which has its own power to perform in our children. Ultimately, we have the Lord Himself who is for us and for our children.

Being a role model for our children may sound like an unbearable burden, but we were made and equipped by God for it. If there has been failure or if the children were raised before you were a Christian, then they may have developed a value system that corresponds to the philosophies of this generation. But all is not lost, for God is the great restorer. However out of control, or part of this world, a child may have become, he is not outside of God's saving power.

We truly have the advantage. Where the world experiences only despair, we have hope. The Lord can make the crooked straight. There is no valley that cannot be filled, or mountain that cannot be brought low, or rough place that cannot be smoothed. There is no punk or junkie, no homosexual or fornicator, that is beyond the transforming power of Christ.

The authority given to a Christian father to be head of his house is given directly from the throne of God. The name of Jesus, and our prayers in that name, will bring under God's control all that is out of control in our homes. God alone can restore what has been wasted. His arm is not too short to save. His ear is open, and He delights to save to the uttermost.

They went out from us, but they were not really of us.
1 John 2:19

Those Who Leave the Church

John gives some clearly defined yardsticks to measure against. The reason he gives for "them" departing is that they were not of us. He says the same thing from another direction, stating that if they had been of us, then they would have remained with us. The "us" is the church.

Unlike the fragmented church of our generation, the church of John's day was identifiable in a city. Christians may leave one church and join another in our day, but this passage refers to *the* church.

Although we are to hold fast to the Head, the Lord Jesus, we are not to deny the body of Christ. To leave the members of the body is to leave the members of Christ. Jesus is not decapitated; therefore, it is deception to think of having a relationship with Christ without being involved with His body, the church. The church is the fulness of Him who fills all things. To be outside of the church is to be outside of Christ and His fulness.

We were all baptized by one Spirit into one body. If we do not remain with the body, it is because we were never truly a part of it. Not all who stay in the company of the church are actually of it, but those who leave manifest clearly that they are not of it.

Jesus will never dispense with the church. He will perfect her and remain her Head. To view the church as God sees her will alert us to our intrinsic involvement with her. You cannot say of another member that you have no need of him. The church is indispensable for your personal growth. Jesus still loves the church. Do you?

Not as Cain, who was of the evil one, and slew his brother.
1 John 3:11-19

Survival or Sacrifice

These verses present a contrast: the spirit of Cain and the Spirit of Christ. Cain was of the evil one and wanted to survive at all costs. The cost of his survival was the sacrifice of his brother. This attitude contrasts with the Spirit of Christ, who for our survival, sacrificed Himself. He laid down His life for us while we were His enemies. Cain hated and murdered his brother. If we hate our brother we are murderers who abide in death. The proof of our having passed from death to life is that we love the brethren.

John by being practical makes it easy for us to assess our condition. "If we have this world's goods and close our heart to our brother's need, we do not have the love of God abiding in our hearts." Love is in deed and truth, not mere words. Jesus demonstrated His love by laying down His life for us, and He tells us to love each other as He loves.

When we put a brother down in order to make ourselves look good, then we fall into the spirit of Cain and of survival, our survival at the cost of our brother's. When we cover our brother, even if it makes it appear that the problem is ours, then we act according to the Spirit of Christ, the spirit of sacrifice.

Personal insecurity will manifest itself in the spirit of survival; whereas, those who know their identity in the Lord can afford to sacrifice for the sake of others. The world and the spirit of the world hates Christians. Even so-called Christians may hate us, but we are to love, not only our brethren, but our enemies. Those who are so disposed have confidence in God.

Beloved, now we are children of God. 1 John 3:2

We Are Children of God Now

There are some things for which we have to wait, but we do not have to wait to be the children of God. We have our mortal bodies **now**, while our immortal bodies are yet to appear. We are to manifest the life of the Lord Jesus in our mortal bodies. These earthen vessels have the treasure of the excellency of the power of God within them. The Spirit that raised Christ from the dead has also quickened our mortal bodies.

In his prayer for the Ephesian church, Paul prays that the Father of glory will give them a spirit of wisdom and revelation in the knowledge of Him, and that the eyes of their understanding may be enlightened so that they might know what is the surpassing greatness of His power towards us who believe, in accordance with the working of the strength of His might which He brought about in Christ when He raised Him from the dead. Now we can know that power. Now we can be raised to walk in newness of life, because now we are the sons of God. If we were to lose sight of that fact, then we could put off manifesting Christ in our mortal flesh until Jesus returns.

John states what we are now in order to give us the impetus not to sin. The revelation of who we are now will motivate us to be that. Paul uses the same reasoning when he says that we are to clean out the old leaven so that we may be a new lump, even as we are in fact unleavened. Fact is defined as "the quality of being actual."

If in fact you are now a child of God, then you can think, speak and act accordingly. You have the authority and the ability now.

We are afflicted in every way, but not crushed; perplexed, but not despairing. 2 Cor.4:8

Perplexed, but Not Despairing

The Bible describes Elijah as a man of like passions, or with a nature like ours. It is comforting to know that such men of God had feelings with which we can identify. Paul is another such comfort. He had fears within as well as fightings without. He was perplexed sometimes, but although he was puzzled he never despaired. The same Greek word for perplexed is used elsewhere as doubt and at a loss to know.

The reason Paul's perplexities did not lead him to despair was the same as Job's, who although bewildered by what had happened, trusted God's sovereignty. Paul, while being perplexed, writes lucidly of our resources in Christ, the nature of faith and the benefits of developing trust and patience.

God ordains circumstances that are a trial of faith and trust. Job responded to his perplexity by saying that though God slayed him yet he would trust Him. Faith comes by hearing the word of God, but trust is exercised when there is no word. However bewildering circumstances may be, we can rest assured that God is in control.

All things do work together for good to those who love God. We may search for an explanation for what appears to be going wrong, but when we find none, God is worthy of our trust. Learn the secret of contentment in all circumstances.

Never give way to the temptation to accuse God. Worship Him when you are perplexed. When you fail to understand why something is happening, praise Him. To despair is to lose all hope, but God will never abandon you. You are never outside of His great love and caring heart.

He rules by His might forever. Ps.66:7

The Sovereignty of God

There was a time when there was nothing but God—no creature, no creation, no angel, nothing but the infinite, almighty and eternal God, glorious beyond imagination, beautiful and awesome, existing in the mystery of His *eternality* and the splendor of His self-sufficiency. His word was the only word, His thoughts the only thoughts. Unexampled in all His attributes, He existed before all things.

Jesus is the word that was with God and was God. "With" denotes the distinction within the Godhead, and "was" indicates the unity. From His own counsel, all that came into being in the invisible, eternal realm and the visible, tangible universe was by Him and for Him. He purposed what was to be and set the timing of every event according to His own good pleasure and will.

Nothing went wrong; He never had to change His plans; and when finally everything is rolled up, He will be the one doing it.

There are many mysteries, including the mystery of God and of his will, the mystery of iniquity, and God's mystery, Christ. Sin is a mystery, but in the ages to come, sin will not enter a second time. The redeemed, in their perfection, will not sin again in thought, word or deed. That is how conclusively God has dealt with sin through Jesus Christ.

God rules by His might forever and has never stopped, nor will He ever cease, to rule. God is infinite, transcending all. Satan is but a created being whose time is appointed. He is totally subject to the sovereign will of God. God has determined and predestined the outcome of all things, and He has never been even a second late.

"For My thoughts are not your thoughts, neither are My ways your ways," declares the Lord. Isa.55:8,9.

God Transcendent

The Bible declares itself to be the word of God. Within its pages God communicates truths concerning Himself, one of which is that He alone is God. There is none like Him, none beside Him, none who can compare with Him. He is self-revealed in plurality and unity: the Father, the Son and the Holy Spirit each having differently defined functions while remaining indivisibly one.

We must never attribute to any being or force what alone belongs to God. All things are from Him, by Him and to Him. Jesus is equal with God because He is God, but God has not created any being that is in any respect His equal.

Whatever power anyone possesses has been given to him by God who alone grants it. The devil cannot act outside of God's sovereign rule. What he does, he does by divine permission and purpose. When the Bible teaches us that Satan had power to overcome the saints, it prefaces that fact with the clear statement that it was GIVEN to him to make war with the saints, UNTIL...! God gives the power for appointed times and purposes.

God cannot be excelled; neither does He have a rival. Our generation knows more about the dimensions of the universe than any former generation. It is as though the physical universe is tangible evidence of infinity. Yet God cannot be restricted within its limits. The heaven of heavens cannot contain God. He created all things, fills all things and transcends them all.

All things are possible with God, and He does what pleases Him in heaven and earth. No purpose of His can be thwarted, and no one can pluck out of His hand, because no one is stronger than God.

Behold, O Lord, Thou dost know it all. Ps.139:1-6

God Omniscient

Omni means all, and science means knowledge. God is all knowing. He knows everything about everything. He cannot be taught, because there is nothing He does not know. Whether it is past, present or future, He cannot be informed, for such would presuppose that there is something He does not know, and that cannot be. His foreknowledge is not His ability to look into the future, for He produced the future. All His ways are known from the beginning.

Before the first angel was created, before the physical universe, when there was nothing and nobody else, there was God. All that came into being, all that has happened, that is happening and that will happen—all is according to His timing and purpose. The end, like the beginning, was finished in God before it began.

David thought upon the omniscience of God and was overwhelmed by it. God knows our rising up and our sitting down. He knows our thoughts afar off. He is not afar off, for He is ever near, but He knows our thoughts that we have not yet thought. He knows our next word, before we speak it. He is intimately acquainted with all our ways.

He counts the dust of the earth and the very hairs of our heads. He alone knows the hearts of all men, and His infinite capacity is never overloaded.

He made man in His image, but we must never put man's limitations upon Him. The prophets provide proof of God's foreknowledge, and the book of Revelation confirms that the future is the outcome of what God had counseled before the world was. Jesus came and will come again according to the will and the timing of God.

Where can I go from Thy Spirit? Or where can I flee from Thy presence? Ps, 119:7-12

God Omnipresent

There is no place where God is not—no reaches of the universe and no atomic structure that are outside of His presence, no opium den or brothel, no hell. There is nowhere to flee from His Spirit. God is even in Sheol because hell does not belong to Satan; it is God's hell. The Dark Ages represented hell as where Satan and demons tormented damned souls, but that is a fallacy.

The Lord declares of Himself that He fills heaven and earth. He cannot be confined, for He fills all things, yet He is not contained even by the heaven of heavens. He does not have to be sent in order to come to a place, for He is already there. His eyes are everywhere, and nothing is hidden from His scrutiny.

He cannot be avoided. The light and dark are alike to Him, and He is not limited by physical senses. He is totally aware all the time. Everything that happens to us happens in His presence.

He will never leave us nor forsake us. His eyes run to and fro throughout the earth that He may strongly support those whose hearts are completely His. What a comfort for those who love Him, that even before they call He will answer. The confidence generated by such knowledge of God produces peace and security for those who delight in His presence.

The Lord desires us to know His presence at all times and the joy that is in His presence. The ultimate experience of life is to know Him continuously and increasingly. He is not a God who is far off; He cannot be nearer. Wherever there is a here, He is there.

O Lord, Thou dost exalt Thyself as Head over all...and Thou dost rule over all. 1 Chron.29:10-13

God Omnipotent

God is the all-powerful one, almighty, of infinite strength, who rules by His might forever. He does what He pleases in heaven and earth, and no on can gainsay Him. He cannot be overcome, and there is no power that anyone has that has not been given to him by God. When Pilate tried to intimidate Jesus by saying that he had power to release or crucify Him, Jesus responded by saying that he had no power except what was given from above.

Before He ascended to heaven Jesus made the glorious statement "All authority has been given to Me in heaven and on earth." As a man, He conquered everything there was to be overcome: the world, the flesh and the devil. Now as victor over death, He reigns as Lord, Lord of all lords, King of all kings. God, His Father, has subjected all things to the Son, and finally, the Son will subject all things to Him who subjected them to Him, and God will be all in all.

After Job's trial, when he was confronted by the Lord, he declared of God that He could do all things and that none of His purposes could be thwarted. As God intends so it happens; as He plans so it stands. None can deliver or pluck out of his hand because there is no one greater than God.

There is no question of His purpose being fulfilled. History unfolds according to God's timing. All that He has said through the prophets has been, is, or will be fulfilled. He reveals and conceals according to His pleasure, and He gives gifts individually as He wills. This omnipotent God is our Father, Savior and lover of our souls.

He who listens to me shall live securely, and shall be at ease from the dread of evil. Prov.1:33

Listen to God and Live Securely

God is contrasted with dumb idols because He speaks and He alone is the living God. He desires to be known and has communicated Himself through His own creation. He spoke to and through the prophets and has in these last days spoken to us in His Son.

Jesus said that His sheep would hear His voice and that the Holy Spirit would teach us all things. God spoke creation into being and alone can speak life to the dead. Such is the power of His word.

As His children we live by faith—faith that comes through hearing the word of God. The word that came to the children of Israel was not mixed with faith in those who heard. To those who hear and observe what He says comes the wonderful promise that they shall live securely and be at ease from the dread of evil.

Listening implicitly contains the idea of doing, as when a father says to his child that he should have listened to him. It was not that the child had not heard, but that the words were not heeded or obeyed. Man is to live by every word that proceeds from God's mouth. Many voices clamor for our attention—multitudes of vain philosophies and the arguments of so-called science—but God's voice is the only one by which we live, not merely existing, but living securely and abundantly.

He speaks peace to His people, but by neglecting to heed His voice we become dull of hearing. Tragic consequences result when we spurn His wisdom and reproofs. By obedience our hearing becomes more acute, and our discernment grows. Give God time to speak. Listen all the time, and live to the full.

The fellowship of your faith may become effective through the knowledge of every good thing which is in you. Phile. :6

Effective Communication of Your Faith

The key to becoming effective communicators of our faith is to give full acknowledgement to every good thing that is in us in Christ. Knowing the full extent of what is in us in Christ is a progressive revelation, the full knowledge of which will be unveiled in the ages to come.

Some foundational things we can immediately appreciate. One is the mystery hidden from past generations that is now made known through the provisions of the new covenant which is Christ in us. When we give full credence to that fact, we have little problem sharing our faith.

Paul exhorts the Corinthians to examine themselves to see whether they are in the faith. He then confirms the truth that Christ is in them, unless they fail the test.

There is only one faith, the faith of God. Christians live by the faith of the Son of God. Do you know that another good thing in you in Christ is His faith?

Mark records that Jesus exhorted His disciples to have faith in God, but in fact the text is better rendered "have the faith **of** God" (Mark 11:22).

The Holy Spirit abides **in** the born-again believer. Jesus said that He would be with us and **in** us. With Timothy, we are reminded that we have received the Spirit of power, of love and of a sound mind. To live in the light and revelation of what is in us in Christ is to be effective communicators of our faith.

To be bound by what we were naturally is to deny our death in Christ's death. When Christ is our life we can do all things through His strength, and what was naturally impossible is now possible.

Enjoy life with the woman whom you love all the days of your fleeting life which He has given you. Eccles 9:9

Enjoy Life with Your Wife

God ordains marriage to be enjoyed all the days of our life. Although that may sound too idealistic, it has been and still is true for many. The breaking up, or down, of a marriage usually occurs because enjoyment has gone out of the relationship. When a husband and wife enjoy each other, they want to be together. It takes little to separate us from what we do not enjoy.

What then causes the loss of enjoyment? In short it is sin. The way we treat each other indicates the relationship that we have with the Lord.

In our western society, systematic rejection of God's commandments is causing an eroding of God-consciousness. This process leads to moral and spiritual collapse. The same principles apply in a marriage. Godly laws are the foundation and fiber of a peaceful and prosperous society. The less we give credence to God's laws the more lawlessness abounds. Because iniquity abounds the love of many grows cold. Satan, thedestroyer, is out to degrade and destroy humanity. He is influencing men, women and children to ignore God and Hiscommandments, and to substitute human philosophy with its lusts.

The outcome of such substitution proves the insanity of man. Injustice, anxiety, despair and death are the traumas we then experience instead of righteousness, peace and joy in life.

If the enjoyment has gone from your marriage, then heartfelt repentance and singleness of heart towards God and the wife He gave you is required. The Holy Spirit will teach you how to restore love and enjoyment to your home.

And we know by this that He abides in us, by the Spirit whom He has given us. 1 John 3:24

The Witness of the Spirit

The Holy Spirit witnesses with our spirit that we are the sons of God. In union with our spirit He makes known to us two aspects of our relationship with Him: one, that He abides in us; and two, that we abide in Him. True believers have the witness in themselves. Both objective truth and subjective experience are necessary. The word and the Spirit agree.

The kingdom of God is not in word only but in power and demonstration. The power is the power of the Spirit, which Jesus said would come upon His disciples as promised by the Father.

Having been made alive by the Spirit we are to continue walking in and by the Spirit. We have the same spirit of faith, by which we are to live. Faith comes by hearing the word of God, not as an external influence only, but also within us. Hearing the voice of the Lord can occur from without and from within. Being led by the Spirit involves discerning His voice, and the final conviction of discernment must be a matter of one's own conscience. Obedience sharpens our discernment just as disobedience dulls it.

Vested interest and selfish ambition hinder sensitivity to the voice of the Spirit. Living by the witness of the Spirit with our spirit may sound dangerous, but it is essential. Ultimately, living by the word does not conflict with living by the Spirit. These two aspects form a tension of truth. The letter of the law can be dead, but subjective experience can be led astray without the word of God as the source of faith. The Spirit is the Spirit of the word, and the word is the word of the Spirit.

No one who is born of God practices sin, because His seed abides in him, and he cannot sin, because he is born of God. 1 John 3:9

Born of God

Jesus Christ knew who His Father was and that He had come forth from His Father. His was not a natural birth, for He was conceived in the womb of Mary by the Holy Spirit. Jesus revealed the nature of God in flesh and blood. When He rose from the dead He told His disciples that He was ascending to His Father and their Father, to His God and their God.

At a normal birth the delivery of the head of the baby is where the labor and travail intensifies. When the head comes through the whole body follows with ease. This is a beautiful picture of what happened spiritually in Christ our Head. The anguish and travail was with our Head, and when He came through to resurrection life, the whole body, the church, was raised with Him.

We are born again to a living hope by the resurrection of Jesus. To be born of God one must be crucified, buried and raised with Jesus. The seed of God, which is Christ, gives us our birth from above. As God's children we now relate to Him as our Father. His Spirit bears witness with our spirit that we are the sons of God, whereby we cry from our innermost being, "Abba, Father," for so He is.

When we are born of God we become partakers of the divine nature and are naturally spiritual. John elaborates on the evidence proving those who are born of God. They do not practice sin, but righteousness. They love God and each other. They overcome the world, and the wicked one. Like Jesus, they are of God, not of this world. They have the ability not to sin, and to be obedient. The Holy Spirit inspired John to write that as Jesus is, so are we in this world.

And He made a scourge of cords, and drove them all out of the temple. John 2:14-17

Cleansing the Temple

At age twelve the Lord Jesus was found in the temple doing His Father's business. He knew that the temple was His Father's house and that temple business was God's business. After becoming subject to His mother and so-called father, Joseph, Jesus appears in no record until the age of thirty. His first miracle was to turn water into wine, denoting the change of covenants from that which cleanses the outward man to that which cleanses internally.

One of His earliest works was to cleanse the temple. He made a small scourge of cords and drove everyone and everything out of the temple. His disciples remembered that it was written that the zeal of the house of the Lord consumed Him.

Do we have such a zeal for His house? We are His house. Our bodies are temples of the Holy Spirit, and Jesus is still zealous about keeping His temple clean.

Nehemiah threw Tobiah's belongings out of the house of the Lord so the vessels of the Lord could be returned there. Paul tells us to cast out the bondwoman and her son so that the son of the free woman alone might be heir. We do not need to cohabit with the old man. We should cast off all that is foreign to Christ in us His temple.

Jesus drove the mercenary men out. Nehemiah threw a foreign man out. Paul instructs us to cast the old man out. Every vestige of the old man has to go. We are now a holy habitation of God by His Spirit. The Lord will thoroughly purge His floor and purify the sons of Levi. Either join the Lord in cleansing His temple by judging yourself, or be severely scourged.

Fervently love one another from a clean heart. 1 Pet.1:22

Our Responsibility to One Another

The most common admonition concerning our relationship with each other is to love one another. The standard is *as Christ has loved us*. Peter adds the proviso of fervent love from a pure heart, which is not unobtainable for those who have purified their hearts by faith.

Our relationship with each other should include, but go beyond, friendship. Our love surpasses even kinship as brothers and sisters, for we are members one of another.

When God poured out the Holy Spirit on the early church, no one had a need that someone else did not meet. They were of one heart and soul, and no man considered what he had his own. By one Spirit they had been baptized into one body and had become members of one another. Although each individual holds fast to the head, each also has an essential placement and function in the body.

The outworking of our love for each other is very practical. By love we serve one another, esteeming and honoring others above ourselves. By love we are devoted to one another, looking not only to our personal needs but also to the needs of others, bearing one another's burdens, forgiving and receiving one another. If we bite and devour one another we shall consume each other.

Accountability to one another is a safeguard in the body. Confessing our faults to each other is a neglected but effective way to overcome them. We will display a marvelous testimony of Jesus when we show the same care for each other. The way we treat each other is how we treat the Lord. As we do it to the least of His brethren, we do it to Him.

He made known to us the mystery of His will. Eph. 1:9

The Mystery of His Will

God's will is surrounded with mystery. It is not His will that any should perish, but many do. He does all things according to the good pleasure of His will, but much happens that does not please Him. We can only bow before Him and declare with the apostle Paul, "Oh the depth of the riches both of the wisdom and knowledge of God! How unsearchable are His judgments and unfathomable His ways" (Rom. 11:33).

Jesus Christ came to do the will of His Father. He delighted to do His will and always did those things that pleased Him. However awful the rejection of Jesus and His agonizing death may appear, He was fulfilling the predetermined will and counsel of God. Peter reminds us that if God wills for any of us to suffer, the faithful Creator is doing right as well as those who suffer (1 Pet. 4:9).

God's will is good, acceptable and perfect. It is the best thing that can happen to us. If we pray that His will be done on earth, then we of all people should fulfill that prayer. We have spent sufficient time in the lusts of the flesh. Now we live for the will of God. Our sanctification, the process of life that conforms us to Christ, is the will of God. Therefore, we must not be foolish, but understand what the will of the Lord is.

Not everyone who calls Him Lord shall enter the kingdom, but he who does the will of the Father. Doing the will of God from the heart pleases God, and that is most important. Ultimately everything else is vanity, and all that is done by way of disobedience to His will shall be burned up as wood, hay and stubble. But he who does the will of God abides forever.

God is our refuge and strength, a very present help in trouble.
Ps. 46:1

Our Refuge, Strength and Help

If there is anything we need in these troublesome times, it is a place of refuge, somewhere to go for safety and assurance, someone to help us and allay our fears. The Lord is that refuge. No shelter into which we can escape the perils pursuing us compares with the Lord. The traumatic conditions and events that Jesus described as prevailing at the end of the age correspond to verses two and three in this psalm. There will be signs in the heavens, dismay among the nations, perplexity at the roaring of the sea and the waves, and men's hearts failing them for fear at the expectation of the things coming upon the world.

Jesus exhorts us to pray in order that we might have the strength to escape all these things. God alone is the unshakable foundation and rock of our salvation. Those who trust in the Lord shall be as mount Zion which cannot be removed. Everything else in heaven and on earth will be shaken.

Wives and children are looking for husbands and fathers who as heads of their families are unshakable—men who in the face of the great distress that is to come upon the world will display that God is their refuge and strength, men who will not fear the earth being moved and the mountains quaking.

Those who trust in God's sovereign power will be examples that inspire others to find the same peace and joy. There is nothing to fear when the Lord is our refuge, our strength and our help, because He is very present and will be exalted among the nations.

If we confess our sins, He is faithful and righteous to forgive us our sins. 1 John 1:9

Forgiveness

The availability of forgiveness is an integral part of the good news of God. As hopeless debtors to God we stood condemned and justly deserved the penalty, but God out of His great love sent His Son to become the sin-bearer and sacrifice for sins. Now forgiveness of sins is preached in the name of Jesus. No one is beyond the pardon of God.

When we receive the forgiveness of God it is incumbent upon us to forgive others. Of all the wonderful themes in the prayer that the Lord taught us, our Lord refers back only to the issue of forgiveness. If we forgive men their transgressions, our heavenly Father will forgive us. If however we do not forgive men, then our Father will not forgive our transgressions.

There are serious implications for the unforgiving. In the parable of the man owing his creditor a considerable sum which he could not pay, Jesus tells us that the creditor had compassion on the debtor and forgave him his debt when he fell down and begged for mercy. That same debtor came across a man who owed him a comparatively small sum and who likewise pleaded for mercy, but his plea was met with hostility and hardness of heart, and he was sent to prison by the one who himself had recently received such forgiveness. A witness to these events reported it to the original creditor, who called back the man he had forgiven and upbraided him for his callous behavior. He then took his forgiveness back and sent the man to prison and to the tormenters.

Bitterness and gall accrue with unforgiveness. Forgive and be forgiven and free. The alternative could mean God giving the unforgiving to the tormentors.

You tithe mint and dill and cummin, and have neglected the weightier provisions of the law. Matt.23:23

Weightier Things

Jesus gave scathing rebukes to the scribes and Pharisees for majoring on minors and neglecting the weightier provisions of the law. In their perverted minds they were more concerned with outward appearance before men than with the condition of their heart before God. Jesus called them whited sepulchers that shone white in the sun but inside were dark and full of rotting flesh.

It is not without significance that those who major on outward observance—touch not, taste not, observance of days, and the like—betray a neglect of true inward faith.

The teaching of Jesus put the emphasis where the word of the Lord had always asserted it, on the heart. He accentuated the secret rather than the public. Unlike pharisaical service, true service to God is a matter of heart and is done in secret. Whether it is praying, fasting, giving, or showing mercy, all is to be done for His pleasure and not for public acclaim.

We are to abstain from every appearance of evil but must remember that our hearts appear before the Lord at all times. If our motivation is to create an impression that does not correspond to the condition of our heart, then we are pharisaical.

It is not the testimony of Jesus to abstain from things that God has given to be enjoyed with thankfulness, and at the same time to have a critical spirit or pride in one's outward observance. God is more concerned with justice, love, mercy and faithfulness from the heart than with appearing to be religious before men. Are the weights on your scales man's or the Lord's?

Because this widow bothers me, I will give her legal protection.
Luke 18:5

Importunity

The Lord Jesus gave the clearest teaching on this neglected aspect of prayer. Importunity means to be persistent and press in, even when it seems inconvenient to the one being importuned. In the parable of the unjust judge and the widow, she became inconveniently persistent until the judge was worn out. Because of her importunity, he gave her what she requested. Our Lord upholds her as an example to imitate in our prayer life.

Again, a man who kept knocking at his friend's door would not take "no" for an answer. His friend knew that he would have no rest until he granted him his request. The Lord asks us to give Him no rest until He makes Jerusalem a praise in the earth.

Importunity does not betray a lack of faith, but on the contrary, it demonstrates a suppliant's tenacious belief in the provider. To ask in faith does not contradict importunity; otherwise, importunity would be taught as a lack of faith, a demonstration of unbelief not to be imitated.

Importunity has in its application the element of *seeking*. To seek does not mean to look briefly and then stop looking, but to keep on looking. God does not need our importunity as much as we do. It takes us beyond the superficial and may even call for wrestling with God.

Jacob wrestled all night and prevailed with God. That experience did something in him that a quick answer would never have achieved. Jesus ever lives to make intercession for us, and the final outcome will be the church in all her glory. The great lesson in all the examples of importunity is that it gets final results.

But wishing to justify himself, he said to Jesus, "And who is my neighbor?" Luke 10:29

Who Is Your Neighbor?

This question, which occurred as a lawyer was seeking to justify himself to Jesus, was the occasion for the parable of the good Samaritan. The impressive thing about the Samaritan was that the Jews despised his people and treated them with contempt. The Jewish priest and the Levite passed by on the other side of the road, and the unfortunate victim, a fellow Jew who had put Samaritans on the *other side,* found himself attended to by one.

The Samaritan's compassion transcended enmity, and he cared for the Jew. Having illustrated the point so vividly, Jesus asked the Jewish lawyer, "Which of the three was neighbor to him?" The lawyer could hardly deny the obvious and answered that it was the one who had shown mercy. Jesus in His inimitable way told him to go and do the same.

Loving His enemies is a facet of God's nature. If we are partakers of the divine nature, then we too can demonstrate such love. Start with loving your wife, your family and fellow believers, and then move on to your enemies. The challenge is to view men and women with love even if they are antagonistic.

In union with Christ we can reach out to the unlovely, to the poor, and even to those who persecute and curse us. We were not God's friends when He commended His love to us. We were His enemies, yet He had compassion because of our lost condition and brought us salvation in all its glorious power.

What He has been to us He desires that we be to others. What you have freely received you are to freely give. Doing good to those who spitefully use you is really being neighborly.

*If we have food and covering, with these we shall be content.
1 Tim.6:8*

Contentment

Paul wrote to Timothy about men of depraved minds, void of truth, who supposed that godliness was a means of gain. Not being content with the great gain that godliness in itself was, they were eager for the gain of riches. Paul reminds Timothy that we brought nothing into the world and can take nothing out. Having food and covering is enough with which to be content. Such a notion is foreign to our western materialistic culture. Paul gladly suffered the loss all things in order to gain Christ. There is no greater gain than Christ.

When Christ is manifested in our mortal body, then we have gained our soul. If gain for us means earthly riches, then we will fall to temptations and snares that plunge men into ruin and destruction.

Seductions to gain more and more natural things abound. Men of God who ought to know better encourage the carnal trait of greed by telling us to name it and claim it, or to visualize it and go for it, all under the guise of faith. Jesus taught us differently by His own lifestyle. In His encounter with the rich young ruler He told him to sell what he had, to give it to the poor and to follow Him. We cannot be His disciples unless we forsake all relationships and everything we have, including our own life.

If God for His own purposes makes us rich, then we are to be rich in good works. Paul was instructed in how to be abased as well as in how to abound, and he learned to be content with all circumstances.

Riches are uncertain, but God is trustworthy. Trust in the Lord and His sovereignty in your life. Contentment is a valuable secret and must be learned, if you are to live in peace.

Always having all sufficiency in everything. 2 Cor. 9:8

Self-Sufficiency?

The question of self-sufficiency needs to be examined, for there is a wrong and a right self-sufficiency. We are not sufficient of our selves, but our sufficiency is of God. It is wrong to consider ourselves adequate apart from God, but if our adequacy is in God then we are truly adequate.

Peter and John are examples of this apparent dichotomy. They encountered a lame man at the gate Beautiful and said, "Look on us." Then in response to the beggar's expectation for money Peter commented that they had no silver or gold but what they had they would give him. "In the name of Jesus Christ... walk" was the gift they could give. When referring back to that incident, Peter replied, "Why do you gaze at us as if by our own power we had made him walk?" He then instructed them concerning faith in the name of Jesus.

We may be earthen vessels, but that does not deny the excellency of the treasure within us, which is of God. Paul uses a word for sufficiency with the prefix *aut* which means self as in automatic. The word literally means self-sufficiency. It does not deny our dependence upon the Lord but rather promotes the fact that Christ in us is our total sufficiency.

Christ being our life gives us an inbuilt adequacy that makes us sufficient from within ourselves. There is no situation with which we are inadequate to cope. We have the sufficiency of God with which we can overwhelmingly conquer in all eventualities. This fact does not underestimate our need for the body, but rather, it gives every member the ability for maximum function.

The first man is from the earth, earthy; the second man is from heaven. 1 Cor.15:47

Two Men

In God's economy there are only two men, the first man Adam and the second man Jesus. We are all born naturally and bear the image of the earthly Adam. All men can trace their lineage back through Noah to Adam. The Lord Jesus taught the necessity of being born again from above by the Holy Spirit. The new birth is not by natural seed but by incorruptible seed, the seed of God. God Himself fathers the new birth, and the life we receive by His Spirit is the life of Jesus, the seed of God.

The born-again believer is categorically no longer in the flesh but in the Spirit, if the Spirit of God dwells within him. Our old man has been crucified and buried with Christ, and we now share in the newness of the resurrection life of Jesus. Christ is our Life. We are seated with Him in heavenly places because we are inseparably joined to Him as one spirit, partakers of the divine nature.

As heirs of God and joint heirs with Christ we are not to live in a duality of expression, the old man with the new man. Let it be either good or evil, not both together. Either Adam or Christ is to be our life.

Pilate gave the people a choice, Barabbas or Jesus. There is no better example of fallen Adamic nature than Bar(son of)-abbas(the father). He was a rebel and a murderer. Jesus also was the Son of His Father, and in reality the choice was "Who shall I release, the son of the father or the Son of the Father?" Who will you crucify, and who will you release? You can live in the flesh or in the Spirit, in the old or in the new, in Adam or in Christ, but do not live with one foot in each.

A people for His own possession, zealous for good deeds.
Titus 2:14

Works

In His letters to the seven churches, the Lord Jesus made it clear that He knew everything about them including their works. We cannot work our redemption, because by works of the law no one can be justified. Then again, we were created in Christ Jesus for good works, which God prepared beforehand that we should walk in them. The erroneous teaching of justification by works has unfortunately produced a reaction against the need for works. Paul commands believers to be careful to maintain good works.

The Lord Jesus taught us to live in such a way that the world might see our good works and glorify our heavenly Father. They should see in us a caliber of life that could only be attributed to God.

Jesus gave Himself for us that He might redeem us from every lawless deed and purify to Himself a people for His own possession, **zealous for good works**. We were created for good works just as Jesus went about doing good works. He is our example.

Faith without works is dead and useless. We are known by our works, for deeds that are good are quite evident, and those that are otherwise cannot be concealed.

The Scriptures are given to thoroughly furnish us for every good work. Ultimately we must all stand before the judgment seat of Christ to receive those things **done** in the body. Each man's work will become evident.

There will be those who will profess that they knew Him but whose works will have denied Him. Jesus calls them workers of iniquity. It is not those who say, "Lord, Lord," who enter the kingdom of heaven but those who **do** the will of the Father. Simply work out what God is working in.

Let your character be free from the love of money. Heb.13:5

Our Attitude Toward Money

We are exhorted to let our way of life, or character, be free from the love of money. It is the Lord Christ whom we serve, not mammon. What we serve not only masters us, but also indicates where our heart is focused. Where your treasure is, there will your heart be also. Western opulence has generated greed rather than satisfaction, and such a love for money is the root of all evil. The Pharisees were lovers of money, and lovers of money head the list of the signs of the end times.

Affluence is not a sin, for the Lord makes the rich as He does the poor, but it is our attitude toward riches that counts. The Scriptures warn against desiring to be rich. Jesus warned against greed and instructed us that the life of a man does not consist in the abundance of possessions. He taught on the nature of true riches and treasures in heaven, and His own relationship to this world's goods is our example.

The last church to be addressed by the Lord was the church of Laodicea. Their own commentary on themselves was that they were rich and increased in goods and had need of nothing. Their deception is seen in contrast to the truth that the Lord Jesus records concerning them.

If most of the Western church is lukewarm, is it not possible that we have a deceptive assessment of ourselves and our wealth? Our hope is not to be fixed on the uncertainty of riches but on God who richly supplies us with all things to enjoy. The rich are exhorted to be rich in good works, to be generous and ready to share. Our generosity is the measure of our attitude toward money.

God's purpose according to His choice. Rom.9:11

Election and Predestination

Some would like *predestination* and *election* to be removed from our vocabulary, but it must be understood that apart from the Bible there is no other source for these doctrines. Augustine and Calvin are not responsible for originating these controversial words. The apostles who wrote in these terms were inspired by the Holy Spirit as instruments of divine revelation.

Jesus, by the same Holy Spirit, enunciated emphatically the doctrine of election. We must sometimes differentiate between what is palatable to human reason and what is taught by the word of God. Paul knew that his teaching would provoke questions and actually addressed them preemptively. If our doctrine does not pose such questions as "Is there unrighteousness with God?" or "Why does He find fault?" or "Who has resisted His will?" then we must question our doctrine.

On the question of whether God chose me because I chose Him, the Scripture is quite clear, saying, "You have not chosen Me, but I have chosen you." We love Him because He first loved us.

To appreciate the necessity of being elected, one has to understand the extent of man's depravity and how dead we were. If God did not predestine and elect, no one would be saved, because there is not one who seeks after Him. God is not taking anything away from anyone when He does not give him eternal life. Those to whom He gives repentance and faith receive them by His grace.

Although His will is a mystery, He alone is God. We cannot solve the mystery with carnal logic, making ourselves the initiators instead of God. Let the elect of God praise Him for His grace.

Let us cleanse ourselves from all defilement of flesh and spirit.
2 Cor. 7:1

Do It Yourself

The great doctrines of redemption make it obvious that we cannot save ourselves. Apart from God's grace we would remain dead in our trespasses and sins. While we had nothing to do with our birth, our growth and maturity are dependent upon our cooperation. As those born of God, we are required by the Lord to begin to do things for ourselves. We are to do nothing apart from Him, because without Him we can do nothing, but through the indwelling Spirit we have the ability to apply our great salvation.

If Christ is our life, then the Scriptures exhort us to wake up to righteousness and sin not. They further exhort us to clothe ourselves with Christ, shake ourselves from the dust, loose ourselves from the bands around our neck, deliver ourselves and cleanse ourselves from all filthiness of the flesh and spirit.

We are to perfect holiness in the fear of God. We are to keep ourselves in the love of God and to keep ourselves pure and unspotted from the world. Furthermore, we are to purify ourselves and walk as Jesus walked, being righteous as He is and Holy as He who has called us is holy.

Natural parents initially do most things for their children, but they gradually encourage the children to do things for themselves. As God's children we are to grow up in Him in all things, and He therefore requires that we do what is expected of us so that we can mature. Doing things for ourselves is nothing less than applying the grace of God and being obedient. It is written that the bride of Christ made **herself** ready.

Out of Zion the perfection of beauty, God has shone forth. Ps.50:2

Zion, City of God

Glorious things are spoken of Zion, the city of God. When we come to Jesus, the mediator of the new covenant, we also come to mount Zion, the city of the living God. He has desired Zion for His habitation, for it is His resting place forever. God's people are the mountain of His holiness, the mountain of the Lord that in the last days will be established on the tops of the mountains.

Daniel prophesied that the stone that struck the image and pulverized it grew into a mountain that filled the whole earth. God is taking the church on to perfection. Out of Zion, the perfection of beauty, God will shine. The church will be a worthy bride for the Son.

Predestination takes the called through justification and on to being glorified together with the Lord Jesus. The church is not yet the joy of the whole earth that it will be. Jesus will build His church, and nothing will prevent that. Nations will come to the brightness of her rising and kings shall see her glory. Her righteousness will shine as brightness and her salvation as a lamp burning in the darkness. There will be glory in the church by Christ Jesus.

The vision of a gloriously effective church that becomes the envy of the nations is to be our goal. Goals discipline us towards their fulfillment. The things that militate against the goal of a glorious church must be put off.

You are responsible for your part of the body. If God is to rest in Zion then He is to rest in you. All that grieves Him must be laid aside with only those things that please Him being pursued.

But God being rich in mercy, because of His great love. Eph. 2:4

God of Mercy

God is the God of mercy. He is revealed as being rich and great in mercy. Mercy, like grace, comes from Him, and no one extends it to Him. We were hostile toward God and enemies in our alienation, yet God extended His mercy towards us. In His mercy He brings the sinner to a place of conviction where he cries for mercy. Of the two men who stood and prayed in the temple, the one who smote on his breast and cried to God for mercy was the one who found mercy and who went down to his house justified.

In giving the truth about our fallen state, Paul interjects with one of the wonderful "but God" quotes: "But God...rich in mercy." God's rich mercy that comes out of His great love for us, even when we were dead in our transgressions, has made us alive together with Christ.

The necessity of God's mercy is absolute. We were debtors owing an incalculable debt with nothing to our credit, but God had mercy upon us and out of His great kindness and compassion paid our debt by giving up His own Son and freely forgiving us.

The merciful are blessed, for they shall obtain mercy. Since we have become recipients of His great mercy, the Lord requires that we show mercy towards others. God loves cheerful givers, and we are exhorted to give mercy with cheerfulness. The world is looking for men of mercy, men whose homes exhibit the godly qualities of love and mercy, where grudges, grievances and malice have no place.

Appreciate how much mercy has been extravagantly conferred upon you by God, and be motivated to be an instrument of mercy towards others.

But the Lord stood with me, and strengthened me. 2 Tim.4:17

The Lord Stands with Us

Paul wrote these words at the end of his life. He had fought a good fight, finished his course and kept the faith.

Yet no one stood with him, for all had deserted him despite his former popularity. In expressing this sorry state of affairs to Timothy, he interjects an ingredient that gave him his buoyancy: "but the Lord stood with me."

Where there is a consciousness of the Lord, deficiencies in all other areas dissolve into insignificance. That is why walking with the Lord in an awareness of His presence is of supreme importance. We experience life in its fulness when we enjoy His presence.

How did Paul have the strength to be poured out as a drink offering, to endure hardship, hunger, deprivation, beatings and persecutions, and to bear the burden of the care of all the churches? He knew the Lord and knew that the Lord knew him. He was able to write from prison a letter of rejoicing. Despite His incarceration he instructed the Philippians to rejoice always, repeating as a command the admonition that they should rejoice.

He had already counted all things but loss in view of the surpassing value of knowing Christ Jesus his Lord, for he counted all that he had as rubbish in order to gain Christ.

Although Paul would have acutely felt the pain of being deserted, the Lord His Shepherd stood with him, and he lacked nothing.

Christ was the prize of his path; Jesus was all in all to him. Such awareness of the Lord is available to all believers. Do you know the reality of the Lord standing with you? What the Lord was to Paul, He desires to be to each one of us.

Do you know the reality of the Lord standing with you?

*I will also rejoice in Jerusalem, and be glad in My people.
Isa. 65:19*

Responding to God

The right response to God will always produce in us its benefits. For instance, true repentance will produce the knowledge of forgiveness, with an accompanying lightness of spirit. The burden of guilt is removed, and the grief of God's Spirit is replaced by His pleasure. That sort of transaction can be felt.

We ought not to limit the work of God within us to that which does not affect us emotionally. God has emotions, and we were made in His image. Jesus had emotions and feelings. When He felt sad His body chemistry produced tears, and when He felt glad He rejoiced with at least a smile.

He was not only a man of sorrows, but He was also anointed with the oil of gladness above His fellows. After the seventy returned with joy, He told them to rejoice that their names were written in heaven. Then He rejoiced greatly in the Holy Spirit. The word used for rejoicing as related to Jesus is different from the word used regarding His disciples. Their word means be glad, while His word means to exalt and leap much for joy.

His body was the vehicle used to express His emotions. When He was *moved* with compassion the word used is *mot* from which we get *emotion*. He was always in control, yet He expressed His feelings.

Our text uses an unusual word for *rejoice*, one that is translated "to spin around under the influence of violent emotion." It is God who does that. The Bible teaches us that God shouts, laughs, sings and dances. He commands us to shout for joy and to shout in triumph. Have you ever done that? How is it possible to obey this command without showing it?

He made Him who knew no sin to be sin on our behalf. 2 Cor.5:21

He Was Made Sin for Us

It is difficult to imagine how utterly pure was the nature of Christ, conceived by the Holy Spirit as the Holy Son of God. After His life on earth He was known as "He who knew no sin." His original purity was never tarnished. He remained the spotless Lamb of God, the beauty of holiness in the form of a man with a glory that could be seen. Yet it was written of Him that He had no beauty that we should desire Him. His visage was marred more than any man's to the point where we hid, as it were, our faces from Him.

What caused such a change in His countenance? In the garden of Gethsemane Jesus wrestled with the full impact of being made sin. He threw Himself on the ground and cried out with strong crying and tears to Him who was able to save Him from death. He began to sweat great drops like blood, and He said that His soul was troubled unto death. An angel was sent to strengthen Him because He nearly died in the garden as He contemplated the implications of the cup he was about to drink.

His pristine purity and unbroken fellowship with the Father was about to be affected by His being constituted sin, not just my sin but the sin of the whole world of all generations. The utter filth and defilement of every imaginable evil was to be laid on Him. He then endured a mockery of a trial and was scourged twice; once by Pilate's men and once by Herod's soldiers.

He was nailed to the cross and despite His weakness threw off principalities and powers and openly triumphed over them. After His great travail He gave up His spirit, and His body was laid in a tomb. He was accepted as the offering for sin because of His purity, and was raised again from the dead, that we might be made the righteousness of God in Him.

That we might become the righteousness of God in Him.
2 Cor.5:21

Becoming the Righteousness of God

Jesus became identified with His bride in her sin before she could be united with Him in His righteousness. He was dead in trespasses and sins that were not His, but ours. What He took upon Himself He became so that we might become what He was in His righteousness. The gift of righteousness that we receive is not something that we hold apart from us. The gift is that we become, or are constituted, righteous.

Jesus was "born again" from the dead that we might be born again by His resurrection, born of God by His seed. The seed is Christ, incorruptible seed which abides in us. The blood of Jesus justifies, and His resurrection brings us new life.

After His resurrection Jesus called His disciples His brethren, saying that He was ascending to His Father and their Father. He was born of God by the Holy Spirit, and so are His brethren. His brethren, the church, are now joint heirs with Him and the habitation of God, for He who is joined to the Lord is one Spirit.

As God's children we are made as righteous as He is. That is why we are exhorted to be holy as He who has called us is holy. It may be difficult to comprehend that we who possessed sinful nature are now partakers of the divine nature. New birth, by the Spirit, creates us new. The new creature has a new heart and a new spirit in union with His Spirit, with all things new and all things of God.

The Lord purified unto Himself a people for His own possession who share His nature. Therefore, wake up to the fact that you are righteous, and stop sinning. Being made righteous gives us the ability to live righteously.

*He who has My commandments and keeps them...I will love him
and disclose Myself to him. John 14:21*

Experiencing God

God is the great communicator. Making Himself known to
man has been His intention in many and varied ways through the
ages. Creation is a vehicle to make God and even His eternal
Godhead known to us, but the ultimate revelation is in His Son,
the Lord Jesus.

As infinite as God is, His delight is with the sons of men.
As finite as we are, by His grace we can become partakers of the
divine nature. Thomas Aquinas, a scholastic theologian of the
middle ages, attempted to prove God's existence by what logi-
cally could be deduced from the world around us. He became the
author of much of the present theology of the Roman Catholic
Church, but he undermined the truth of experiencing God. At the
end of his life, while he sat on the side of a well, the Holy Spirit
came upon him in power. He sewed a record of the experience
inside his garment, including this commentary on his life: "All my
life is straw." He had expounded for many years the logical de-
duction of God, but God Himself finally overwhelmed him. This
experience of God made his former logic and denial of feeling like
straw in the day of reckoning.

Whatever can be inferred from creation cannot be compared
with experiencing God in personal intimacies. Jesus said that
those who loved Him and kept His commandments would be loved
by Him and His Father, and He would disclose Himself to them.

He still manifests Himself and speaks to His own. The ability to rejoice with joy unspeakable and to cry from our innermost
being, "Abba Father," comes from an overwhelming experience
of Him.

This is the victory that has overcomes the world—our faith.
1 John 5:4

Faith for Overcoming

John lays the groundwork for our faith in the Lord Jesus as the ultimate overcomer. That faith gives us victory over the world. Jesus overcame the world, the flesh and the devil. When we partake of Christ we share in His life, which has already conquered. Jesus in us is greater than he who is in the world, and we overwhelmingly conquer through Christ who strengthens us.

Paul asks us to examine ourselves to see whether we are in the faith. If Christ is in us, then we have the faith of Christ, but if He is not in us, then we fail the test. When we live by the faith of the Son of God, we can resist the devil, and he will flee from us. Through our union with Christ we have superior power over sin and the powers of darkness. We face a defeated foe in the power of the conqueror.

The exploits of those who by faith gained a good report under the old covenant are recorded in the Scriptures. How much more ought we, under the terms of the new covenant, display strength and take action. Overcoming cannot be conceived of as passive. Put on God's armor, fight the good fight, wrestle against principalities and powers, and prevail.

Jesus has broken our fetters and freed us to bind their kings with chains and their nobles with fetters of iron. The judgment has already been written; execute that judgment. All saints have the honor of implementing the provisions of Christ's triumph. Do not be subject to old habits and seducing spirits. By faith in who you are in Jesus, and who Jesus is in you, take dominion, and be numbered with the overcomers.

Whenever you fast, do not put on a gloomy face. Matt. 6:16

An Expression of Self-Control

One obvious pitfall in a society where food is plentiful and money available is overeating. When Paul referred to buffeting his body, he was not alluding to a buffet, or eating place; although the way we eat may betray that we are more disposed to that ludicrous interpretation.

One discipline in the area of self-control is fasting. Our Lord fasted and taught on the subject. He said, "When" not "If" you fast. Furthermore, He told us how to do it unobtrusively. When and how are the operative words. The Holy Spirit who teaches us all things will tell us when and how to fast. The residual power of the flesh in our bodily appetites can overrule the voice of the Spirit. If we have not fasted for a long time, then we may have seared our consciences in that area.

Fasting because of the intensity of a burden can be a liberating experience. It will certainly prove our ability to make slaves of appetites that once mastered us. We were created to rule and subdue. We have no satisfaction when we are dominated by lusts in their various forms, but we have deep personal fulfillment when we rule from our spirits.

Not only do we benefit enormously from self-control, but we also defeat spiritual powers. The purposes of God are worked out, angels dispensed and powers of darkness overthrown through prayer and fasting. In place of the excesses of the flesh, our moderation should be known to all men, but beyond everyday moderation God calls us to the abstinence of a fast. If it were not necessary, the Lord would not teach us how to fast.

The mind set on the Spirit is life and peace. Rom.8:6

The Mind Set on the Spirit

A tragedy in much of Christian experience is that having been made alive to the things of the Spirit, we do not set our minds on the Spirit. The renewal of the Spirit is not superficial, it includes a renewal of the mind. New birth constitutes us spiritual to the extent that we are no longer in the flesh but in the Spirit. We are under no obligation to the flesh to fulfill its lusts, because we are now able to walk in the Spirit.

We have a new mind, one set on things above where Christ is. We set our thinking on the Spirit and upon whatever is true, honorable, right, pure, lovely and of good repute. Our minds are to dwell on these things, and we are to walk accordingly.

Being led by the Spirit requires listening to His voice. Becoming dull of hearing is the outcome for those who hear and do not obey, for the voice of the Spirit becomes diminished by the clutter and clamor of every other voice. Those who mind earthly things miss out on the heavenly things. The deep things of God, His intimacies and His secrets, are made known by His Spirit.

All the treasures of wisdom and knowledge are in Jesus. Unspeakable insights, breathtaking revelations that make our spirits leap, are ours as the Holy Spirit makes Christ known to us. The overwhelming knowledge of His presence dissolves our fears and anxieties and causes us to rejoice with a joy unspeakable.

Jesus came that we who formerly lived alienated from the life of God might have life and peace abundantly by His Spirit. Set your mind on Him.

You are fellow citizens with the saints, and are of God's household.
Eph. 2:19

Joint Citizens with the Saints

Paul addressed the Ephesian church as fellow citizens, for he was unveiling to Gentiles the mystery of their relationship with the Jews who were in Christ. A partition no longer divided them, for Jesus had come and reconciled both in Himself by one Spirit into one body. All Christians, whether Jew or Gentile, have the same Father, with Jerusalem above as their mother.

Our heavenly citizenship is more fundamental than the country of our natural birth. Patriotism toward our earthly and temporal nation is subservient to our citizenship above. We have a different relationship with fellow Christians in our earthly country than we do with unbelievers. We are God's family, and because of this our relationship with fellow Christians in other nations differs from our relationship with unbelievers in our own nation. We join a company that no man can number from every nation, kindred, tribe and tongue.

The *called out* ones are the church, the body of Christ. All true Christians are members one of another, each is a part of the whole building, which is being fitted together and is growing into a holy temple in the Lord.

Those who are joined to the Lord are one spirit, one body and one soul. Oneness of soul is a neglected emphasis. The term translated *one accord* or *united in spirit* in some versions is better translated *one in soul* or literally *joint soul* (Phil.2:2). Our natural country of origin is of a temporal, not an eternal, status. Being in Christ separates us out of every nation as God's holy nation.

If they had been thinking of that country from which they went out, they would have had opportunity to return. Heb.11:15

Abuses and Excuses

God has His own way of revealing what is in our hearts. He will even provide us with what appear to be legitimate reasons not to go on with Him. Our excuses may seem valid, but they only prove what was already in our hearts. If it is in our hearts to go back, then God will give us opportunity to return. If we seek a better country, then despite any abuse, we will go on.

The church may fail us, a pastor may let us down, a fellow believer may betray us—and if we are looking for an excuse not to pursue God with His people, then we will have one. If we need an excuse not to be baptized with the Holy Spirit or to receive His gifts, then we will believe the horror stories of people swinging from the chandeliers and cursing God in Chinese.

Our spiritual condition today is nobody's fault but our own. We can blame nothing and nobody for not going on with God. Pointing the finger will not absolve us from responsibility. Nowhere in the Scriptures are the guilty discharged from their punishment because another is held responsible for their sin. We may blame the devil, the church, circumstances and so on, but it is of no avail, for we only manifest what is in our hearts.

The Lord Jesus had every excuse because of the abuses He encountered to give up on men, but for the joy that was before Him He endured the cross and despised the shame. The promises of God are for those who encounter opportunities to return yet overcome them and press on. The abused who forgive and refuse the excuse to return will be led forward in triumph.

I buffet my body and make it my slave, lest possibly...I myself should be disqualified. 1 Cor.9:27

Controlling the Body

The importance of controlling our bodies is set forth clearly in the New Testament by the number of references to the subject. Paul states that the alternative to being in control is to risk being disqualified or even a cast away. The body was created as a vehicle to express our spiritual life in union with God.

The fall alienated us from the life of God, and the lusts of the flesh became manifested in our bodies of sin. It was as though the fall reversed the roles in our personal trinity in which spirit should rule soul and body. Bodily appetites now became the dominant feature over our lost soul and dead spirit.

New birth by the Spirit of God restores us to our union with Christ and to our ability to live by the Spirit. When Paul refers to God sanctifying us, he prays that our spirit, soul and body may be preserved complete and blameless until the coming of our Lord. If the Spirit that raised Jesus from the dead dwells in you, then He will quicken your mortal body.

Sin no longer reigns; therefore, we can now reign or control from our spirit. The body is a temple of the Holy Spirit in which we can glorify God. We must allow nothing to master us again, however lawful. Our body is the Lord's, and now the life of the Lord Jesus is to be manifested in our mortal body.

It will take severe discipline to keep our thoughts and actions under control, but remember the alternative. Paul buffeted his body and kept it in subjection rather than being enslaved to it again. Present your body as a living sacrifice to God, controlled by His Spirit and His love.

September 9

The kings of the earth take their stand...against the Lord and against His anointed. Ps.2:2

Godly Practice in an Ungodly State

The world, the flesh and the devil oppose God and His anointed ones. If men rejected Jesus, then little wonder that all men hate His followers. A basic antagonism exists between men of the flesh and men of the Spirit. The flesh and the Spirit resist each other. The persecution of the early church set the tone for the relationship between Christians and the world.

Not some, but all who live godly according to Jesus Christ will suffer persecution, but the Lord pronounced blessing upon those who suffer for the sake of righteousness. He clearly stated that in the world we would have tribulation, and He told us to be of good cheer because He had overcome the world.

Although God commands Christians to be law-abiding citizens, our submission extends only up to the point of conscience, beyond which obedience to God must defy the State. Many martyrs and prisoners have testified to the fact that we obey God rather than man, and for their obedience they are commended by God.

Under the prevailing sovereignty of God, the world lies in the power of the evil one, so Christians must expect conflict. A true Christian is a testimony of Jesus, the light of the world, shining brightly among a wicked and perverse generation. Compromising with the world enables us to be accommodated by the world but makes us God's enemies. We do not wrestle against flesh and blood; therefore, we do not fight with carnal weapons. The victory that overcomes the world is an uncompromising faith.

As for God, His way is blameless. Ps.18:30

God's Way Is Perfect

One of the consequences of Adam's fall was his expulsion from the garden and from the way to the tree of life. Man was turned out of the way because he had turned to his own way. Everyone born since then has been lost, except Jesus who was born of the Holy Spirit. He declared Himself to be the way, the truth and the life. His Father, in word and through works, bore witness of Him that He was the means by which we who were lost could be found and reinstated in the way. The early church was known as the Way (Acts 9:2). True Christianity represents the way of Christ.

Jeremiah prophesied that God would give them one heart and one way, and Jesus is that way. God's way is perfect, and those who follow Him have their way made perfect. He instructs sinners in the way. He teaches the meek and humble His way. The man who fears the Lord will be instructed in the way he should choose. These are valuable lessons when we are faced with choices of direction.

Man forsook the way of peace. Jesus invites us to come to Him, the Way, to find peace. The way that leads to eternal life is narrow because there is only one name given among men whereby we must be saved, the Lord Jesus. The multitude of other ways that seem right to man end in death.

Backsliders will be filled with their own way, finding themselves empty and lacking satisfaction. The broad way leads to destruction, but Christ has opened up the way to immortality and life.

Those who follow the Lamb wherever He goes shall not walk in darkness but in the light of life and in the way of righteousness where there is no death.

If anyone wishes to come after Me, let him deny himself, and take up his cross daily, and follow Me. Luke 9:23

Following the Lord

Following the Lord involves us not only in deep water, but also in fiery trials. Just as the water does not overflow us, so the fire will not consume us but will extract the dross of carnality from us. God designs our way to conform us to Christ. Even situations that loom as mountains and impasses can be made a way. "I will make all my mountains a way," says God in Isaiah. The one who desires to do the right thing has the promise that the righteousness of the righteous shall rectify, or smooth, his way.

Paul knew that if he were mistaken the Lord would reveal it to him. When he mistakenly wanted to visit the churches in Asia, he was close enough with God to be forbidden by the Holy Spirit. He made the same mistake about Bithynia and was again forbidden, the Lord then directing him in a dream to Macedonia.

The way of holiness has to do with the inner man continually being renewed even though the outward man is perishing. Our life is hidden with Christ in God; therefore, the wicked one does not touch us who walk in the way of the Lord. In Bunyon's Pilgrim's Progress, the lions were alongside the path but were chained so as not to be able to reach the path. As Pilgrim walked on the path, he felt the wind of their claws and the heat of their breath, but they were unable to touch him.

How blessed is the man in whose heart is the highway to Zion. God has set His way in our hearts, and if we turn to the left or the right we shall hear a voice behind our ear saying, "This is the way, walk in it." It is the voice of the shepherd saying, "Follow Me."

There is an appointed time for everything. Eccl.3:1

An Appointed Time for Everything

Times and seasons are under the sovereign hand of God. He does the appointing. David had that revelation when he declared that his times were in God's hands. Jesus knew His timing down to the hour, stating, "My hour has not yet come." He was sent in the fulness of time, and the time of His return is known by the Father. Satan knows that his time is short because God has determined his end. God has determined the appointed times of every nation, even to the boundaries of their habitations. Empires rise and fall at God's behest.

Neither Satan nor man appoints, but it is God who changes the times and seasons, who sets up or sets down. Promotion comes from nowhere else but the Lord. He is the author of our personal times and seasons. The infinitely intricate details of our circumstances are orchestrated by God to produce the life of Christ in us and rid us of our old carnal man. Whether we need abasing or abounding, He knows and ordains works in which we are to walk.

When all has finally been fulfilled, then it will be accredited to God that all His works were wonderful and that everything was beautiful in its time.

However ugly the incident or season, in God's overall plan and eternal perspective, it will be seen to be beautiful. All His works shall praise Him, even the wrath of man. We misunderstand our problems and become disappointed when we lose sight of God's sovereignty in our lives.

Rest assured that all things truly work for your good if you love Him. If God is for you, who or what can be against you?

For we are His workmanship, created in Christ Jesus for good works, which God prepared beforehand. Eph.2:10

We Are His Workmanship

There are works of the flesh, the things of which unregenerate man is capable, and there are the works of Satan and of darkness, which Jesus came to destroy. Then there are the works of God. From the infinitesimal to the supercolossal, creation bears witness to the mighty and awesome power of God. The exquisite beauty of form and structure in a crystal, a butterfly, an atom or the countless rolling spheres that speed through His heavens—all make known the Creator's infinite capacity to work amazingly.

With all we know of God's ability, the fact that we are His workmanship created in Christ Jesus should once and for all cure Christians of low self-esteem. The true church is God's chosen dwelling place, the perfection of beauty out from which God will shine.

When a man is born again by the Spirit of God, he becomes a new creature. All things become new, not some or most, but all. The image of God that was marred in man because of sin is renewed into a true image of Christ. We are now God's sons. We are now partakers of Christ, partakers of the divine nature. Not only are we His workmanship, but He is now at work in us both to will and to do His good pleasure. We have the inestimable privilege of working out what God is working in.

He takes us through various circumstances to rid us of every vestige of our old man. As we express Christ in our mortal body we are conformed to His image. If we knew heaven's perspective and what our perfecting requires, we would complain less and entrust ourselves more to a faithful Creator.

Reprove a wise man, and he will love you. Prov.9:8

Accepting Correction

The effect correction has upon us is a gauge of our maturity in the Lord. Defensiveness betrays insecurity, which comes from immaturity. Correction can cause us to feel belittled, undermined or rejected, resulting in embarrassment and offense as pride takes yet another blow.

When a plumbline is put at the side of what we have done, we can either straighten up, move away from the plumbline or insist that the plumbline is crooked. Yet to grow up necessitates change. If we are wise we will welcome correction, but a scoffer will hate the one reproving him.

All Scripture is profitable for instruction, reproof, correction and rebuke, but reading a reproof stirs up less of our defensiveness than a verbal admonition. We are exhorted to admonish one another, and part of the function of a shepherd is to rebuke, sometimes sharply.

It would probably astonish us to know how many Christians have left churches and have broken fellowship because they refused correction. Yet, how else can we be changed and conformed to Christ. It is for our temporal and eternal benefit to be adjusted. How much of what is wrong with us do we want to live with? Are any of us already perfect? Paul told the Philippians that he had not yet attained to the resurrection and was not yet perfect.

It is wise to appreciate criticism and to be grateful for having our attention directed to what could have robbed us of eternal glory. We will be rewarded neither for carnality nor for shutting our ears to correction. Reproofs for discipline are **the** way of life.

Not everyone who says to Me, "Lord, Lord," will enter the Kingdom of heaven, but he who does the will of My Father. Matt. 7:21

Prayer: No Substitute for Obedience

God's house is to be called a house of prayer for all nations. We must view prayer as a priority, for the word commands us to pray always and to be devoted to prayer. But as great as is the need for prayer, even prayer can be sin. Obedience is better than sacrifice. Obedience is also better than prayer if prayer is used as an excuse not to do what needs to be done.

Prayer can be a form of procrastination. Putting off doing by praying is sin. Many prayers ask God for what He has already given. In our prayers, "May we" is often a cop-out for declaring that "We will." An example is praying for opportunities to witness but never witnessing. Life is full of missed opportunities.

Are we willing to be instruments that God uses to answer our prayers? "Lord, increase our numbers" can be a sinful substitute for preaching the gospel. "Bless the poor" should involve us in giving, in being the embodiment of the answer. Is there a need for more gifts of the Spirit? It may be good to pray for them, but better to exercise them.

If you want the Lord's work to be done, remember the words of the old chorus, "Mine are the hands to do the work, my feet shall run for Thee, my lips shall sound the glorious news, Lord here am I send me."

The terrible lack of prayer in the lives of God's people is exceeded only by the lack of obedience. It is through your obedience that the life of Jesus is manifested in your mortal body, whether in praying or in outworking prayer. Shining as a light in this wicked and perverse generation has to do with your good works, that people may see and glorify God.

For me to live is Christ, and to die is gain. Phil.1:21

To Live Is Christ

This glorious truth is not just an objective and legal matter, but it must also be a subjective experience for all born-again believers. Paul gives his personal testimony, but he uses it to include all true Christians when he talks in terms of Christ being our life. Paul had no special covenant for himself. When he said, "I live, yet not I but Christ lives in me," he was testifying to what is true of all who are Christ's.

Being joined to the Lord involves every aspect of our lives. No department of life is alienated from Him. We are inseparably bone of His bone and flesh of His flesh, one in spirit, heart and soul. Even our bodies are the Lord's, and we ourselves are members of His body.

When Christ becomes our life we are renewed in the spirit of our minds. All our feelings, emotions, and longings, our intellect, our aesthetic appreciation—everything involved in our hearts and minds now operates in conjunction with Christ. We can love and hate with the heart of Christ if our old heart has been circumcised. If we have received a new, pure heart, one in which the love of God has been shed abroad by the Holy Spirit, then we can be controlled by His love.

We must understand that Christ is the life, and apart from Him there is no life. We could live according to the course of this world, but we lived like that when we were dead in trespasses and sins. Jesus said that He came that we might have life and have it more abundantly. If you have the same Father as Jesus, then what Jesus has made possible, you can experience as actual.

Go therefore and make disciples of all nations. Matt.28:19

He Who Sends Us Will Lead Us

Being sent by God is different from being sent by anyone else. We never leave His omnipresence. He will never leave us nor forsake us. He sends us to fulfill His purpose, but also leads us and goes with us. He never leaves us to ourselves, but we rob ourselves of the knowledge of His presence if we refuse to listen to His voice.

The Bible definitively says that those who are led by the Spirit of God are the sons of God. The whole Bible is there for us to learn of God and be taught principles of conduct, but to be led by the Spirit we must have a relationship with the Principal as well as His principles.

The Bible is essential as the basis for testing all doctrine and practice, but it also teaches about men and women who encountered God, heard His voice and knew Him when they were not looking at or thinking of the Bible. Before the Scriptures were written men walked with God. Enoch even prophesied the second coming of Christ. He heard from God and walked in a way that pleased God.

The Bible is the word of God, but if it were removed, the Lord's presence would remain with us. Solitary confinement with its lack of outside stimulus has been the place of intimate fellowship with the Lord for many of the persecuted.

We must insist not only upon sound doctrine and Biblical inerrancy, but also upon knowing the Lord's presence, hearing His voice and being led by His Spirit. Doctrine and experience are not mutually exclusive. The Lord desires that we know His word, share His life and walk in His Spirit.

The Queen of the South...came from the ends of the earth to hear the wisdom of Solomon...something greater than Solomon is here. Matt.12:42

A Greater Than Solomon

The spectacle of Solomon and all that attended him overwhelmed the queen of Sheba to the point where there was no more spirit in her. She commanded no mean resources, for her retinue was very large, and she had brought great riches; but hers was no match for the opulence that God had lavished upon Solomon. She had heard what she had thought an exaggeration, but she openly confessed that the half had not been told. She said of Solomon's men that they were blessed, and how blessed were his servants who stood before him continually and heard his wisdom.

When Jesus, the Lord of glory, was on the earth, He rebuked the Pharisees and scribes for their unbelief and rejection, and He cited the queen of Sheba and her encounter with Solomon. She had come from the ends of the earth to hear the wisdom of Solomon, but now a greater than Solomon was here. Jesus, the King of kings, in whom are hidden all the treasures of wisdom and knowledge, had come.

We should go to any length and any expense and whatever might appear to be an inconvenience to seek out the Lord Jesus and to hear Him. What can be said of those who become His servants? How blessed indeed are His men. If Solomon's servants were blessed, how much more the servants of Christ.

Those who continually stood before Solomon to hear his wisdom were blessed as no men had ever been, but a greater than Solomon has come. Solomon was a mere type and shadow of great David's greater Son, whose kingdom is everlasting and who reigns forever. The servants of Jesus have been given garments of salvation and can know His abiding presence, and can hear His voice.

To all who are beloved of God...called saints. Rom.1:7

Beloved of God

This term of endearment means to be dearly loved. It is from the basic word *agapo*, which is used for God's love as opposed to both sexual love and brotherly love. It is a quality of God who is love. The Father uses this expression in reference to His Son, the Lord Jesus, when He says, "My beloved Son." Our Lord prayed that the love which the Father had for Him would be in us. He said that the Father loves us just as He loves Jesus, and that He Himself loves us just as He loves the Father.

Paul addressed the Roman Christians as beloved, which applies to all believers. We are all dearly loved, the apple of God's eye. God will never stop loving those who are wrapped up in a bundle of life with Him in His Son. No one can pluck us out of His hand, and the beloved of the Lord shall dwell securely because we dwell between His shoulders.

Whether we think in terms of being carried in His bosom with His everlasting arms underneath, or walking with Him with His hand upon us, He is our Father, and we by His grace and love are His children. God is exceedingly jealous for us (Zech.8:2), and what is done to the least of the brethren of Jesus is done to Him.

If we give good gifts to our children, how much more will our loving heavenly Father give good gifts to His children. Knowing that we are so dearly loved of the Father should give us great security. As representatives of our Father, we should in turn express His love to our children. We may have been abused and neglected by earthly fathers, but by new birth we can now enjoy true fatherhood as expressed by God Himself. His banner over us is love, beloved.

Master, we worked hard all night, and caught nothing.
Luke 5:5

Worked Hard and Caught Nothing

Labor in the Lord is never in vain, but "in the Lord" is the operative phrase. Labor can be in vain when we do what God is not doing. At the bidding of Jesus, the same men in the same boat on the same lake let down the same net, and what had been a futile exercise all night became a bountiful catch. It was at His bidding that amazing results ensued.

Unless the Lord builds the house, they labor in vain who build it. The Lord teaches that without Him we can do nothing. He does not mean that we are paralyzed, but He means that what we do without Him amounts to nothing. If we build anything that He is not building, it will either be torn down, or it will eventually fall down.

Working the work of God requires faith, and faith comes by hearing the word of God. The key is to be in a place of fellowship with the Lord where we can hear His voice. Selfish ambition and wrong motivation make us dull of hearing.

Peter and his companions toiled all night, but the result was frustration. The Lord spoke His into their situation, and despite former failure, they obeyed and marveled at the outcome of simple obedience. Jesus taught us to work, not for the food which perishes, but for that which endures to eternal life. The results of obedience are not always seen in the terms that man calls success, but the one who works the works of God will be fed by the Lord with eternal food.

True success means being current with the Lord, willing what He wills and laboring as a fellow worker with Him. Such labor is never in vain.

Work out your salvation with fear and trembling. Phil. 2:12

Work Out Your Salvation with Fear

It is because God almighty, the infinite and sovereign Lord, is at work in us, that we should with fear and trembling work out what He is working in. Perfect love casts out the fear of the consciousness of sin because our sins have been forgiven and taken away. Still, fear of the Lord and fear of the consequences of sin are part of the new-covenant promise God said He would put in our new hearts.

The fear of God is His treasure, and if God treasures it, we are rich when we have it and poor when we lack it. This fear is a gift of God, and is to be a delight. Jesus delighted in the fear of the God, as Isaiah prophetically speaks of Him. The Spirit of wisdom and revelation is also the Spirit of the fear of the Lord. God has put His fear in our hearts for our good and for our children's good, and to stop us departing from Him. If our love for the Lord fails to produce obedience, then the fear of the Lord is a safety valve to keep us from committing sin.

As it grew, the early church continued in the fear of the Lord. Paul spoke of knowing the terror of the Lord, and with that in mind he persuaded men. Peter tells us to pass our time here in fear. Jesus told us whom to fear: not man, but Him.

Some recent translations translate the Greek word for fear as *reverence*. This is unfortunate. The word for fear means knee-knocking fear, associated with trembling. If men depart from evil by the fear of the Lord, then obviously workers of iniquity do not have the fear of the Lord, even though they refer to Jesus as Lord. It is better to fearfully depart from evil than to have to depart from the Lord.

The effective prayer of a righteous man can accomplish much.
James 5:16

A Righteous Man

Although we are responsible as men to provide for our families, we should not be anxiously preoccupied with how we are going to do that. Jesus said that our heavenly Father knows what we need, and He gives much more responsibly than we do. He will supply out of His great love and fatherly care. Instead of the cares of this life, His kingdom and righteousness must be the priority of our focus. Having been made righteous by faith in Jesus, we are to actually be righteous. A righteous man is one who lives righteously **now**, not one who was once righteous.

Maintaining righteousness is a matter of living by faith, a faith that hears the word of God and does it. Seeking His righteousness involves the inner quest to discover more of Him who is our life. How diligently we seek determines the measure of what we find. We must be convinced of the necessity to seek. The reward of finding the Lord in different revelations of His being should motivate us.

The Lord makes Himself available to the diligent seeker, for He promised that we will find Him when we seek Him with our whole heart. Halfhearted and disinterested seekers will not persevere, nor will they find.

God has introduced us to Himself and to His kingdom, and we have now embarked upon an adventurous calling that could not be more high or rewarding. It involves getting intimately acquainted with the eternal, sovereign Lord and having the mystery of His nature disclosed to us. He gives such revelation for the purpose of our becoming an expression of His righteousness.

For all who are being led by the Spirit of God, these are sons of God. Rom.8:14

Fads or Revelation?

Being fashion conscious is a byproduct of an affluent society. The rapid changes in fashion create a pressure for anyone who wants to keep up with the in thing. The poor spiritual condition of an affluent church makes it vulnerable to bandwagons and fads. God is outworking a linear purpose, one from beginning to end. There is a vast difference between gearing up for the latest fad and receiving ongoing revelation in the purpose of God.

Bandwagons substitute for being led by the Spirit. When we languish in stagnation, a faddish new emphasis can appear as a panacea for all ills. However this sort of remedy, like any fashion, is always short-lived and has no long-term gains.

The children of Israel wandered in the desert for forty years. The miracles that occurred everyday—the manna, the fiery cloud, the shoes and clothes that did not wear out—did not prevent them from moving in circles.

Some Christians convey their doctrinal emphasis with the claim that they move in certain circles. That is what the children of Israel did for forty years. A fad will take us no further than a circle. We may change to a different circle, but still we may fail to progress along the line of God's purpose.

The remedy for stagnation is an inflow and an outflow. The inflow is the inspiration of the Holy Spirit. The outflow is the outworking of the inflow.

Jumping on a bandwagon is like wearing someone else's clothes. The *well-dressed* Christian wears only the clothes that his Father provides for him, and they fit him perfectly in his personal history.

Pray to your Father who is in secret, and your Father who sees in secret will repay you. Matt. 6:6

Your Father Who Is in Secret

The consequence of man's fall was alienation from the life of God, producing a basic insecurity with which everyone is born. This inner insecurity moves us to find temporary alleviation in externals. So we naturally seek the applause of men, relishing the recognition and accolades of others and finding ourselves deeply wounded by criticism or rejection. We must guard against the inordinate desire to appear before others for the purpose of gaining their approval.

The Lord Jesus defines how we ought to live, and His way involves doing things in secret. This demands an attitude of living to God for His approval however unknown or misunderstood our efforts may appear to men. Jesus said that the men-pleasing Pharisees already had their reward. Like them, we deny ourselves our heavenly Father's reward if we do things with the motive of being seen and applauded by men.

An apparent contradiction exists: letting our light so shine before men that they may see our good works, but not letting what we do to be seen of men. Jesus made it clear that it is a matter of motive. The Pharisees lived to get applause from men. Christians live to give applause to God.

If our lives are the light of the world then they cannot be hidden, but God will be glorified, not us. What we are in secret and in heart will one day be rewarded openly.

Be a man of the secret place because your heavenly Father is in secret. The more we do in secret the more secure we become. Giving, praying and fasting in secret teach us to live our lives in every respect to God alone. Security comes from secrecy.

If by the Spirit you are putting to death the deeds of the body,
you will live. Rom.8:13

Death to the Deeds of the Body

The truly born-again believer has been crucified, buried and raised with Christ. His old self has been put to death in the death of Jesus, so it can be said of him that he has died and his life is hid with Christ in God. The life of Christ in which we share, is hidden in God. It is spiritual life, or life in the Spirit. The same Spirit that raised Jesus from the dead, raised us from the dead, and quickened our mortal body.

Our mortal body was an instrument of sin, but the power of the cross and the blood and the death of Jesus dealt with that. Now, by His Spirit we can present ourselves to God as alive from the dead, and our bodies as instruments of righteousness. By the same Spirit, the deeds of sin that once were manifested in our bodies can now be put to death. This is what living in the Spirit is all about.

Do not undermine the power of your new life. It is not fragile, but it is robust, strong and of the eternal essence, enabling you to live unto God.

Obedience to what has been received from Christ causes spiritual fruit and growth. Our new heart and new spirit give new motives and desires, new intentions and new appetites.

Since death can occur through neglect or starvation, we must take care to express our new life by starving the old ways, and their power will die through neglect. Thoughts, words and actions should progressively prove the old man dead and the new man alive in the Spirit. If you believe that Christ is your life, then translate that belief into a manifestation of His life in your mortal body. You are equipped for overcoming the world, triumphing over the flesh and conquering the powers of darkness.

Take heed to the ministry that you have received in the Lord, that you may fulfill it. Col.4:17

Fulfilling Your Ministry

Paul encouraged Archippus to take heed to the ministry that he had received in the Lord, to fulfill it. This message applies equally to all members of the body of Christ. The proper working of each individual will produce a collective impact beyond our imagination. It is the whole body that fulfills the work of the ministry.

Unless we become what God has called us to be, we will remain unfulfilled. No other pursuit will enable us to live a truly full life. Time is a limited commodity, and it is running out. What we waste is lost forever. If we are not fulfilling what God has called us to be, then we are not living by faith, and that which is not of faith is sin.

Many so-called Christians who appear to live good lives are workers of iniquity if they are not working the works of God specifically assigned them.

We often undermine the extreme seriousness of sin. Sin is knowing what to do and not doing it, and doing what the conscience says is wrong. A single sin caused the fall of man and resulted in death. As the sin-bearer Jesus agonized and died to free us from sin and its power. Living in sin is not limited to unmarried couples living together. Living in sin is living for one's own interests and not Christ's.

Paul tells us to wake up to righteousness and stop sinning. John writes similarly, saying that he writes so that we may not sin. The importance of fulfilling your particular service to the body of Christ cannot be overstated. Any other life is sinfully wasted.

But realize this, that in the last days difficult times will come.
2 Tim. 3:1

Difficult Times Will Come

Difficult times will characterize the last days. The condition of man, far from evolving him into a more perfect being, is deteriorating. The Bible vividly and shockingly portrays the extent of man's depravity, describing the frightful prospect facing us of people who are self-lovers and haters of good, treacherously perpetrating their deceptions. We can adequately confront the difficulties of the last days by rightly equipping ourselves.

The truth of the Scriptures introduces us to salvation in Jesus and grants us insights into His wisdom. Regrettably, a deplorable ignorance of the Scriptures abounds in Christendom. It is scandalous to have the word of the Lord available and fail to take advantage of it.

An erroneous conception relegates the study of the Scriptures to pastors. Further, many pastors themselves do not understand the truth of the gospel and the provisions of the new covenant, and many actually deny the contents of the Bible. Therefore, many who consider themselves Christians have not in fact been born again. Many do not believe in the baptism of the Holy Spirit, and many deny that the gifts of the Holy Spirit and miracles of power are for today. All these conditions are the result of satanic strategy to deny Christians their power to resist him, and to demonstrate Christ's kingdom.

Jesus said that not everyone who calls Him Lord will enter the kingdom of heaven, but he who does the will of His Father. Discernment comes from knowing the Lord and obeying His word. Ignorance of the written word is a major cause of failing to hear the inner voice of the Lord. Becoming familiar with the whole counsel of God will help you to avoid deception in difficult times.

But where sin increased, grace abounded all the more. Rom. 5:20

Abounding Grace

The ever-increasing amount of sin with its accumulating weight of evil can never exceed the abounding grace of God. Even though darkness covers the earth and gross darkness the people, the Lord will arise on His people, and His glory will be seen upon them.

Light is unimaginably more powerful than darkness. God is light, and He is unimaginably greater than all. His abounding grace never excuses us to continue in sin, but it powerfully encourages us to overpower sin. God extends grace, not to help us accommodate sin, but to free us from its dominion. The grace of God instructs us that, denying ungodliness and wordly lusts, we should live soberly, righteously and godly in this present age.

Whatever my mountain of difficulty might be—my besetting sin or my natural traits or weaknesses—God's grace abounds to free me from its dominion. God is able to make *all grace* available to us (and that is a lot of grace) enabling us to be sufficient for every eventuality.

God is not running short of grace. He does not merely balance us up with grace equal to our problems, but He lavishes grace upon us. Daily He loads us with benefits. He gives pressed down and shaken together and running over, not just enough, but more than enough.

Jesus came to give us life more abundantly, not begrudgingly or sparingly. God is the God of infinite abundance and of unlimited grace. Sin no longer reigns, but grace now reigns through Jesus, the righteous overcomer. He gives His grace to you so that you might reign with Him and prove His grace to be abundantly sufficient.

Stand by and see the salvation of the Lord. Ex.14:13

Stand Still

Standing still is one of the most difficult things to do. This command came to God's people in the context of their enemies about to overwhelm them. They were to do nothing but stand still, for God needed no human agency to help Him do what He was about to do. The enemy would encounter God directly as all God's people stood by and watched.

In many instances we must personally engage the enemy in the good fight of faith, but occasionally God sovereignly proves that the battle belongs to Him by directly and unmistakably engaging the enemy while we as stand by and watch His hand at work. A door may be opened or shut, a turn of events may occur, desperate circumstances may yield a miraculous outcome—and we can only bow the knee and worship the God of our salvation.

We often have a problem taking our hands off something God wants to do alone. However there is a time to stand aside and stand still. We create our own frustration when we try to help God out. If God is not building, we labor in vain. If God is not speaking, we must keep quiet. It is no less an act of obedience to stand still and do nothing at His command than it is to arise and thresh or build. We still shine whether we obey His word to arise or to sit down.

God wants to do much through us, but He is more interested in doing much in us. Obeying His word to be bystanders and onlookers works something of God's character in us. It can work impatience and self-reliance out of us, as well as enhance our sense of dependence upon Him. Be patient, wait on the Lord, and see what He will do.

I will put My laws into their minds and write them upon their hearts. Heb.8:10

Sentimentalism: Friend of Carnality

The dictionary defines sentiment as a mental feeling, a tendency or view based on or colored with emotion, a tendency to be swayed by feelings rather than by reason. It is emotional weakness, and the nursing of the emotions.

Nothing is wrong with the fact that we have emotions. God made us in His image, and God has emotions. When Jesus was on the earth, compassion moved Him to tears. The word *moved* contains the Greek root word *mot*, the basis of our word emotion. God created us with emotions, but like every other quality comprising God's image in man, emotions have been disrupted and perverted by sin.

One promise of the new covenant is that the Lord will put His word in our hearts. We also have the witness of His Spirit with our spirit. His word in us must be the basis of the faith by which we live. His word formulates the doctrine, which objectively lays out the principles of conduct by which the Holy Spirit subjectively leads us.

Objective truth will witness with the Holy Spirit who wrote it in our hearts, and will guard us from being moved by carnal emotions. It is common to be influenced by sentimentalism, especially for those ignorant of sound doctrine and not accustomed to being led by the Spirit of truth.

To be taught of God one must give time to listen to God. Correction and adjustment of our emotions and feelings will save us from being sentimental. Sentimentalism can wrongly sway us when hearing of someone's troubles and can generate sympathy that opposes God's dealings with them. When our sentiments conflict with God, we are siding with sin.

Conduct yourself in a manner worthy of the gospel of Christ. Phil.1:27

Walk Worthily of the Gospel

Paul's appeal to conduct ourselves in a manner worthy of the Gospel is one of six such exhortations. They parallel the admonitions to be holy as He who has called us is holy, to love as Christ has loved us and to be perfect as our heavenly Father is perfect. These references prove the power of the cross to put to death the old man. They also prove the power of the resurrection to enable us to walk in newness of life.

In Revelation, Jesus alone is worthy to open the book and loose its seals, so worthy that all who have faith in Him are made worthy to be joined to the Lord. Being made worthy through justification is one thing, while walking worthily requires the application of our faith.

We are no longer subject to the dominion of our old flesh, but we are in the Spirit (if indeed the Spirit of God dwells in us) and are capable of standards that were once unobtainable.

This new life is not one of mindless automation, but it is natural to us. A Christian can sin and live in the flesh; although, he ought not to do so. He can build with wood, hay and stubble upon the glorious foundation of Christ, but he ought to build precious things that the fire only refines.

God's word urges us to comply with the life of Christ in us by reckoning ourselves dead to sin and alive to God.

Christ in us enables us to walk in this present world as He walked. If such a gospel is not preached, how will it be believed? We are made worthy in order to live worthily, and we live worthily not to somehow become justified by works; Jesus did that for us. We must, however, work out what God is working in to prove His great power to transform.

*Whatever is true... honorable... right... pure... lovely...
of good repute, if there is any excellence and if anything worthy
of praise, let your mind dwell on these things. Phil.4:8*

Set Your Mind on Better Things

Anxiety is the thief of peace. The Lord Jesus instructs us not to be anxious and gives us the reason why, for we have a loving heavenly Father. The cares and worries of this life can consume us, robbing us of our peace. There can be no joy where there is no peace. Knowing the nearness of our God and His fatherly care dispels our fears. We have an ever-present good Shepherd and Comforter.

If we determine to set our minds on things above, where Christ is seated and where we are seated with Him, then His assurance will dissolve our anxieties. Peace is powerful and will guard our hearts and minds. Thinking on things that are pure, lovely, noble, excellent and worthy of praise must be a decision of our will. The world is geared to fill our thinking and even do our thinking for us. As a result our minds can dwell on unprofitable, unhelpful, ungodly and unnecessary things. The lack of peace and joy among Christians betrays as much.

Technology provides multimedia visual portrayals of every sin under the sun, but we must think on different things, for we become like what we spend our time thinking about. A battle for the mind certainly exists, but it starts in the heart. Where your treasure is there will your heart be also. You can tell where your heart is by examining where your treasure is. If you spend most of your time thinking on the things of this world, you value the world the most. The mind set on the flesh is death, but the mind set on the Spirit is life and peace. Set your mind on the better things of Christ, and be at peace.

I have learned the secret of being filled and going hungry, both of having abundance and suffering need. Phil. 4:12

I Have Learned the Secret

God will make known His secrets to those who are in a position to hear. The secret of the Lord is with them who fear Him, and He is intimate with the upright. Paul learned the secret of being content whether he was abounding or being abased. He knew how to get along with humble means or prosperity, for he knew God to be the author of both prosperity and adversity.

Those who deny that God brings adversity deny His sovereignty and ignore the word of God, which explicitly expresses that He makes both prosperity and adversity. They also deny themselves the means of growing up in Christ through the diversity of God-given experiences. They have not learned the secret.

Others grumble at their lot in life and constantly complain, for they have not learned the secret. Some declare that godliness must lead to gaining this worlds goods, for they have not learned the secret. It is godliness with contentment in whatever circumstances that is great gain.

Paul said that he was content with weakness, but many Christians are discontent with weakness because they have not learned the secret. The strength of God is made perfect in weakness; therefore, we can glory in weakness and infirmity because the power of God is made known in and through us. Paul's weakness of body and loss of temporal things were overwhelmingly dominated by his appreciation of his eternal inheritance and present strength of Christ. He learned the secret of contentment for every circumstance, even going hungry and suffering need. The secret is to trust God's sovereignty to totally rule over all.

Jesus Christ will transform the body of our humble state into conformity with the body of His glory. Phil. 3:21

Jesus Will Transform Our Bodies

True Christians are citizens of heaven. Having been born there they now live there seated with Christ as surely as He lives in them on the earth. Although we dwell in the world, we are not of it, for here we have no continuing city. We inhabit earthly tabernacles, or mortal bodies, but the life we share with Christ is the treasure and the power within those bodies.

A moment will come in time when these mortal bodies will be changed to become immortal. This corruptible shall put on incorruption, yielding bodies that are compatible with the eternal life within them. Our mortal bodies belong to the Lord, and He will change these bodies of humility to be conformed to His glorious body. At His coming, in just a twinkling of the eye, He will transform us beyond our comprehension. It is for this that we groan, eagerly awaiting the redemption of our bodies.

What a wonderful hope! We have already been redeemed, but much of what was purchased for us waits to be revealed, the redemption of the body being one of those things.

At this present time we can manifest the life of the Lord Jesus in our mortal bodies, but at His coming our true status as sons of God will be manifested in immortal bodies. The whole creation waits and groans anxiously and eagerly for that manifestation. There will be a generation that will not die in any way. Having been made alive through new birth while still in mortal bodies, they will undergo an instantaneous transformation as they are clothed with their heavenly bodies at the return of Christ. Make sure you are not found to be naked.

For many walk of whom I have often told you, and now tell you even weeping, that they are enemies of the cross of Christ. Phil.3:18

Enemies of the Cross of Christ

Jesus makes it clear to His followers that He expects them to take up their cross daily if they want to follow Him. He was crucified once, for all. While the power of His death puts to death our old man, we must apply that power daily. If we have died with Christ, we need to constantly reckon ourselves dead to sin, and we need to practice righteousness.

Those who receive the forgiveness of God through what He accomplished in the cross of Christ need to apply the cross to their lives daily. Putting off the old man with its lusts and passions while putting on the new man is an ongoing process as well as an initial crisis. Growing up, or becoming conformed to Christ until His life is demonstrated in our mortal body, is a daily working out of what God is working in.

An enemy of the cross rejects the implications of the cross. A friend of the cross daily embraces the cross and its implications. An enemy of the cross refuses to identify himself with the crucified Lord in a daily, practical way even though he believes Jesus died on the cross. Where the carnal nature is not put to death, life remains a continuation of fallen nature.

An enemy of the cross fulfills his own desires instead of the interests of Christ. Anyone not walking in the Spirit by faith, makes himself an enemy of the cross. Jesus said that we are His friends IF we do what He commands. He commands us to repent, to forsake relationships, things, and even our own lives, if we want to be His followers. If you are not His friend, then you are His enemy.

That I may know Him and the power of His resurrection. Phil. 3:10

The Power of His Resurrection

Paul's desire to know Christ and His resurrection power did not come out of complete ignorance. He already knew Christ, for he had received the gospel directly from Him. He had been born again and baptized with the Holy Spirit and therefore knew the transforming work of Christ to bring him from death to life. However, what he knew of His Lord and the power of His resurrection only motivated him to want to know more.

His was not a casual, but an insatiable thirst. Having tasted of the Lord, he now hungered for Him. Nothing could stand in the way of his quest to know his Lord. He counted everything as dung in comparison with the excellency of the knowledge of Christ Jesus his Lord. He laid aside every weight, and he ran, fought, endured, pressed in and forgot things that were behind as he reached forward, ever seeking to apprehend that for which he had been apprehended.

He prayed for the Ephesian church that they might know the surpassing greatness of God's power toward them. This was in accordance with the working of the strength of God's might which He brought about in Christ when He raised Him from the dead. This same power is at work in us, not only to bring us to life, but also to conform us to Christ. We too can walk as those who are alive from the dead.

Are you pursuing the source of life that conforms you to His image? Or have you lost your taste for the Lord? Complacency betrays a loss of appetite for knowing Him, and that will stagnate you. A cry that rises from the depths of your being to know Him will be rewarded with more revelation of Him.

So stand firm in the Lord, my beloved. Phil.4:1

Stand Firm in the Lord

Adam yielded when he should have stood his ground. Through his fall we inherited an inability to withstand the seductions of sin and the powers of darkness. Sin and death dominated us, and Satan held us in bondage. However, a man came to earth, conscious from His early years that God was His Father. He was tempted in all things as were we, yet He withstood every assault that Satan could muster. Jesus was that man. He was approved of God among us. He was stronger than the strong one who bound us, and He prevailed over and bound him. He is the man who reverses what we experienced through Adam. By a man came death, and by a man came also the resurrection from the dead.

Jesus conquered in total victory. He triumphed gloriously and was exalted to the throne of God, having all authority and power subjected to Him. Those who receive Him, with all the implications of faith and repentance, He raises to His throne to be seated with Him. From that vantage point we can stand.

God provides us with His armor to fight a defeated foe who has been disarmed. Satan will not stand against us but will flee if we resist him steadfastly in the faith. Through the strength of the one in us who is greater, we can stand against Satan and the world.

All Christians are soldiers of Christ and have weapons mightier than Satan's, which enables them to overwhelmingly conquer. Jesus in you will always cause you to triumph. No longer let sin or Satan dominate you. Believe what you are in Christ and what Christ is in you, and you will be steadfast and unmovable. Stand firm!

The temple is not for man, but for the Lord. 1 Chron.29:1

The Temple Is for the Lord

David spoke these words to the assembly, inspiring them to follow his example of delighting in the house of the Lord. He said that the work was great, because he knew that the Lord was a great God above all gods.

Paul uses the analogy of the temple, giving it its new covenant application, when he says that our bodies are the temple of the Holy Spirit. The body is not for fornication, but for the Lord. The body and the spirit belong to the Lord; therefore, we are to glorify God in our bodies.

I was asked to speak to the students at Bradford University on the subject which asks, "What is man—animal, machine, or what?" I quickly dismissed the animal and machine to deal more extensively with the or what. God destined man to be His dwelling place. That is a marvelous mystery, inexplicable but nonetheless true. "Don't you know," says Paul, "that your bodies are the temple of the Holy Spirit who dwells in you?"

Individually, our bodies are temples that house the excellent treasure of the Lord Himself. Corporately, the Spirit is building us into a temple, a holy habitation of God. The work is monumental, but the finished product has already been seen: the Bride, having no spot or wrinkle, nor blemish, but who is holy and blameless, having the glory of God upon her. By applying all the provisions of her Lord, the Bride makes herself ready to be presented to Him in all her glory.

As we work out this great work, we need a revelation of the great builder who is at work in us both individually and collectively. Jesus is the ultimate bodybuilder, and through Him there will be glory in His body, the church.

Who then is willing to consecrate himself this day to the Lord.
1 Chron.29:5

Who Will Consecrate Himself?

Who is willing to consecrate himself THIS DAY to the Lord? Just as we need daily bread, we also need to take up our cross daily to follow Jesus. The process of salvation occurs daily even though the crisis of our initial salvation occurred on a certain day. Today is the day of salvation, not only in experiencing new birth, but also in expressing a new dimension of abundant life.

The question posed by David is relevant to us today. Who will reckon himself to be dead to sin today? Who will walk according to the Spirit with an undivided heart today? Who will disengage himself from the deceitfulness of riches and the cares of this life and press on with undistracted determination to serve the interests of Christ today? These questions have countless applications that should remind us that we have been cleansed with the blood of the everlasting covenant and are already consecrated to God.

Consecration does not need to involve the lengthy anguish of soul and cry for mercy that attended our initial repentance. Consecration is an attitude recognizing that because we have already been consecrated we will live consecrated—today. To consecrate ourselves is to devote ourselves, reaffirming our singleness of heart for the Lord. A consecrated lifestyle confirms our virgin purity to Him who gave purity to us.

Present yourself in a very practical and definite way to God as one alive from the dead. Who will do it today? Let the words of Joshua be the reply of your heart: "As for me and my house, we will serve the Lord." How else can it be a day of salvation?

You did well that it was in your heart. 2 Chron 6:8

Is Building with God in Your Heart?

The prophet told David that he did well in wanting to build a house for the Lord. Although David was not allowed to accomplish his desire, he worked toward the vision by contributing invaluably. This principle applies to many different longings we may have. Even though we may not personally experience the ultimate fulfillment, the aim of our hearts gives us fruitful lives.

The Lord gives us goals for which to aim, ultimates toward which we direct ourselves. As we obey the heavenly vision, we not only become the means of furthering its fulfillment, but we ourselves benefit from the demands of the vision. For this reason, goals and aims are of great importance. Without a vision the people dwell carelessly, or perish; whereas, a vision gives purpose and direction to life.

All those who serve God and His purposes in their generation will be welcomed into the joy of their Lord with the commentary "Well done, you good and faithful servant." Living for the fulfillment of God's purpose in our hearts may find us finishing our particular course before the Lord has finished His purpose, but we would have done well to have had His purpose in our hearts.

Our Lord directs us to seek first His kingdom and righteousness. That priority must be in our hearts as a motivating force to channel our thinking, our speaking and our doing. How else will we do well? Bad conduct and unfaithful behavior will be forgiven but not rewarded.

Ask the Lord to unite your heart so that you will be single in your aim. Think well, and then do well.

But they are altogether stupid and foolish in their discipline of delusion. Jer.10:8

Discipline of Delusion

Jeremiah uses these words in the context of worshiping manmade idols. Those who engage in such delusions are "altogether stupid and foolish." Despite rigorous fleshly disciplines that often accompany the appeasement of the gods, unregenerate man can neither achieve power over his flesh nor please the only true God.

Paul wrote to the Galatian church in order to combat the error that certain false teachers had impressed upon it. Under Paul's ministry, the Galatian believers had begun in the Spirit, but had fallen from grace. False teachers had bewitched them into returning to the yoke of slavery from which Jesus had set them free. They had returned to the weak and worthless elemental things—the observance of days, months, seasons, years, and rules such as touch not, taste not, handle not—things destined to perish.

Such legalistic demands are not part of the new covenant but are merely the persuasions of men who do not understand it. These regulations are called self-made religion and are of no value against fleshly indulgence.

While God's grace and the freedom with which Christ has set us free are not to be misused as an occasion for the flesh, neither can the outward observance of self-imposed laws provide a heart that is full of the Spirit. There are indeed disciplines of the Spirit, but they all have to do with the heart.

To avoid disciplines of delusion, seek to understand the true nature of the new covenant. Realize the worthless nature of the beggarly elements of legalism, and comprehend the holy nature of your life, one lived within the veil in union with God.

Considering the reproach of Christ greater riches than the treasures of Egypt; for he was looking to the reward. Heb.11:26

Looking to the Reward

Christians, of all people, should live in the present with respect to the future. Having had our past forgiven and its dominion over us rendered powerless, we now have a new aim towards which we press, the prize of the God's high calling in Christ Jesus. The singleness of our heart is proved by the singleness of our goal.

Paul said that he did one thing, and that was to forget the past, and to reach forward to what was ahead. Maturity is achieved not by being affected by the past, but by being affected by the future. The past should affect us less and less as the future increasingly develops us.

Goals discipline us! What we aim for determines how we live. If we do not anticipate being held accountable, then we will live differently than if we see ourselves standing before God one day to give an account.

The Scriptures exhort us to set our aim on Jesus and the heavenly realm. That focus disciplines us toward that goal. It enables us to run the race set before us less encumbered. We gain mastery in the good fight not by looking back but by looking ahead.

Moses was able to disdain the riches of Egypt and enjoy the reproach of Christ because he was looking to the reward. We can have a better or a worse resurrection according to how we live. Justification is not the issue here. Jesus alone is that foundation. At issue is what we build upon that foundation. At issue is the neglected doctrine of rewards. Christians have the honor and the opportunity to look to Jesus and to be conformed to Him.

I baptize you with water for repentance, but He...will baptize you with the Holy Spirit and fire. Matt.3:11

The Baptisms of John and of Jesus

John was great, but Jesus was much greater. John was a prophet of the Most High, while Jesus was the Son of the Most High. John was the forerunner of Jesus, declaring that Jesus was mightier than he and that Jesus was preferred over him because Jesus was before him. John preached a baptism of repentance for the forgiveness of sins, but he pointed to Jesus and to another baptism with the Holy Spirit and fire.

Paul made it clear to the Ephesian disciples that although they had received John's baptism they needed to be baptized both in the name of Jesus and with the Holy Spirit.

There is one baptism, and it has three aspects. Being crucified, buried and raised with Christ is being baptized with Christ's baptism. Being baptized in water in the name of Jesus is the practice of the church for believers. Receiving the baptism of the Holy Spirit is a clearly defined experience apart from the former two.

When Peter saw that his hearers were baptized with the Holy Spirit before baptism in water, he commanded that they also be baptized in water.

Apollos, mighty in the Scriptures, was accurately proving that Jesus was the Christ, but he was only informed concerning John's baptism. Priscilla and Aquila took him aside and explained to him the way of God MORE accurately.

There are still many Christians who know accurately the things concerning Jesus, but who do not know a baptism beyond the baptism of John for repentance and forgiveness of sins. To know more accurately is to know Jesus the baptizer with the Holy Spirit and fire.

I fear no evil, for Thou art with me. Ps.23:4

Thou Art with Me

David was confident even when walking in the valley of the shadow of death that he would fear no evil. He knew that the Lord was with him. Under the provisions of the new covenant, the Lord is not only with us, but in us. The fact that the Lord is in us gives a new dimension of meaning to Him being with us. When nobody stood with Paul, he too was able to convey his confidence, saying, "Nevertheless the Lord stood with me."

The Lord desires us to know His presence. James exhorts us to draw near to God, with the encouragement that when we do, He will draw near to us. It is not that He is elsewhere, but we can lose the sense of His presence and feel distant. We may know the truth of His omnipresence and believe Him to be with us, but the Lord wants us to know Him and the sense of His nearness.

Do we who have come to know Him have more consciousness of His presence now than when we were alienated from Him in our sin?

We have been made alive unto God and should pursue an increasing awareness of His presence. Nothing and no one can compare with the sure knowledge of His presence. All fear subsides, anxiety dissolves and apprehension evaporates when we become conscious that He is with us.

The Lord has fitted us for fellowship with Himself. Having cleansed and forgiven us, He has reconciled us to Himself in Jesus Christ. We were created for union with God to enjoy Him forever. Therefore, we must avoid all behavior that spoils such intimacy. To know His presence is to luxuriate in ultimate pleasure.

*Have this attitude in yourselves which was also in Christ Jesus.
Phil. 2:5*

Jesus in the Philippian Letter

No matter where the apostle directs our attention in this letter, he always returns our focus to the Lord. The first chapter alone mentions the Lord over twenty times. Paul's all-embracing statement that for him to live is Christ expresses a relationship with the Lord that has been provided for all believers.

Paul expresses his aim that Christ be magnified always in his body, whether by life or by death. Death to him is gain, a far better state to be desired beyond this mortal realm.

The Philippian letter highlights the pursuits of Christ's interests as opposed to selfish interests, contrasting selfish ambition with the supreme example of Christ's humility. Although He existed in the form of God, yet He humbled Himself, making Himself of no reputation and suffering the ignominious agony of death by crucifixion. But God raised and exalted Him, giving Him a name above every name, that all might bow to Him confessing that He is Lord.

Paul exhorts us to have the mind of Christ. If He is indeed our life, then we must think according to His mind. Our attitude must demonstrate His attitude, for only then can we truly rejoice in the Lord. In a sweeping statement, Paul repudiates all things and counts them as rubbish in view of the more excellent attainment of Christ Jesus his Lord.

He sets Jesus before us as the one to be desired with a hunger and a thirst that exceed all other appetites. Christ our life—our mind, our aim—is then presented as our strength and source of supply for all our needs.

No one, after putting his hand to the plough and looking back, is fit for the kingdom of God. Luke 9:62

Putting Your Hand to the Plow

When we make a commitment to follow the Lord, then we have no acceptable excuse for turning back. Our Lord Jesus stated that no man after putting his hand to the plow and looking back is fit for the kingdom of God. He spoke these words to a man who said that he would follow the Lord, but who wanted permission to do something else first. To another Jesus made it clear that there would be a cost involved, that of not having a place to lay one's head. There is always a cost to be counted, and having made the decision to follow, there must be no turning back.

To plow a straight furrow, the plowman must look straight ahead and aim for a target. The Lord Jesus is the target upon whom we fix our gaze. Looking to Jesus enables us to plow in the right direction. Our vision must contain the vital elements of God's goals for us. He has called us to be conformed to the image of His Son. All short-term goals must point in the direction of God's ultimate goals.

If we pursue the Lord, we will apprehend that for which we have been apprehended by God. If we are not conforming ourselves to Christ, if we are not changing, if we are not growing, then we must be looking back.

Part of Satan's strategy is to divert our eyes from the Lord. Looking back also denotes something in the heart that has never been crucified. Are your interests the interests of Christ? Jesus set His face like a flint. He will likewise strengthen us to walk or to run, to fight and to overcome, and finally to finish the course.

My God shall supply all your needs according to His riches in glory in Christ Jesus. Phil. 4:19

God the Source and Supply

Paul testifies of his contentment in whatever circumstance he finds himself. He then attributes his ability to do what is required to Jesus who is his strength. Out of a confidence wrought by proving the grace of God in extremities of experience, he encourages the Philippians, telling them that his God is their God. They also may experience their needs being met from the boundless resources of God in Christ Jesus.

The circumstances that God in His sovereignty puts us through are intended to enlarge our faith. Our trust and obedience cause us to grow in faith, in likeness to Christ, and therefore, from glory to glory. Peter reminds us that the Spirit of God and of glory rests upon those who suffer for Christ's sake. What we see as an inglorious situation may in fact be the very revelation of God's glory upon us. His grace abounds to us for every eventuality.

His strength is made perfect in our weakness, and His glory is an unseen presence in our infirmity. Whatever the need—be it for grace, strength, peace or the necessities for life—God will supply according to His riches in glory in Christ Jesus. Nothing that we will ever encounter will find us without help. God is our refuge and strength, a very present help in trouble. We will not be moved, because we know that He will help us, and that right early.

The delays we experience (according to our timetable, not necessarily His) stretch our capacities, enabling us to grow. Even when we are perplexed we are not in despair, knowing that our times are in His hands.

The people who walk in darkness will see a great light. Isa.9:2

A Great Light

When darkness surrounds us, the appearance of a light, however small, encourages the heart. The appearance of Jesus was to those who dwelt in darkness a GREAT light. He was the light of life, unmistakable, illuminating, scattering the darkness and lighting the way. All other glimpses of light that had come were surpassed by this great light.

During the Indonesian revival, a whole village of sun worshipers capitulated to Christ because He appeared in the heavens at the time of the midday sun. They said that He who outshone the sun was greater than the sun. He is the radiance of the Father's glory. His life is the light of men who dwell in darkness. This great light is the true light, which coming into the world enlightens every man.

Physical light and darkness represent the higher truth of spiritual light and darkness. Unregenerate man is not only in darkness, but is darkness (Eph.5:8). The sun could neither pierce the gloom of our darkened spirits nor illumine our darkened understanding, but the Son of God appeared as the light of the world to lighten our darkness. Those who follow Him shall not walk in darkness but shall have the light of life.

Those who receive Him and His great work of redemption are translated out of darkness and its terrifying dominion into the kingdom of light. By becoming partakers of Christ, we who were formerly darkness are now light in the Lord. Walk as children of light, because He who is light has conferred upon you this honor: "You are the light of the world."

For Ezra had set his heart to study the law of the Lord, and to practice it, and to teach...in Israel. Ezra 7:10

Study, Practice and Teach

Ezra set his heart to study the law of the Lord, to practice it and to teach it to Israel. Similarly, our Lord Jesus began to do and to teach what He had learned from His Father. What He taught was founded upon what He did, and He did only what He knew to be His Father's will. Learning from the Lord is the basis for doing, and doing is the necessary basis for teaching. Teaching by example is more effective than teaching by hypocrisy, that is, teaching without doing what one is teaching.

Israel asked Moses to speak with the Lord, promising that then they would hear and do what he commanded, but they failed to follow through. The Lord said that they had done well in what they had spoken; but then came an utterance of deep yearning from the heart of God, expressed in the word *Oh*. God knew their heart. He longed for them always to have an obedient heart because then it would be well with them and their sons forever.

They were, however, a people who drew near with their lips, but whose hearts were far from Him, and they did what their evil hearts dictated.

Ezra had a heart SET to study the word of the Lord, SET to practice it and SET to teach it. The good hand of God was therefore upon him, causing him to prosper and to find favor. He became a respected and effective teacher because he practiced what he taught, and he himself had been taught by the word of the Lord.

You must be careful from whom you learn, and what you teach and how you teach it. Only as you practice what you have received from the Lord can you teach with authority.

Now with all my ability I have provided for the house of my God.
1 Chron. 29:2

Now with All My Ability

David's delight in the house of God proved itself in his wholehearted provision for it. He spared no expense in laying up materials for the building of a house for God. Even though he knew that he would not actually build it, he had a heart to build it. So he helped Solomon, the next generation, by his own planning and preparation. The final product would one day find its completion through what David had contributed.

Although we may desire our generation to be the one that receives the coming King, it may not be. However, we must still play our part and prepare ardently for it. If our sons are to be that generation, then they should bear the indelible marks of our provision and investment. To "leave it to them" would be to abdicate our responsibility and to prove our disinterest.

The spiritual nature of the house involves every generation in its building. We are being built by the Spirit into a temple, a holy habitation of God. The zeal of the Lord for the house of the Lord was made known by Jesus. It ate Him up. That same zeal should possess us, inciting us to drive out from the temple of our bodies all that is foreign to His house. Are you making provision for the house of God with all your ability?

God is a builder who is working at this moment. You can work with Him by working out what He is working in you. Through Christ Jesus there will be glory in the church. You can play your part in your generation by glorifying the Lord in your life, thereby laying up a spiritual heritage for the next generation.

Blessed is the man that has made the Lord his trust, and has not turned to...those who lapse into falsehood. Ps. 40:4

Lapsing into Falsehood

There is no truth in the devil. Lies started with him. He is the great deceiver who blinds the minds of the unbelieving. Nevertheless, truth has never ceased, because God is the God of truth, Jesus Himself being the embodiment of truth. Falsehood is the contradiction of truth. It is misrepresentation made with intent to deceive.

When what is incorrect replaces what is correct, when the right is substituted by the wrong, then the kingdom of darkness is at work in lying, deception and all that is spurious.

To be truly saved is to be delivered out of the kingdom of darkness, out of the whole realm of the false. It is Jesus who is the truth who sets us free indeed.

As we conduct ourselves in the truth we find ourselves engaged in a war with lies. Wicked lying spirits seduce not only the unconverted, but also unbelieving or disobedient Christians.

According to the Concise Oxford Dictionary, to lapse is to "fail to maintain a position or state for want of effort or vigor, to fall away into an inferior or previous state by failure of conditions." That definition speaks for itself. One of the devil's schemes is to cause Christians to lapse into falsehood. Those who seek to know the Lord and do His will are led into all truth. Those who lapse into falsehood betray their sin.

Having a relationship with the Lord vicariously through someone else's ministry opens us up to their error. Always search the Scriptures to see if a teaching complies with the truth. If you confess and renounce the false, the Lord will reinstate you into the truth.

To him who orders his way aright I shall show the salvation of God. Ps.50:4

Ordering Our Way Aright

It has been said that order is the first law of heaven. Be that as it may, we do know that God is not the author of confusion, which is another word for disorder. Ordering our way aright parallels the exhortation to make straight paths for our feet. As we clear the way before us, we make a way for the Lord. Putting things in order and keeping them in order manifests self-control, a fruit of the Spirit. A disorderly home and a disorderly life reveal one who is out of control, or who is controlled by disorder.

Order is not a quality that is dependent upon a certain standard of living. I have visited truly poor people who have orderly homes, as I visited comparatively wealthy people who have most disorderly homes. Ordering our way aright has to do both with discipline, which is the hallmark of a disciple, and with diligence, which is the hallmark of the industrious.

To order our way aright is to persistently apply what we have learned from the Lord to our lifestyle at all levels. Ordering our way aright involves us in disallowing our old ways and instating new codes of conduct, not because of legalism, but because of new appetites. There is a promise to him who orders his way aright: God will show him His salvation. Salvation is much more than being initially saved. It is a whole process experienced by one who is continually being saved from what he was as he is transformed into Christ-likeness.

God promises more revelation to those who apply the revelation already received. He promises to disclose Himself to them.

If the foundations are destroyed, what can the righteous do?
Ps.11:3

Destroying the Foundations

Satan is a thief who comes to steal, kill and destroy. He has, in a short time, changed the very foundation of Western civilization. We have seen the eroding and annihilating of Biblical law as the basis for morality and judgment. There is no longer any valid appeal to the Bible for precedent. Such is to be expected of a secular society, but more serious is the effect secular thought— higher criticism, liberalism, modernism, rationalism—has had in the church. History has been relegated to myth. The supernatural has been rationalized and dismissed. Sound doctrine has been reduced to existentialism for interpretation.

Webster's Dictionary defines existentialism as "the doctrine that maintains that the source and elements of knowledge have their existence in states of mind... personal decisions in the face of a universe without purpose." For instance, if one asks for a definition of a Christian, he can find as many different answers as people questioned. Another vital question asks for a definition of a church. These foundational concepts have been changed— and in some cases destroyed—as far as the revelation of Scripture is concerned.

The Bible has widely been shelved and theological ignorance has become rampant among Christians. The denial of every sacred doctrine and the practise of every sin common to man are both found in the church. True foundations must be unearthed and relaid with clarity in our generation. We must contend earnestly for the faith once delivered to the saints.

They turned back in the day of battle. Ps. 78:9

Turning Back in Battle

God in His infinite wisdom has incorporated fighting in the outworking of His purposes. It is a mystery: He who rules by His might forever is the God of war—not that anyone could overcome Him, but He fights and we fight for our good. God uses the battle to try our faith and expose our hearts.

Some people never question God until tragedy strikes at their door. As far as they are concerned, there was a God until their circumstances made them question His existence. They fail to understand that what happened to them has happened every day for thousands of years to others, but unlike those others, their faith had remained untried. In their day of battle they turned back only to prove the unreality of their faith.

Untried faith is unproven faith. To be unproven is to be unqualified. The unqualified become qualified when their proving has taken place. The unqualified become disqualified when they fail the test. Jesus said that no one who puts his hand to the plow and looks back is fit for the kingdom of God. Looking back is a disqualifying act for those who are to press on into what God has set before them. We have need of endurance so that when we have done the will of God we may receive what was promised.

If we shrink back, His soul has no pleasure in us. Those who shrink back, do so to destruction, but those who exercise faith in the battle overcome by faith and preserve the soul. The Lord Jesus overcame, and through faith in Him we too can overcome the world and all that the enemy can bring upon us.

Passing through the valley of Baca, they make it a spring...
Every one of them appears before God in Zion. Ps.84:6,7

They Make Weeping a Spring

Those whose strength is in the Lord, who have a heart set in God's direction, transform situations. The valley of Baca was the valley of weeping. The balsam trees oozed their gum like tears. This figurative language points to the change possible in those who are strong in the Lord. They make the valley of weeping into a spring. Tears fall down, and a spring springs up. Instead of being overwhelmed, they well up from within and overflow.

Such strength adds more strength. "Every one of them appears before God in Zion" (Ps.84:7). Their consciousness of God takes them from faith to faith, translating them from one degree of glory to another. They behold the Lord as they look at their circumstances. They appreciate the way of the Lord as their way unfolds, and they bring to bear the strength of God upon even their most depressing plight.

God transforms us from within so that we ourselves can transform our outward environment. Jacob laid his head down in a desert place, but through a revelation of God he called it Bethel, the house of God. What is your desert place at this time? What is your valley of Baca?

All our springs are in the Lord. He makes the thirsty ground into springs of water, and He wants us to do the same through His strength. He gives us His Holy Spirit to be a well of water springing up to eternal life.

By the Holy Spirit, we can overflow in whatever dry and arid places we find ourselves. Make your prison a setting for praise. Bring your light into the dungeon and your joy into the place of tears.

That you may not be sluggish, but imitators of those who through faith and patience inherit the promises. Heb.6:12

That You May Not Be Sluggish

Contrasted with the sluggish are those who through faith and patience inherit the promises. Faith involves patience, but the waiting does not diminish the activity of faith. When we are exhorted to redeem the time, we are reminded to be actively engaged in using the available time doing the will and work of the Lord.

The word of commendation from the Lord to the wise steward is "Well **done**, good and faithful servant." Time well spent is time spent in active faith, even though obedience may involve waiting on and for the Lord. The slothful and the sluggard are featured in Proverbs as shipwrecks and are set as warnings to be avoided. We can come short of the promise of His rest. We must be diligent to enter that rest.

What is the alternative to "well done"? If we have not done well, then the Lord will not say that we have. The sluggish spirit is not the Spirit of God. The sluggard procrastinates, putting off what should be done now. Time will pass and often the opportunity with it. If the promises are not inherited, then what is? Regrets, remorse and the ruing of wasted time are the inheritance of the sluggish.

If an engine runs sluggishly, it is time for some maintenance. Change the plugs, adjust the timing and replace the oil. Is it time for your personal maintenance? Let the Holy Spirit give you an overhaul. Repentance will reinstate you in God's timing and resensitize you to the Spirit of love, power and sound mind. Be filled with the Spirit of zeal, and be hot.

Being conformed to His death, in order that I may attain to the resurrection from the dead. Phil.3:10,11

Attaining to the Resurrection

Preaching a deficient gospel produces a substandard Christianity. Easy-believism—the neglect of repentance and identification with Christ in His death on the cross—has resulted in an anomaly. While new birth should cause people to live new lives, they now "get saved" and live their own lives. They are willing to accept the work Jesus wrought for them, but they deny the work that the Holy Spirit wants to do in them.

The relationship between justification and sanctification is clouded in their thinking (if it exists at all). The notion that everything will be alright if you believe in Jesus needs to be qualified and clarified. While it is true that only the blood of Jesus can justify, it is also true that God makes us worthy that we may in fact walk worthily. If we are known by our fruit, then walking in the flesh could prove a lack of new birth.

When Paul speaks of not yet having attained to the resurrection from the dead, he is referring not to his justification but to his laying hold of that for which he was laid hold of by Christ: living by the faith of the Son of God, pursuing the prize of the high calling of God in Christ IN ORDER to attain to the resurrection from the dead.

The doctrine of rewards is a neglected focus. Ignorance of this doctrine will result in many Christians being saved, yet so as by fire. They will suffer loss because they built their own works of wood, hay and stubble upon the foundation of Christ. The fire will try the quality of each man's life. Your works as a Christian are nothing less than who you are.

The precious possession of a man is diligence. Prov.12:27

The Precious Possession of a Man

Diligence is a commendable character trait that a wise man possesses. It involves being persistent in effort, steady in application, attentive to duties and hearty in work. Although it is a hallmark of good stewards and servants, we are told that the hand of the diligent shall rule. Two aspects of the status of God's sons are serving and ruling. Jesus diligently served and ruled. He is our Lord and Master, and our service to Him should be characterized by diligence.

Being diligent is the opposite of being lazy, slothful and apathetic. The persistence of the diligent keeps him militant against all hindrances. Steadfastness allows no pressures to disillusion or distract. The diligent overcome and maintain the rule. God wills that His sons rule and reign with Him. Sin will have no dominion over the diligent in heart.

We serve God acceptably by diligently ruling over the world, the flesh and the devil. No man can serve two masters. When we serve God we rule over mammon. Peter reminds us to apply all diligence in adding to our faith moral excellence, knowledge, self-control, perseverance, godliness, brotherly kindness and love. These qualities will be ours and increase only as we are diligent. Peter then tells us to be all the more diligent to make our calling and election sure.

The alternative is blindness, shortsightedness, forgetfulness, and continuation in sin, corruption and worldly lust. For this reason diligence is a most precious possession.

Behold the bondslave of the Lord; be it done to me according to your word. Luke 1:38

Be It to Me According to Your Word

The heart behind these words is one of a bondslave. The statement suggests both submission and affirmation. It ascribes to the word of the Lord the authority to govern one's life. There is no vested interest to prohibit the Lord from having His entire way; no self-preservation or self-serving to limit His divine will. With such a serving heart the Lord is well pleased. Jesus Himself knew not His own will but the will of the Father who sent Him. He delighted to do the will of His Father.

Mary's submission occasioned the Redeemer, and the Redeemer's submission produced redemption. What great things God accomplishes through submitted hearts. One act of righteousness effected justification of life to all men. The obedience of one will result in many being made righteous.

It takes only a little leaven to leaven the whole lump. That little leaven can be the leaven of the Pharisees, of which we must be wary, or the leaven of the kingdom of God. However little we perceive ourselves to be, when we submit to God for His word concerning us, our "little" can feed a multitude or provide sustenance for many days. Remember the little lad's loaves and fishes, the widow's last meal of oil and grain, the cruse of oil that never failed.

Those born of God neither bargain with nor demand of Him. Rather, they like their elder brother and Lord submit to God the blank sheet of their future, with their signature at the bottom. In other words their response to their master is as Mary's: "Be it unto me according to your word."

The horse is prepared for the day of battle, but victory belongs to the Lord. Prov.21:31

The Victory Belongs to the Lord

No might or power can effectively be brought against the Lord. He, the Almighty, treads down His enemies, laughing them to scorn. Preparing for battle is futile unless we consult with and follow the Lord. Just as the race is not to the swift, so the battle is not to the strong. The battle and the victory belong to the Lord. When the weak are strong in the Lord, He causes them to triumph over the strong.

The Lord Jesus has gloriously triumphed as a man. The enemy has been defeated. Righteousness has triumphed over all evil. Jesus is head over all things to the church. if we hold fast to the Head, then we ourselves are able to be the head in our lives and not the tail: that is, we can reign through Christ in our sphere. We were born again to reign with the Lord.

He loves us and loves to see us avail ourselves of His victory. God delights in His children taking up His armor and His mighty weapons of warfare and implementing the defeat of the powers of darkness. The record of David's defeat of Goliath has thrilled the hearts of every generation and encourages us in the name of the Lord to come against what appear to be impossible odds.

Have you ever shouted to God with the voice of triumph? We are exhorted to do just that. We are not to let sin reign over us. We are not to let anything master us. This life of ruling is ours through Him who strengthens us. Seated with Christ in heavenly places is our present status. Let us be to principalities and powers a revelation of the mystery of the reigning Christ in us.

Do not lay up for yourselves treasure upon earth...but lay up for yourselves treasure in heaven. Matt.6:19,20

Treasure on Earth or in Heaven

We can ask a simple question to test our hearts: Where is our treasure? Where our treasure is, there will our hearts be also. Jesus was always cutting through appearances and revealing the heart of matters. What He said about the eye had a deeper application to the heart. An evil eye corresponds to an evil heart, and blindness of eye corresponds to blindness of heart.

Serving is a matter of heart. We cannot serve God and mammon (riches). The mixture is unacceptable to God. We must hate and despise the master called mammon, and love and hold to God.

The world eagerly seeks for material things, but Christians are to seek first the kingdom of God and His righteousness. Then all the things we need will be added to us. As our heart exercises our allegiance to God, He calms anxieties. Our heavenly Father is Jehovah Jireh, God our provider. The most important place to have treasure is in heaven. This world and all its lusts will be burned up, but he who does the will of God abides forever.

We can lay up deceitful temporal treasure or true eternal treasure. The riches of this life are worthless in the Spirit. Where we lay up treasure betrays where our heart is focused.

In keeping with His principle of telling us how not to behave before telling us how to behave, Jesus tells us not to lay up treasure on earth, but to lay up treasure in heaven, where there is neither corruption nor loss. Obedience to God at all cost on earth lays up gold, silver and precious stones in heaven.

*I want you to understand that Christ is the head of every man,
and the man is the head of a woman, and God is the head of
Christ. 1 Cor.11:3*

Cultural or Creational

The Bible is cosmopolitan in its appeal. Although the Old
Testament is largely a record of God's chosen people, the Jews, it
was not written exclusively for the Jews. It relates to all parts of
the world, and it is applicable to every culture.

Jesus fulfills all the types and figures of the old covenant
and institutes the new covenant, which is to be preached to every
creature. To reject any of the New Testament as cultural bias,
therefore making it irrelevant for today, is to misunderstand.

In the passages that deal with the roles of men and women,
neither culture nor the fall is referred to as a basis of the teaching.
Creation is the basis of reference.

Man was created first and then woman. The man was not
created for the woman but the woman for the man. The fall is no
more responsible for man being head of the woman than it is for
man being the glory of God and woman the glory of man. This
divine order is neither the result of sin nor a mere cultural phenomenon.

To blue pencil the passages in the New Testament that differentiate between the role of a man and the role of a woman on
the basis of the philosophy that we are to bring in the values of the
age to come is illicit. John warns of those who "go beyond." Not
all that Christ accomplished in His death, burial and resurrection
will be evidenced in this age.

Jesus told the Sadducees that in the resurrection we neither
marry nor are given in marriage, but are like angels who are in
heaven. We are not there yet. We must return to the clearly
defined New Testament roles of man and woman.

For the Lord God helps me, therefore, I am not disgraced; therefore, I have set my face like flint. Isa.50:7

Set Your Face Like Flint

The Lord Jesus was determined to accomplish that for which He had been sent. He would not be disheartened by rejection or distracted by attempts to make Him king. He was always conscious of the eternal realm and continually remained in vital communion with His Father. He was aware of His destiny, of what lay ahead, and for the joy that lay before Him, He endured the cross and despised the shame. He made Himself of no reputation, but He maintained His integrity.

From His youth He cultivated an attitude of setting His face like flint. At the age of twelve He knew that He should be about His Father's business, and He never wavered. We too must set our face as flint in order to fulfill the purpose to which God has called us.

The enemy sought to disqualify our Lord Jesus, and he has the same design towards us. The antidote to his wiles is a perpetual consciousness of our Lord and the hope He has put before us.

The future that God has for you should be your motivation to live in a way that apprehends it. Jesus was glorified not on the basis of His birth alone but on the evidence of His life. We are born again to a living hope. If we suffer with Him, we shall also be glorified with Him. How we live with Him does affect our reception into glory and our status in the age to come.

Look again to Jesus. Set your affections on Him, and you will not be distracted with another focus. When you are conscious of your living intimacy with Christ, discouragement will not overtake you. Be steadfast, immovable, always abounding in God's work.

By the word of God the heavens existed long ago and the earth was formed out of water and by water. 2 Pet.3:5

The Word of God

Never lose the sense of wonder at the mighty power of God's word. He spoke, and worlds came into being. The very words "let there be" contained all the infinite resources of the Creator, and that which did not exist came into being. The heavens and earth are kept—that is, they function—by that same word.

We are born again by the word, we are cleansed by the word, we undergo the washing of regeneration by the word, and we live by every word that proceeds from the mouth of God. If His word abides in us, then we can ask what we will, and it shall be done. Faith comes by hearing the word of God, and we are to live by faith. We must be men of the word, letting the word of Christ dwell in us richly.

Sin came by a contrary word. A time existed when there was no word other than the word of God. Everything was in harmony with God's word until a wrong motive produced a wrong word. That contrary word contradicted God's word and ultimately resulted in the fall of man. Man listened to the contrary word, but the eternal word took human form, and the word that was God became flesh.

As a man, Jesus, the incarnate Word, prevailed over the contrary word and its source, providing for the elevation of man from fallen innocence to eternal righteousness. That is a powerful word.

How vital it is to hear the word of God, to give time to read His word and to listen to His voice. There are many sources of the contrary word that vie for our attention. Shut off and shut out the contrary word. Hear, obey, live and speak the word of God.

Do not judge lest you be judged. Matt. 7:1

Be Careful How You Judge

The tension of truth is never more relevant than in the subject of judging. Jesus tells us not to judge, but He also tells us how to judge. We are to try the spirits and prove all things. Growing in discernment is nothing more than becoming acutely aware of God's assessment. We have choices to make and verdicts to reach that necessitate the exercise of judgment.

Matthew emphasizes not passing judgment as a critic who is faultfinding, censorious, and hypocritical. God forbids us to make judgments on the way others behave when we are not in possession of all the facts and certainly when we are not aware of God's perspective. The priorities of God in dealing with one man can be very different from His priorities with another. In matters that do not apply generally to all men, our personal convictions must not be imposed on others.

We need wisdom to know when to judge and when not to judge. Some issues requiring correction need to be addressed, but other issues must be left to God. At times we are to be governed by another's conscience, while at other times we are to exercise our own convictions.

Although Paul's liberty was judged by others, he instructs us not to pass judgment on opinions of others. We have a critical faculty given to us by the Holy Spirit for discerning right from wrong, but the Lord is against gossip, belittling, backbiting and judgmental attitudes that harm and put down others.

You are blessed if you do not condemn yourself for what you allow and you do not condemn others for what you disallow.

They went far from Me and walked after emptiness and became empty. Jer. 2:5

Becoming Empty

What a contrast there is in the results of seeking the Lord as opposed to pursuing vanity. God is the God of fulness, and He desires that we be filled. Jesus gave us His joy that our joy might be full. He sent us His Spirit that we might be filled with the Spirit. The church is the fulness of Him who fills all in all. We receive of the fulness of Jesus, and with all saints attain to the fulness of Christ, and are destined to be filled with all the fulness of God.

The focus of our hearts determines what we receive. The one who pursues evil will bring about his own death, whereas he who pursues righteousness and loyalty finds life, righteousness and honor. However filled a man may become with material wealth, there is an emptiness within him that remains empty. There is a void within us that is the result of our separation from God, and only reconciliation with God will fill that emptiness. We were created to be filled with God. The pursuit of substitutes to satisfy the inner longings will result only in further emptiness.

Just as the natural hunger of a man cannot be satisfied with reading about a meal, so the spirit of a man cannot be reached with material and tangible substance. Those who hunger and thirst after righteousness shall be filled. Seek the Lord while He may be found, and you will find the God of fulness, and the days of your emptiness will end.

If you drink of the water of life that Jesus gives, you will never thirst again. The Lord invites you to open your mouth wide, and He will fill it.

They are dismayed and caught; behold, they have rejected the word of the Lord. Jer. 8:9

Rejecting the Word of the Lord

The question that follows this statement proves the insanity that is in the heart of man. "What kind of wisdom do they have?" When men reject the word of the Lord, they reject true wisdom. Deception and folly are a poor substitute for truth and wisdom.

Unregenerate man can be expected to act degenerately, but incredibly, many voices in the church proclaim their rejection of the word of the Lord. From unconverted ecclesiastical office holders to evangelicals and charismatics, men relegate clear Biblical teaching to outdated culture, and esteem selected Biblical truths as irrelevant to modern society.

The Bible is a unique source of God's word, without which there would be no record of God, creation, the fall of man, God's dealings with His ancient people, countless prophecies of things that have come to pass and of things that have yet to happen, the incarnation and the person of Jesus Christ, the gospel and the early church. The list continues, with teachings on topics such as the new covenant, the Kingdom of God and judgment to come.

When God's word is set aside or discounted then nothing less than the contrary word of Satan takes its place. To teach contrary to the word of God is to become a purveyor of fool's food. Why give the counterfeit when the original and true can be given? Contend for the faith, and do not contradict it. To reject the word of the Lord is to hold fast to deception. Receiving and observing the word of the Lord is to live. Think about the alternative to the way of life, and avoid it by living according to His word.

The way is broad that leads to destruction...the way is narrow that leads to life. Matt.7:13,14

Which Gate and Which Way?

Most of mankind has lived, and continues to live according to the different faiths and philosophies of this world. This multitude of ways of living comprise what Jesus calls the *broad way*. In contrast, He also speaks of the *narrow way* that few find. It is narrow because of its singularity, for Jesus alone is the way. He is the only door through which men may go and be saved.

Much of the persecution that comes to Christians is a result of the uncompromising and unaccommodating stance taken that Christ is the only way. Criticism comes even from those who profess Christianity, who in their misguided liberality deny that Jesus is the only savior and His name the only name given under heaven whereby we must be saved.

Our generation is repeating the apostasy of Israel. Having forsaken the Lord and His word, every man is doing what is right in his own eyes. *Live and let live* may be the rule of the day, but it is not God's rule. Like the traditions of the Pharisees, man's value systems nullify God's values.

We must teach children the only good news of salvation for all men. To teach it we must learn it, but not from those on the broad way. It must be proclaimed to those on the broad way in order to turn them from their way to God's way.

Our children are immersed in influences that oppose the wisdom of God. We can forestall and counteract by being the first to affect their consciences as we constantly reinforce their ability to repel the seductions of the broad way. Those who travel the narrow way, Christ the only way, find abundant life.

The devil has come down to you, having great wrath, knowing that he has only a short time. Rev.12:12

Satan's Time Is Short

The Scriptures teach us that the devil has great wrath because he knows he has only a short time. As his time runs out, God's sovereign hand will allow his anger and activity to intensify; powers, signs and lying wonders with deceptions will increase. God Himself will send strong, deluding influences upon those who do not receive the love of the truth so as to be saved.

In our day, iniquity and deceptions abound; however, where sin abounds grace much more abounds. The antidote to falling away and having our love grow cold is to grow in grace and in the knowledge of Jesus our Lord.

We must guard against becoming dull of hearing and falling victim to deception. The ability to discern between good and evil belongs to the spiritually sensitive, those who have set their minds on the Spirit and by reason of use have their senses exercised to discern good from evil.

Our time is also short, so we must turn our affections from worldly pursuits and the gratifying of the flesh, to Christ. We redeem our time by vigorously applying ourselves to seeking the Lord. We must give time for pursuing God and His word.

We have been called to overcome Satan by the blood of the Lamb and the word of our testimony. Jesus sent the Holy Spirit so that His disciples could be testimonies of Him. God has given us His armor and the sword of the Spirit, which is the word of God.

The provisions for your victory have been made. Instead of letting your love grow cold, be on fire for the Lord. Display your love by living in righteousness and holiness, and by defeating Satan's strategy for your fall.

Everyone who hears these words of mine, and acts upon them, may be compared to a wise man, who built his house upon a rock. Matt. 7:24

The Responsibility of Hearing

Our Lord describes our response to hearing His words in terms of building a house. The outcome is either a house that stands or one that falls. We are all building a house! We must be careful how we build. The Lord has shown how superficial and unfounded is a profession of His Lordship without the accompanying obedience. That sort of discrepancy is as precarious as a building without foundation.

Building upon sand is a complete waste of life, because what is built **will** collapse, resulting in missing out eternally. To hear and obey is to build wisely. Luke adds, "who dug deep and laid a foundation upon a rock." We cannot work our own justification, for Jesus is that foundation. However, just as we must strive to enter by that narrow gate, we must also dig deep to find that foundation. The tools of repentance and faith moved by the conviction of the Holy Spirit will unearth the rock of our salvation.

The substance of the buildings may appear to be the same, but the fact that one has a foundation which the other lacks will become evident when either the storms of life assail them or the final great storm of judgment bursts upon them.

Many Christians hold to the false security that once they are saved everything will be alright at the judgment. The quality of what we build will be judged, and Christians can suffer loss. If we hear and do not obey, then we build upon the sand, not Christ. What good is it to enjoy the word and not heed it? Herod did that, but when he found himself under the pressure of having his reputation put at stake, his pride ruled him, and his end was destruction.

It is not those who know God's word who enter the kingdom of heaven, but those who do His word.

Catch the foxes for us, the little foxes that are ruining the vineyard.
Song 2:15

Little Foxes Ruin the Vineyard

There are always dangers that accompany blessings. Self-sufficiency, spiritual pride, complacency and losing our first love, to name but a few, can creep in unawares. The antidote to regression is progression. We must have a healthy appetite that makes us hungry for more of the Lord. The pursuit of God must be a quest engaged in from the heart as a continual exercise.

Losing one's first love for the Lord usually occurs gradually, even imperceptibly. The Lord Jesus has to send messengers to tell His people what their condition is because they no longer hear His voice.

To search out and discover more of the Lord Jesus in deeper experience, to explore the treasures of wisdom and knowledge that are in Him—these are life indeed, abundant life. The small foxes that spoil the vine are as destructive as ever. They succeed when we let our guard down, either through busyness and fatigue, or when the edge goes from our zeal.

How is it that front-line Christians become fringe people? Those who were once committed are numbered with the uncommitted, and the flow of spiritual life in service for others ebbs to a halt. A cavity in a tooth starts from a little neglect that becomes a careless disregard. What was a tiny area of plaque, if unchecked and allowed to persist, will corrupt the tooth and finally destroy it.

There is a power greater than that of corruption, and that is incorruption. A child of God is born again of incorruptible seed and can grow up into Christ in all aspects. How shall we escape if we neglect so great a salvation?

Cursed be the one who does the Lord's work negligently.
Jer. 48:10

Neglecting the Work of the Lord

Under the terms of the new covenant, the work of the Lord is not something apart from our personal livelihood. The work of the Lord is to be our life's work. Whatever we do, we are to do it unto the Lord wholeheartedly.

The church has been sold down the river with the pernicious doctrine that relegates everyone who is not clergy to having a secular job. Secular means worldly, not sacred, not spiritual. No Christian should have a secular occupation. Every Christian should see his livelihood as his vocation in which he serves the Lord. Our very bodies are to be living sacrifices, presented to God for His will and pleasure.

Loving God involves our entire being and strength. The commandment to love God totally, which under the old covenant was a condemnation to us, is fulfilled under the terms of the new covenant. The Lord promised that He would circumcise our heart to love Him with all our heart and all our soul. He gives us a new, pure heart into which He sheds His love.

Christ in us is still the same zealous Christ who fervently loves and works. No one can accuse the Lord of being negligent, for it is His zeal that performs His purposes. Carelessness and neglect are not evidences of the Spirit of God, but they can gradually creep in until there is a disregard for Christ's interests.

David danced before the Lord with all of his might, and he laid up for the house of the Lord with all his might. We are exhorted to be fervent in spirit, serving the Lord. Whatever you do, do it heartily, and with all your might.

Therefore, since we receive a kingdom which cannot be shaken, let us show gratitude, by which we may offer to God an acceptable service with reverence and awe. Heb.12:28

Showing Gratitude

One of the character traits of men in the last days is ungratefulness. We must guard against such an attitude because, sadly, what is going on in the world so often influences the church. The ability to render thanks is in itself furnished by the grace of God. That same grace enables us to offer to God acceptable service in a spirit of fear and awe.

God has provided grace for us to apply practically. That grace has made us recipients of an unshakable kingdom. Those things that can be shaken will be shaken when God will shake not only the earth but also the heaven.

It is His pleasure to give us the kingdom. Having made us partakers of Christ, He has freely given us all things with Him. We are not only heirs of God but **joint heirs** with Christ. Little wonder that the word *therefore* precedes the statement *let us show gratitude*. It is because of all that God has provided for us by His grace.

Lay hold of grace and show how grateful you are by offering yourself as a living sacrifice. Is it not reasonable to do just that? Dare we show contempt. Dare we neglect so great a salvation? Can we remain unmoved or complacent in the light of such love and grace? An extra incentive follows: God is a consuming fire. Remember Aaron's sons who offered unacceptable offerings and were consumed by the fire of God.

In the new covenant God has dealt with our hearts. We can now serve the Lord continually, from new hearts in which He has written His law. With such a demonstration of gratitude God is well pleased.

In order that the requirements of the law might be fulfilled in us, who do not walk according to the flesh, but according to the Spirit. Rom.8:4

God's Requirements Fulfilled in Us

We can misconstrue the message of grace. Grace is not grace to sin. Grace enables us to walk in the Spirit and not fulfill the lusts of the flesh. The Spirit of the Lawgiver has given birth to all born-again believers. In the new covenant God provides a new birth, a new heart, and a new spirit, which comprise the new creature. Unlike the old heart, the new heart has His law written in it, enabling us to fulfill the will of God from the heart. Obedience now becomes more natural than disobedience. We must believe that of ourselves.

We have received the same spirit of faith as God, which is why Jesus could say that we are to have the faith of God. The same Spirit that raised Jesus from the dead now dwells in us and gives life to our mortal bodies. The love of God has been shed abroad in our hearts by that same Spirit. We cannot enjoy the benefits of the new covenant relationship with the Lord if we do not believe that our old heart has been removed. God promised to remove it. We must believe that He has done that. God promised to give us a new, purified heart. We must believe that we have received it.

When the old heart of unbelief raises its ugly head, reckon it dead, for the power of the cross renders it powerless. Reckoning is faith in action. Reckon yourself alive unto God, and you will live by such faith. When you exercise faith in the cross over your old man and in the resurrection for the new man, then you can experience the power of death and the power of His resurrection.

If what God requires of you is written in your heart, then by His grace fulfill it.

I came that they might have life, and might have it abundantly.
John 10:10

Abounding in Restriction

In the context of telling us that the thief comes to steal, kill and destroy, Jesus discloses one of the reasons He came: "that you might have life and have it more abundantly." However, the life that He gives does not depend upon physical resources, nor is the abundance comprised of material things men possess.

Jesus forewarned the disciples that in the world they would have tribulation, persecution and great distress, yet all the while have abundant life.

Paul is an example of one who enjoyed the life that he shared with the Lord, but whose circumstances were often what we would call restrictive. When jailed and fettered he sang praises and wrote letters exhorting others to always rejoice. Our ability to rejoice and to be exceedingly joyful should not hampered by restrictive circumstances and pressures.

The life that we receive from the Lord is His life, which cannot be touched by the tangible world. Our life, since it is hidden with Christ in God, is eternal and incorruptible.

Drawing upon Christ, who is our life, as the source of our joy can even be enhanced by outward affliction. Being placed in circumstances that hem us in and appear to be limitations does not restrict our ability to abound in the abundant life.

The key to living abundantly is to know Him who is your life and to be aware of your union with Him. That awareness goes beyond the mere knowledge of physical and temporal life to where the reality of your spiritual and eternal life are prominent. Only then will you know the unrestricted flow of abundant life.

As Christ was raised from the dead by the glory of the Father, so we too might walk in newness of life. Rom. 6:4

All We Have to Do Is Walk

The new covenant provides for us to become new creatures. As such, we should walk in newness of life. The life that we now live in our mortal bodies should be lived by the faith of the Son of God. Christ has faith for us to walk by His Spirit. When we exercise that faith, we walk in the Spirit and make no provision for the old, sinful self.

Believing that our old man was crucified with Christ does not mean that we never engage in the conflict of the flesh and the spirit. It does mean that the power and dominion of the flesh is nullified and that we can decide not to sin. It is as easy as that! The power of the life of Christ within gives us not only the ability to refuse sin, but also the desire to do the will of God from our new heart.

The yoke of Jesus is truly easy. We are given life. All we have to do is live. We are made upright. All we have to do is walk uprightly. God is at work in us. All we have to do is work it out. We were made worthy to walk worthily.

The very highway to Zion is programed into our new hearts along with everything else God has written there. This enables us to do all that we do heartily—with a whole heart—unto the Lord.

We were separated from God because of our sin, but now He has freed us from our sins and reconciled us to Himself. All we have to do is abide in Him and stand fast in the liberty with which we have been freed. The grace in which we stand is not grace to walk in the flesh, but grace to think like Christ, to speak like Christ, to live like Christ, to walk even as He walked.

*For the law of the Spirit of life in Christ Jesus has set you free
from the law of sin and of death. Rom.8:2*

The New Covenant and the Law of Sin

The Holy Spirit uses the apostle Paul as an instrument to
instruct us in the mechanics of the law of sin. When we were in
the flesh (the old, carnal, unregenerate man) the sinful passions,
which were aroused by God's law, were at work in the members
of our bodies to bear fruit for death. We were of the flesh, sold
into bondage to sin. Sin, the indwelling master that overpowered
us even beyond our convictions, was performing its work in and
through us. We were prisoners of the sin which ruled in our members. Even if our minds concurred with God's law that it was
good, we had no power to perform it. However, that wretched
state of bondage has now been dealt with by our Lord Jesus Christ.

He came in flesh and blood as a man and conquered sin and
death, providing for us deliverance and freedom from sin. By
repentance, faith and regeneration, a new law comes into our
members. It is the law of the Spirit of life in Christ Jesus, and it
sets us free from the law of sin and death.

Our old man is crucified with Christ, and the Spirit that
raised Jesus from the dead makes us alive, quickening our mortal
bodies. We are no longer in the flesh, but in the Spirit, if indeed
the Spirit of God dwells within us.

We now have the superior power of the conquering Spirit
of Christ in union with our spirit to give us the ability not to sin.
Sin shall no longer be master over us. Being dead to sin and
alive to God is a living reality. Christ did not pay such an
immense price for it not to work. We are no longer slaves to sin,
but God's slaves, and our faculties have become instruments of
righteousness.

One thing have I desired of the Lord...that I may dwell in the house of the Lord all the days of my life. Ps.27:4

Dwelling in the House of the Lord

David's one desire and petition was to dwell in the house of the Lord, to behold the beauty of the Lord. Surely there is no greater experience, no more rewarding and utterly fulfilling encounter, than to look on the beauty of the Lord. God in His grace and mercy has provided for us to be fitted for His presence. The cleansing and regeneration that occur by the blood of Jesus and by the power of the Holy Spirit enable us to dwell with the consuming fire.

Dwelling forever with the Lord includes all the days of our life on earth. If David enjoyed dwelling in the house of the Lord all the days of his life, how much more should we who are under the new covenant know His abiding presence.

We have been birthed into a union that joins us to the Lord and makes us one spirit. We do not need to wait until we "go to heaven" to dwell with the Lord. We know by faith and by the Spirit He has given us that He dwells in our hearts. Through the love we display, the abiding presence of God is expressed in and through us.

David not only wanted to behold the beauty of the Lord, but he also desired to enquire of the Lord. The Lord Himself invites us to petition Him: "Ask and it shall be given." Often, we do not have, because we do not ask.

The Lord desires to dwell with you and commune with you. The reason Jesus knocks at the door is to be let in. He wants to dine with you, and for you to dine with Him. What response does His fervent desire for you generate within you? Do you thirst for the Lord as the deer pants for the water? How blessed are those who dwell in His house.

Wretched man that I am! Who will set me free from the body of this death. Rom. 7:24

Who Will Set Me Free?

This question is the cry of someone trapped in bondage and slavery. The taskmaster is sin, and the fetters are corruption and death. It is the one who is so imprisoned, driven and dominated who in desperation cries out beyond his wretched self for a deliverer.

Israel cried out concerning her cruel bondage, and God sent her a deliverer, Moses. The things that happened in those days are examples of what was to come, when God would send His Son to be the Savior who would deliver sinners from their sins.

Israel was baptized into Moses through the cloud and the sea, and Pharaoh and all his army were destroyed in the same sea. Through His death, Jesus has disarmed and destroyed Satan and the powers of darkness. Their extension of activity is limited to an allotted time. The fact that we can resist Satan and have him flee from us proves his defeat through the greater One who now dwells in us.

When we are baptized into Jesus, we are baptized into His death. The death of our old man in the death of Christ sets us free from the dominion of Satan, sin and the fear of death. Death itself cannot touch the incorruptible seed which has given birth to us. The Spirit that raised Jesus from the dead not only brings us to life and liberty, but leads us in life, proving that we are the sons of God.

Who shall set me free? The answer is Jesus Christ. If the Son sets you free, then are you free indeed, free to enjoy the glorious liberty of the sons of God. The mystery and the power of Christ in you will give you the knowledge of what to do and the freedom to do it.

As for me and my house, we will serve the Lord. Josh.24:15

As for Me and My House

Joshua made this classic statement before Israel as a testimony that he and his house would serve the Lord. He, the head, refers to his wife and children as his house. In the New Testament, one of the qualifications for an elder is that he must rule or manage his own house well. The reason given is that if a man does not know how to manage his own household, then he cannot take care of the church of God.

Such instruction is unacceptable to a generation that has rejected God's word in favor of its own philosophy, but there are numerous instructions concerning the different roles of men and women in the word of God. These declarations of divine order reinforce the need for godly men to be able to speak for their families.

The breakdown of God's beautiful order for the family makes it difficult, but not impossible, to rebuild. Any man who embarks on the course of reinstating the Lord's structure into the family has the power of God working for him.

Each must prayerfully apply himself to extracting from the word of God the salient passages dealing with God's revealed will concerning the role of the man, the woman and the children. Having seen where he personally has failed, each man should confess and repent before the Lord—but not leave it there. He must enlist the help of his wife by openly admitting his failings and seeking her forgiveness, doing the same with his children as well.

Hurts take time to heal, and trust must be earned, but God can move in a family in which the head makes himself available to God.

You were made to die to the law through the body of Christ, that you might be joined to another. Rom. 7:4

The Law of God and the Law of Sin

The law has jurisdiction over a man as long as he lives. Death alone can release him from being bound by the law. God uses the analogy of marriage to help us understand how we relate to the law and to Christ. Before Christ came in the flesh we were bound, as in marriage, to the law. Although the law is good, holy, righteous and spiritual, it serves only to manifest the exceeding sinfulness of sin in us.

Just as partners of a marriage are not permitted to marry others unless one of them dies, so for us to be free to be joined to Christ, either we or the law had to die. The law cannot die, so we had to die.

Jesus came and fulfilled the law, then offered Himself up in death so as to effect our death. Those who have been crucified with Christ are dead with Him. The old, unregenerate man—which instead of living by the law was only condemned by it—has been put to death in the death of Jesus. But the same Spirit that raised Jesus from the dead quickens the mortal bodies of those who have been crucified and buried with Him. Only those so joined to Christ in His death can be joined to Him in His resurrection and bear fruit to God.

Jesus did not do away with the law, for He came to fulfill it. The moral law represents the desires of the lawgiver. We are not under it as a means of our justification. Rather we are under grace, which gives us the ability to fulfill all righteousness.

Through the body of Christ you died to the law. Through that same body you were raised from the dead, in union with Him who is the head of His body, the church. Jesus lives, and now by the law of the Spirit of Life you also are alive.

The woman whom You gave me to be with me, she gave me from the tree, and I ate. Gen.3:12

The Woman You Gave Me

A characteristic that resulted from the fall is the tendency to blame others for our mistakes. Reluctance to admit faults is commonplace. Adam pointed to Eve and to God, and Eve pointed to the serpent, but God judged both Adam and Eve. No matter whom we blame for our mistakes, God holds us accountable. The fact that all die proves that blame is not transferable. "She made me do it." "The devil made me do it." These are unacceptable excuses.

God commands repentance without excuses from all men. The man who bowed his head in shame under the conviction of sin, beating his breast and crying out to God for mercy—this man, rather than the self-righteous man, was justified by God. A man only adds to his sin when he tries to transfer the blame for his problems. Further, it is cowardly for men not to take responsibility for problems in the home.

Jesus helped his wife out of her troubles even to the point of taking them upon Himself. He loved her and bore her sins in His body on the tree. So husbands ought also to love their wives. A man is more of a man when he sees his wife make a mistake and comes to her side to help, even cleaning up the mess himself. Instead of jumping all over her or the children when an accident occurs, he embraces them, comforts them and helps them out. You were created as a man to do just that.

Express your God-given manhood, and let your strength support your family, rather than allowing your bad temper to compound the problem. Admit your faults, and help others out of theirs.

For he who loves his neighbor has fulfilled the law. Rom.13:8

He Who Loves Fulfills the Law

The new covenant proclaims a new commandment, which instructs us to love one another as Jesus loves us. The carnal nature rendered us incapable of such love, but our carnality has been replaced by a new heart in which the love of God has been shed by the Holy Spirit who was given to us. The faith and love of Christ should now be the controlling factors of our lives. The whole law is summed up in this saying: You shall love your neighbor as yourself.

Far from being rejected, the law has been fulfilled with a righteousness that continues to be fulfilled in those who walk according to the Spirit. When love controls us, we find ourselves loving God and keeping His commandments. We do not envy, are not jealous and do not steal or kill. We have a caring rather than a self-seeking heart. Those who walk in love will fulfill all the good contained in the law for their neighbor.

When we walk in fellowship with the Spirit, we walk in love. The witness of the Spirit with our spirit opens up dimensions of God's love toward us. Such knowledge constrains us to exhibit His love toward others, even our enemies. As we express the love that has been poured into our hearts, we manifest Christ in our mortal bodies.

The heart of the lawgiver never changes. Our aim should be to please Him, and to please Him we must do the things that please Him. Jesus said, "I always do those things that please the Father." Out of His love He fulfilled the law as a man in order that we might know the same ability to love Him and to keep His commandments.

Put on the Lord Jesus Christ, and make no provision for the flesh in regard to its lusts. Rom.13:14

Put on the Lord Jesus Christ

Putting off and putting on are daily exercises. In the natural we would not think of putting clean clothes over the top of soiled ones. Neither can we put on Christ until we have put off the old man. Our former manner of life with its evil practices is linked with our old self, which we are told to lay aside and reckon to be dead. The new self, which in God has been created in true righteousness and holiness, is to be put on.

Now, for us to live is Christ. It is no longer we as what we were who live, but Christ in union with us lives in us. The life that we now live in the flesh we live by the faith of the Son of God. The fact that He has the faith should encourage our faith. He has told us to take up our cross daily. Paul knew that experience, for he said that he died daily. Perhaps we would more easily experience the reality of Christ as our life if at the beginning of every day we put off the old man and put on the new man as a definite act of faith. Then, during the course of a day, when the flesh lusted against the Spirit, we could lay aside the deeds of darkness while reminding ourselves that we had put on Christ and could make no provision for the flesh to fulfill its lusts.

Truth is to be very practically applied, and going through the physical motions often enforces the spiritual truth. It is like presenting oneself to God as alive from the dead: it simply needs to be done. How enjoyable it is to put on Christ, to stand or bow before God literally presenting yourself to Him as one who is alive from the dead.

He commanded them not to leave Jerusalem, but to wait for what the Father had promised. Acts 1:4

What the Father had Promised

Baptism in the Holy Spirit is part of the new covenant. Jesus calls it *the promise of the Father*. Controversy about the subject rages despite the clear statements about it in both old and new covenants. Peter uses the terms of Joel's prophecy to explain what happened on the day of Pentecost: the outpouring of the Holy Spirit was to be evidenced by prophecy, visions and dreams in the lives of sons and daughters, slaves, and young and old men. As the book of Acts unfolds, whenever the Holy Spirit comes upon people something tangible appears.

Joel speaks of prophecy occurring, and Acts speaks of prophecy and—even more frequently—of tongues occurring. Both Cornelius and his company and, much later, the Ephesian disciples spoke in tongues after the Holy Spirit came upon them. The point being underscored is that the "experience" of the outpouring of the Spirit is the promise of the Father for all who have been born-again.

A simple way to test the experience of any who say that they have received the promise is to see if their experience conforms to the infallible record of what happened in the New Testament. Evidence of the Holy Spirit's power was certainly manifested in prophecy and tongues then. On what basis do we relegate the scriptural accounts as irrelevant for today?

The testimony of Jesus is the spirit of prophecy. The Bible was never given as a substitute for the gift of the Holy Spirit and fire. The promise is still being poured out, and people are still becoming testimonies of Jesus.

I shall find out, not the words of those who are arrogant, but their power. 1 Cor.4:19

Not Words But Power

There is a form of godliness that denies the power of true godliness. Jesus promised the disciples that they would receive power after the Holy Spirit had come upon them. The word *dunamis* (power, dynamism) occurs seventy-seven times in the New Testament. Paul uses it as the measure for assessing what type of Christian is being so arrogant against him, giving notice that he will find out whether their power matches their words. He then makes a classic statement of principle: "for the kingdom of God does not consist in word only, but in power." Peter uses dunamis in Acts 10:38, where he talks about Jesus whom God anointed with the Holy Spirit and power.

Jesus began His ministry when the Holy Spirit came upon Him at His baptism. When He returned from the wilderness, where He had defeated Satan in the power of the Spirit, He was dynamic, doing good and healing all who were oppressed by the devil. The dynamite of Jesus was of a much greater magnitude than that of Satan. He blasted out the devil and gave His disciples His power over all the power of the enemy.

The power of the Holy Spirit makes a Christian a witness of Jesus. It is the promised gift for all believers. It identifies us with Jesus to the extent that we become witnesses of Him and can rightly speak in Christ's name. False teaching, that which denies the baptism of the Holy Spirit and power, in many churches has left thousands spiritually cold and weak, as opposed to hot and dynamic.

What is your power rating? God still gives the Holy Spirit and power to those who ask and obey Him.

It was for freedom that Christ set us free... do not be subject again to a yoke of slavery. Gal.5:1

True Freedom

Sin enslaved us, making us helpless to resist or overcome. The fear of further corruption culminating in death tormented us. We desperately needed deliverance, and in His mercy, God sent the deliverer, Jesus. Repentance resulting from a revelation of Christ as our sin offering releases us from our sense of wretchedness. Joy takes the place of desperation when we experience forgiveness. Freedom from our disrupted personality, once ruled by ungodly influences and self-centered responses, is included in our deliverance. God's answer is complete.

God freed us into perfect liberty. He crucifies us with Jesus and raises us into a new life Fathered by Him. Our identity no longer depends on what we can salvage from our natural birth, but now finds a rock-solid basis in our new status as the sons of God.

As new creatures we are owned and equipped by the Holy Spirit. We are designated specific gifts in which we find ourselves neither deficient nor overloaded. We are free to be what we were created to be—free from the past, free from useless striving, free from regret or complaint about who we are.

This freedom extends to our liberty to enter into the holiest place of all, the presence of God, there to remain in constant union with Him. Being bound to Him is perfect freedom.

The transformation that takes place in those whom the Son sets free proves His power to break every yoke, every chain and every trace of the power of what was our natural personality. Live in that glorious liberty.

So then, brethren, we are not children of the bondwoman, but of the free woman. Gal. 4:31

Children of the Free Woman

Hagar and Sarah represent two covenants: the first from Mount Sinai, which corresponds to the earthly Jerusalem; and the second from Mount Zion, which is from above. Jesus told Nicodemus that unless a man was born of the Spirit, from above, he could not see the kingdom of God. Jerusalem above is free. She is our mother.

Our new birth by the Spirit brings us to Mount Zion, to the city of the living God, the heavenly Jerusalem. We are not of this world. We have been freed from bondage to corruption and to the flesh. Now our citizenship is in heaven even though we walk on earth. Our liberty as children of God introduces us to a heavenly environment, "to myriads of angels, to the general assembly and church of the first born who are enrolled in heaven, and to God, the Judge of all, and to the spirits of righteous men made perfect, and to Jesus, the mediator of the new covenant, and to the sprinkled blood which speaks better than the blood of Abel" (Heb. 12:22-24).

Our natural birth brought us into the bondage of corruption, while our new birth has brought us by incorruptible seed into a liberty that frees us from the necessity and obligation to sin. Our liberty is not meant to give us an occasion for the flesh, but it is meant to free us to be what God has made us to be in spirit and truth.

The power of the cross is the power of death over our old man. The power of the resurrection and the power of the Spirit is the power to live as those alive unto God. We once bore fruit unto death, but now in union with Jesus we bear fruit unto God. Against such fruit there is no law or prohibition.

So shall My heavenly Father also do to you, if each of you does not forgive his brother from his heart. Matt.18:35

Forgive and Be Forgiven

To be ultimately relieved in our consciences we must receive ultimate forgiveness, which comes only from God. Any sense of guilt or condemnation reveals the need for forgiveness. Death itself continually reminds us of the ultimate wages of sin and of our accountability to God. It is little wonder then that under the pressure of traumatic circumstances, when the danger of death is imminent, men and women cry out to God.

How tragic that the last desperate cry for God is so often not accompanied by the relief and serenity that come from knowing God's forgiveness. Such is the stupidity of man. One of man's basic needs, if not the most basic, is to know God's forgiveness. He has proved His great love towards us and His willingness to forgive us by what He has done for us in Jesus Christ and His shed blood. We can live with the knowledge of that forgiveness— or without it. We can know that we are justified by repentance and faith in the Lord Jesus, or we can live a self-condemned life with a nagging conscience that scolds us before God and worries about the fearful prospect of His wrath and judgment.

When God cleanses us from all unrighteousness, the *all* is fully embracing. We must forgive ourselves as God has forgiven us. Then, as we have freely been forgiven, we must freely exercise that forgiveness towards all who have sinned against us. The message is clear: no one has done against us anything that can be compared with what we did against God. If we will not forgive others their sins, neither will God forgive us ours.

But we did not yield to them in subjection for even an hour, that the truth of the Gospel might remain with you. Gal.2:5

The Truth of the Gospel

Paul makes extraordinarily aggressive statements against those who preach another gospel. There were in his day those who defiled the purity of the true gospel and taught an unholy mixture of works and faith, of law and grace for justification. He said that these teachers were to be accursed. Such was his passion for the truth of the gospel.

Jesus Christ, having fulfilled the works of the law, redeemed us from its curse, and in so doing made obsolete such laws as touch not, taste not, and observance of days, months, times and years. These were weak and beggarly elements which only brought back into bondage those seeking to be justified by them.

The purity of the gospel is still being compromised by teachings that add to or subtract from what Christ has accomplished. "Other gospels" are prevalent today. The erroneous plusses are the touch-nots and the observance of days, etc. The minuses are those teachings that, through the employment of other mediators, belittle what Jesus did and what He is.

People who major in external observance betray a deficiency of internal obedience. The obedience of faith is an expression of love from the heart. It was the Pharisees who were the whited sepulchers and who washed the outside of the cup. Jesus upbraided them for hypocrisy, and for their outward observance meant to be seen of men, and He spoke of their being defiled by what came out of their heart.

To walk in the Spirit, one must be rightly related to the Lord in the inner man and be led by the Spirit. Do not put what God has written in your new heart back on tablets of stone.

But before faith came, we were kept in custody under the law, being shut up to the faith which was later to be revealed. Gal. 3:23

The Faith That Was To Be Revealed

The law convinces us of our guilt and of our need for a Savior. If there had been a law by which we could have been made righteous, then Christ need never have died for us. It is faith in the Lord Jesus and His finished work that justifies us and makes us God's children.

Paul refers to the time before faith came and to the fact that faith has now come. There was a dimension of faith that certain men and women exercised under the old covenant, enabling them to live and die in faith. They lived in obedience to God's word, but died without receiving the promises. They saw them and embraced them from a distance, but did not receive what was promised. They could only look forward to what we now experience. They looked for a city whose builder and maker was God, but we have come to that city of the living God. They looked towards the coming of the Messiah, but we who have come to Jesus look back to the Messiah's coming and to all that He fulfilled. Their faith in the promises was accompanied by the observance of requirements that pointed to Jesus.

With the coming of Jesus came the revelation of faith in Him, without the necessity of observing the now worthless elemental things. Jesus fulfilled the whole law and all the types, symbols, gifts, sacrifices and offerings. These regulations were necessary until a time of reformation.

The time of reformation came when Christ appeared, accomplishing all that the Father had given Him to do. We are now justified by faith in Jesus, without the works of the law.

How is it that you turn back again to the weak and worthless elemental things? Gal. 4:9

Weak and Worthless

The apostle enumerates superfluous observances beyond mere circumcision. He feared that believers were returning to things no longer necessary. Jesus had come, faith had come, the Spirit had come. Now the old requirements, which could never make the observers perfect, were redundant. Making a similar point to the Colossians, he informs them that observances such as touch not, taste not and handle not are of no value against fleshly indulgence. Jesus clearly taught that what really matters is that which is happening in the heart.

What comes out of the heart is that which really defiles, not what goes in through the mouth. Jesus declared ALL foods clean (Mark 7:15-19). Likewise under the new covenant, ALL days are holy. To hold one day above another or to abstain from certain meats or other foods is unnecessary.

In Jesus we are now a kingdom of sanctified priests who live continually in the true temple. Our state of holiness is not altered from day to day. If we may not do something one day, then we ought not do it any day. We enter God's rest when we cease from our own labors. God is not more holy on certain days, and neither are we. It is not the day that matters, but the heart.

Outward observance is not only weak, but it is worthless because it is of no value against carnality in the heart. If we have begun in the Spirit, we will not be perfected by the elemental things of the world. All shadows and types have been fulfilled in Jesus. Now that the perfect has come, God will not revert to types and figures, and neither should we.

Cast out the bondwoman and her son, for the son of the bondwoman shall not be an heir with the son of the free woman. Gal. 4:30

Cast Out the Bondwoman and Her Son

Jerusalem above is free. She is the mother of all born-again believers. We are either sons of bondage or sons of freedom. The two must not cohabit. Jesus has set us free from the old self by taking it into death in His death. If we do not cast out the bondwoman and her son, then we remain in a duality dominated by what we were naturally.

The double-minded are unstable in all their ways. Single-mindedness is for those who through repentance have crucified the flesh, and in so doing have cast out the bondwoman and her son. Only then can we enjoy the true freedom of our new nature uninhibited by the old.

In place of indwelling sin we receive the indwelling of the Spirit, which creates a cry from our innermost being, "Abba Father." Where the Spirit is there is liberty. It is a glorious liberty to which we are introduced, a liberty that will finally release us from the mortal and corruptible, from sorrow and suffering and death. Until that day we are to enjoy the freedom that is ours in this day.

Sin shall not dominate us. We are to live in the victory that overcomes the world and the flesh and the devil. Faith makes it all possible, faith in Christ's finished work for us and faith in His ongoing work in us. That same faith will enable us to cast out the bondwoman and her son. In this way we reckon ourselves crucified with Christ and alive unto God. The Spirit reveals the truth and empowers us to apply the word by faith. The outcome is the jubilant freedom of a new creature.

*And not holding fast to the head, from whom the entire body,
...grows with a growth which is from God. Col.2:19*

Hold Fast to the Head

Every member of Christ's body has a direct relationship with
the Head, the Lord Jesus. There are no indirect connections. The
nature of our union with Him ensures that no one is born again
with a disadvantage when it comes to personal access. However,
the Scriptures clearly state that we can BECOME dull of hearing and can even sear our conscience.

Hindrances can arise in our communion with the Lord and
appear to put us out of touch. If that experience occurs, it is of
paramount importance that we spend time seeking the Lord and
searching our own soul for what could have grieved the Spirit.
True repentance always makes us more sensitive to the Lord.
Sometimes a time of leanness in our walk with the Lord is meant
to drive us deeper and more earnestly into Him.

The Lord desires intimacy with us. He wants to come in
and sit down with us personally, even when He has been put outside the door. If any man hears His voice and opens the door, He
will come in and sup with him and he with the Lord. What love!
What condescension!

He jealously desires us. It is true that we can experience
His life through others, but He has not delegated others to be
received and known in place of Himself. Some Christians live a
vicarious relationship with the Lord through others, experiencing
little or no relationship with Him themselves. This is a travesty of
what the Lord desires for each one of us.

We all have the capacity to hold fast to the head. Our personal experience of Jesus produces a heart cry that exclaims, "The
Son of God loved ME and gave Himself for ME!"

Knowing that from the Lord you will receive the reward of inheritance. It is the Lord Christ whom you serve. Col. 3:24

The Reward of the Inheritance

The Oxford Dictionary defines inherit as to receive property, rank and title by legal descent, or to derive quality of character from one's progenitors. The Lord Jesus has by inheritance obtained a more excellent name than angels. He has been appointed heir of all things. All things that the Father has are Christ's, and by His great love and mercy, we are His, and all things are ours.

By faith we become heirs of God, joint heirs with Christ. He is the mediator of the new covenant to us so that we might receive the promised eternal inheritance. The fact of our inheritance should move us to serve the Lord with gladness, with wholehearted love and gratitude. We have been made heirs of the eternal kingdom with an inheritance that is incorruptible, undefiled and fades not away, reserved in heaven for us.

God does not want us to lose our inheritance by sharing our new life with our old, unregenerate self. The provision of death for our old man was made in the crucifixion of Christ for us. We are to put off the old man, because the son of the bond woman is not to be heir with the son of the free woman.

We have the option of positive or negative consequences for the way we live on earth; therefore, we are to beware of losing out and suffering loss. Paul tells us to know with certainty that no immoral or impure person or covetous man, who is an idolater, has any inheritance in the kingdom of Christ and of God.

Jesus warned His church in Philadelphia that they were to see to it that no man robbed them of their crown. Be careful not to lose what you can obtain.

Now the deeds of the flesh are evident,which are: immorality, impurity, sensuality.... Gal.5:19-21

The Fall and Depravity of Man

The colossal extent of the fall is usually minimized, resulting in man mistakenly attributing to himself what is directly the result of God's grace. The grace of God comes in many ways, not the least of which is through the legal system of policing and the fear of punishment. Without the prospect of punitive action the evil heart would express itself in every form of depravity, for all men are intrinsically evil.

When Jesus told His disciples that they were evil, He was not exaggerating. The reason men love darkness rather than light is because their deeds are evil. God has said that the wickedness of men is great, and that the thoughts of their heart is only evil continually.

Left to himself man has a heart that is deceitful above all things and desperately wicked. Jeremiah reminds us that insanity is in the heart of man all the days of his life, and that all mankind is stupid and devoid of knowledge.

There is not one who is good, not one who is righteous, for all are dead in trespasses and sins, all are lost and all are not only in darkness, but are darkness. Such scriptural definitions of our nature are not readily accepted, yet the evidence remains indisputable.

Education, far from eradicating wickedness, has produced more sophisticated criminals. Ecclesiastes tells us that because the sentence against an evil deed is not executed quickly the hearts of the sons of men are given fully to do evil. The importance of knowing one's total depravity cannot be overstated, because he who is forgiven much, loves much.

Let a man regard us in this manner, as servants of Christ, and stewards of the mysteries of God. 1 Cor. 4:1

Stewardship of the Gospel

The main virtue of a steward is faithfulness, because a steward is someone who has been entrusted with what another has given him. Paul's letter to Timothy charges Him concerning his stewardship. He tells Timothy to guard the treasure that has been entrusted to him, as well as to stir up the gift that was given to Him.

Paul himself had been entrusted with the glorious gospel of the blessed God, and was faithfully discharging his own stewardship. The central focus of Paul's fight was the doctrine of Christ, which had become the apostles' doctrine.

Timothy was rather on the timid side, yet Paul urged him not to be ashamed of the gospel, but rather to confront. Rebuking sharply, refuting and even delivering some over to Satan—these are integral ingredients of earnestly contending for the truth of the gospel.

If the church, which is the body of Christ, is to be the pillar and support of truth, then it must be taught the truth and live in truth. The truth of the gospel conflicts with every other gospel.

Poor stewards who want a quiet life have allowed erroneous, confident assertions of false teachers to go unchallenged. Every Christian has a deposit of divine treasure in his earthen vessel and is a steward of that which has been entrusted to him.

Although we are not all called to be teachers, Jude exhorts Christians in general to contend earnestly for the faith once delivered to the saints. Other gospels flourish because some who have been entrusted with God's word remain unfaithfully silent, having buried their talent.

By common confession great is the mystery of godliness: He who was revealed. 1 Tim.3:16

Our Common Confession

The *He* in this verse obviously refers to God. The mystery of godliness has come to us in the person of Jesus, and this verse sums up His appearing. The Word, which was God, became flesh and dwelt among us.

Jesus was born of the Spirit, anointed with the Spirit, spoke words that were Spirit and life, shed His blood, offered Himself up by the Spirit, and was raised by the Spirit. The Holy Spirit vindicated Jesus as the incarnate Son of God.

Angels proclaimed His birth, ministered to Him in the desert at the beginning of His ministry, and strengthened Him at the end in the garden. They declared His resurrection at the empty tomb, and they all worship Him. This gospel is for every creature, and through it those who sit in darkness are seeing a great light. Nations, tongues and tribes all over the world are believing in the Son of God as Savior and Lord. The one who came from heaven has now ascended, returning to the glory that He had with the Father before the world existed. Jesus is glorified and reigns as Lord over heaven and earth.

These truths are our common confession. They are to be believed and confessed by every member of His body, the church, which is the pillar and support of truth. These are foundational truths pertaining to the great mystery of godliness.

God Himself will open the eyes of the blind and the hearts of people everywhere through the gospel we speak. Be a communicator of the good news which declares that Jesus came to earth, completed His work, was received back into glory, and shall return to render judgment to every man.

Thou hast made known to me the ways of Life. Acts 2:28

The Ways of Life

Jesus made it clear that the Christian life would not be a bed of roses. Persecution, tribulation and even death await those who testify to the world of Christ and the way of righteousness. Nevertheless, His way and His will are good, acceptable and perfect. When following the Lord Jesus, we should not be surprised to find ourselves in circumstances similar to those in His earthly experience. Being men of sorrows and acquainted with grief is part of the deep water through which we travel.

God's way leads us through deep water, but the water will not overflow us. He provides a way through the sea, one which teaches us lessons that produce in us thanksgiving for the deep way. His way leads us through the wilderness. The wicked dwell in the wilderness, but going through is different than dwelling in the wilderness. Jesus had His wilderness experience, and if we follow Him we will have our wilderness experience. Our dry and arid times drive us to seek Him for water, to thirst for the living God.

His way leads us through the whirlwind and the storm. When everything is collapsing we find the Lord to be an unshakable refuge. He will remove all props that hinder our complete dependence upon Him. He is the author of the wind, and what He blows upon proves to be for our eternal good.

He instigates our seasons, even our necessary winters. We, as well as our times, are in His hands. He has ordained a way for us in which to walk. Walking in the Spirit is walking with the Lord in the way that we should go. Only then will our way please Him.

For everything created by God is good, and nothing is to be rejected, if it is received with gratitude. 1 Tim. 4:3-5

Nothing Is To Be Rejected

A false doctrine perpetrated by deceitful spirits in the last days is the abstaining from foods. In Mark, Jesus states twice that NOTHING outside of a man going into him can defile him, but it is that which proceeds out of the man that defiles him. Mark observes that Jesus thus declared all foods clean.

Paul instructs the Corinthians twice to eat ANYTHING put before them. Giving further clarity to Timothy, Paul explains why abstaining from foods is a false doctrine of demonic origin. Men who are liars and hypocrites with seared consciences—who want only to appear godly for the sake of gaining an advantage—will insist upon abstaining from foods, which God has created to be gratefully shared in by those who believe and know the truth. Everything created by God is good. Nothing should be rejected, if it is received with gratitude, for it is sanctified by the word of God and prayer.

Eating is a matter of faith. Falling away from faith in the truth of the gospel is referred to as a symptom of the last days. Many branches of the church pride themselves with legalistic demands that have nothing to do with the truth of the gospel. The new covenant is not in outward observance, but in inward holiness that proceeds from a new, pure heart.

Wherever a legalistic gospel of outward commandments is taught, demanding what you should eat or drink, you can be sure that deceitful spirits are at work. No one received more scathing rebukes from the Lord Jesus than the Pharisees. Their traditions nullified the commands of God.

They strained at gnats, swallowed camels, and neglected the matters of the heart.

We have fixed our hope on the living God, who is the Savior of all men, especially of believers. 1 Tim. 4:10

The Savior of All Men

In this letter Paul makes it clear that entreaties, prayers, petitions and thanksgivings should be made on behalf of all men. The reason he gives for praying for all men is that God desires all men to be saved. God gave Himself as a ransom for all and is the Savior of all men, especially of believers.

Jesus commanded that the good news be preached to every creature, but if Jesus did not die for all then how could there be good news for all? The special relationship that believers have does not invalidate the fact that Jesus is the Savior of all men. He is the propitiation not only for our sins, but also for the sins of the whole world.

Peter speaks of false teachers who will secretly introduce destructive heresies, even denying the Master who bought THEM. Their judgment and destruction does not alter the fact that they were purchased by the Savior. Jesus is to be preached to all men as their Savior because He is. Some men reject their Savior, but if He were not their Savior then they could not reject Him as such. Where Jesus is received He is especially their Savior because He becomes their life, but that does not diminish the truth of Christ being the Savior of all men.

Those who do not believe are judged because they have not believed that Jesus is the Son of God, their Savior. The grace of God has appeared and brought salvation to all men. God does not wish for any to perish, but for all to come to repentance. Jesus is the Savior of the whole world. Go and tell everyone, all creation, the good news.

She does not know that it was I who gave her the grain and the new wine, and the oil. Hosea 2:8,9

The Drinking of Wine

This topic elicits much controversy. The Scriptures must be fairly examined to find the balance of truth. As with many other issues, the abuse of wine has led to prohibition in many quarters. Most temperance societies are in fact abstinence societies. However, the Scriptures do not prohibit drinking wine. On the contrary, they teach that God gives wine as a blessing and takes it away as a judgment.

Assuredly, there are clear warnings against being addicted to wine and against drunkenness. The dangers of alcohol dependence are obvious. The Scriptures also admonish us not to cause a weaker brother to stumble. Yet, the Bible never describes such a thing as nonalcohlic wine. The wine of the Bible contained alcohol. Our Lord Jesus referred to the fermentation of wine, turned water into wine and drank wine. He contrasted Himself with John the Baptist, citing the fact that people accused Him of being a drunkard because He drank wine, while they accused John of having a demon because he abstained.

Paul rebuked the Corinthian church for those who got drunk at the Lord's table, confirming that the wine they drank was intoxicating. He even prescribed a little wine for Timothy's infirmities. While we must uphold each other's conscience, abstinence from eating or drinking must not be made a part of the gospel of Jesus Christ. The kingdom of heaven is not meat or drink. This truth must be swallowed by all persuasions. Let each be persuaded in His own conscience by the truth of the Scriptures. Happy is he who does not condemn himself in what he approves.

Sufficient food and choice attire for those who dwell in the presence of the Lord. Isa.23:18

Dwelling in the Lord's Presence

One of the consequences of Adam's sin was that he became afraid of God and therefore tried to hide from His presence. His actions were of course futile and proved that insanity had taken over his thinking processes. God is omnipresent and cannot be avoided. However, dwelling in His presence necessitates being qualified to be there. Certain conditions must be met in ascending the hill of the Lord and standing in His holy place. Only those who have clean hands and a pure heart may dwell in the fire of His presence.

Justification through faith in the blood of Jesus removes from us all of our disqualifications and presents us faultless before His presence. God has reconciled us to Himself by purifying us for His own possession. That reconciliation involves a joining of spirits where we become one spirit with Him. The prayer of Jesus that He would be in us and the Father in Him that we might be one in Them is fulfilled in the new covenant.

In place of indwelling sin, we receive the indwelling Spirit. He abides in us and teaches us that we abide in Him. The presence of the Lord is the habitation of His children. He has set us in His presence forever. An increasing awareness of His presence should be the pursuit of our heart. Setting our mind and affections on things above, where Christ is, is a constant attitude of searching.

The Lord desires us to seek Him and responds by revealing Himself increasingly. There is unspeakable joy and renewed strength in His presence, and His desire is for constant, conscious communion.

The grace of our Lord was more abundant, with the faith and love which are found in Christ Jesus. 1 Tim.1:14

Faith and Love Are in Christ

Paul reminds Timothy in both of his letters that faith and love are in Jesus. It was Jesus who demonstrated the nature of God in flesh and blood and in so doing made divine nature available to man. The truly born-again believer lives by the faith of the Son of God. The faith of Jesus was tried in every respect, and He overcame the world.

John tells us that our faith is the victory that overcomes the world. James instructs us that faith is only valid as it is worked out (in other words, it is not just theoretical). Paul adds the dimension of love to faith when he says that faith works through love.

Jesus worked out His faith by love, love for His Father and love for us. If we have all faith so as to remove mountains but have not love then we are nothing. God is love, and He is the God of faith. Faith is one of three abiding qualities (faith, hope and love), yet the greatest of the three is love.

Working out our faith by love demonstrates that we are God's children. Our first love for the Lord can grow cold, as can our love for anyone else, but it can also be rekindled. If our love for the Lord is merely lukewarm, then what is the condition of our love for our enemies?

Faith is fundamental for salvation and must be taught to accompany the love that validates it. Put on the breastplate of faith and love, which is righteousness in practice. Paul commended the Thessalonians because their faith was greatly enlarged and because their love towards each other grew greater. True growth is characterized by the increase of both faith and love that are in Jesus.

For God has not given us a spirit of timidity, but of power and love and discipline. 2 Tim.1:7

The Nature of Our New Spirit

Knowing what we have received under the terms of the new covenant is essential for living as we ought. We have received neither a spirit of bondage leading to fear again nor a spirit of timidity or cowardice. We have received a spirit of power and love and discipline.

If the same Spirit that raised Christ from the dead dwells within us, then He in union with our spirit will quicken our mortal bodies. The same power that raised Christ raises us from being dead in trespasses and sins, and makes us alive unto God. Then there is the baptism of the Spirit of power that Jesus promised would come upon believers. The same Holy Spirit sheds God's love abroad in our hearts, empowering us to love with the love of God. How else could we love as Christ loves?

Another transforming revelation is that we receive the spirit of discipline, or of sound mind, which renews the spirit of our minds, giving us the mind of Christ. The same root word is used to describe the demon-possessed man, who when Jesus released him was said to be in his *right mind*.

Christ in us by the Holy Spirit gives us the ability to think straight. Our consciences are cleansed and sensitized by the Holy Spirit to discern right from wrong, and as we obey the voice of the Lord we become more acutely aware of His guidance. Fellowship with the Lord becomes unhindered, and we develop discernment that enables us to know His will.

The Lord desires us to know Him more intimately. Such intimacy is achieved by beginning to trust that we can hear His voice and make decisions that are sound, and in love, and to boldly walk accordingly.

For the testimony of Jesus is the spirit of prophecy. Rev.19:10

The Testimony of Jesus

Jesus did not accept testimony from man because He knew what was in man. He did not accept testimony from demons even though they stated facts about Him. Only one could testify of Jesus: the Spirit of truth. The Spirit of truth was in neither men nor demons. But Jesus promised that after the Holy Spirit had come upon His disciples they also would be His witnesses.

Joel prophesied that the outcome of the outpouring of the Spirit would be prophetic utterance. The apostle Peter referred to the outpouring of the Holy Spirit on the day of Pentecost as the fulfillment of Joel's prophecy.

Paul tells the Corinthians that they may all prophesy one by one for the edifying of the church. The book of Revelation defines the testimony of Jesus as *the spirit of prophecy*. To relegate prophetic utterance to the past is to completely miss the meaning of the testimony of Jesus. The Holy Spirit is still being poured out upon men, women and children, making them testimonies of Jesus.

The book of Revelation speaks of the word of God and the testimony of Jesus, for which John was exiled and martyrs were slain, and by which the overcomers prevailed, proving the ongoing necessity of the testimony of Jesus. The testimony of Jesus must become our testimony as it did theirs.

Paul told the Corinthian church that they may all prophecy one by one. By the power of the Holy Spirit coming upon us, we become true testimonies of Jesus according to the Biblical definition.

The ministry I received from the Lord Jesus, to testify solemnly to the gospel of the grace of God. Acts 20:24

Grace (Charis)

The historical development of the word grace stems from its earliest use as charm. Plutarch refers to the charm of Homer's poetry. Aristotle defines grace as "helpfulness towards someone in need, not in return for anything." From kindly and courteous, grace took on extensions of generosity and the willingness to do someone good.

The Amplified Bible denotes grace as unmerited favor. The gospel enriches its meaning and broadens its dimensions, not only adding jewels to the kaleidoscope but also enlarging its mirrors. The gospel is the gospel of God's grace, the grace of Christ and the Spirit of grace. God's grace is true grace because it is freely given—not earned, not even sought.

God loved a fallen world. That is grace. Jesus came to seek and to save that which was lost. That is grace. God will have mercy on whom He will have mercy. That is grace. God took the initiative. He performed the purchase. He applied redemption. That is grace. God directed grace towards His enemies, as demonstrated by Jesus when He asked the Father to forgive those who were nailing Him to the cross. That is grace.

We who are the recipients of His grace stand immersed in this grace, enjoying all the immensity of its provisions. The grace of God has brought us peace and power: peace by way of justification and reconciliation, and power through the Spirit of grace to deny ungodliness and worldly lusts and to live righteously and godly in this present world. There is still more grace to be revealed at Christ's coming and in the ages to come.

Suffer hardship with me, as a good soldier of Jesus Christ.
2 Tim. 2:4

Soldier, Athlete, and Farmer

Paul uses three analogies to characterize the Christian life. Firstly, the soldier does not entangle himself with the affairs of everyday life, but enlists to be a soldier twenty-four hours a day, every day. He does not pursue any other calling or devote his time and energy to any other interests. During World War II if someone wanted something that was extravagant, people would remind him, "there is a war on." Similarly, we must be reminded that a spiritual battle is raging and the warfare is continuous.

Secondly, the athlete has a goal in mind: the prize of conquest. He disciplines himself in the rigors of training in order to achieve peak performance. His self-denial is of no account in view of the glory that comes with victory.

Thirdly, the hard-working farmer ought to be the first to receive his share of the crops. Just as the ox should not be muzzled when it treads the corn, the Lord directs that those who preach the gospel should live by the gospel.

Like the soldier, we should place ourselves unreservedly at the beck and call of our Commander in Chief and fight the good fight of faith. To please Christ who enlisted us, we must focus our lives upon His interests. Like the athlete striving for the prize of the mastery, so we should press on toward the goal for the prize of the upward call of God in Christ Jesus. As the farmer eats of the fruit of his labors, so we will reap what we have sown. We must remember also to make material provision for those who labor in the word and doctrine among us.

For if we died with Him, we shall also live with Him.
2 Tim.2:11-13

The *if* Scriptures

Those who add little weight to the *if* scriptures shall be indebted to them. As glorious as is the doctrine of election, mere intellectual assent is no guarantee of being elect. Certain evidences and fruit exist to confirm or to question such a profession. Paul lists four *if's* and their consequences in our text. We live with Jesus only IF we have died with Him. We shall reign with Jesus only IF we endure. As Jesus Himself taught, IF we deny Him before men, then He will deny us before His Father. The fourth IF declares the faithfulness of God, which endures even when we are faithless.

The writer to the Hebrews states that we are Christ's house, IF we hold fast our confidence and the boast of our hope firm until the end. Also, we partake of Christ, IF we hold fast the beginning of our assurance firm until the end. The Colossian church received a similar warning. Being reconciled through His death in order to be presented holy and blameless and beyond reproach is affirmed only IF we continue in the faith, firmly established, steadfast and not being moved away from the hope of the gospel.

Peter speaks of being diligent to make our calling and election sure. God is sure, and we too can be sure IF the qualities of the Spirit are ours and are increasing. There is a vain and useless faith that calls Jesus Lord and does things in His name, yet is unknown and disowned by Him. IF you are a worker of iniquity, your profession will not save you. IF you lose your life for Jesus and the gospel's sake, you will find eternal life and obtain His glory.

The Lord knows them that are His, and let everyone who names
the name of the Lord abstain from wickedness.   2 Tim.2:19

The Lord Knows Those Who Are His

Being known by God is more important than what we think
we know of Him.   There are those who profess to know Him but
by their works deny Him.   Some call Jesus Lord, and even cast
out demons, prophesy and perform miracles in His name, yet are
told by the Lord that He never knew them.   They are workers of
iniquity who will receive the appropriate penalty.

Paul wrote to the Galatians that they knew God—or rather,
that they were known by God.   Not everyone who calls Him Lord
shall enter the kingdom, but he who does the will of the Father.
Those who love God keep His commandments and do His will,
and if any one loves God, he is known by Him.

God has given a witness of His Spirit within those who are
His that they are indeed His children.   That is how we know we are
owned by God and can call Him Father from our innermost being.

Another way of knowing that we are known of God is to
give ourselves diligently to being approved by God.   Working out
what God is working in us is a lifelong work.   When we finally
give an account for what we have worked, will we be workmen
that are ashamed?

The first part of the seal of the foundation of God is that the
Lord knows those who are His.   The second part is that everyone
who names the name of the Lord should abstain from sin and
wickedness.   These two parts are equally necessary to prove that
there is a foundation of God in us.

God commands us to wake up to righteousness and stop
sinning.   No one who is born of God practices sin, and he who
does not practice righteousness is not of God.   Loving in deed and
truth assures our hearts.

You shall receive power when the Holy Spirit has come upon you, and you shall be My witnesses. Acts 1:8

You Shall Receive Power

The promise of power was the promise of the Holy Spirit. The disciples were not without the Holy Spirit, for Jesus had breathed upon them after His resurrection and said, "receive the Spirit." That was their birth by the Spirit, but they had not yet been baptized with the Spirit. They were to wait for the promise of the Father, and the power they were to receive would be theirs as the Holy Spirit came upon them. Only then would they be testimonies or witnesses to Jesus.

There are many who profess godliness but deny the power. The Bible warns us to avoid them. God has given us a Spirit of power, and He can do exceedingly abundantly beyond what we can ask or think, according to the power that works in us. Our earthen vessels contain treasure: the excellency of the power of God. The power of the Spirit within us works the work of faith with power. The kingdom that we have received is not in word only, but in power and demonstration.

Paul wanted to know not the speech of his critics, but their power. The absence of the power betrays the absence of the Spirit of power. Where Paul detected the absence he asked if they had received the Holy Spirit since they had believed. Have you received the power of the Holy Spirit empowering you to demonstrate the power of Christ and His kingdom?

The gifts of the Holy Spirit are gifts of power, enabling us to do things that we are naturally incapable of doing. We cannot be testimonies of Jesus in power without receiving the promise of the Father. Jesus still gives the Spirit to those who obey Him and ask.

All Scripture is inspired by God and profitable for teaching, for reproof, for correction, for training in righteousness; that the man of God may be adequate.   2 Tim. 3:16,17

The Scriptures: God's Book

There were many writings available to Jews and Gentiles, but only one collection had the peculiar title of "holy." These writings were sacred because the Holy Spirit inspired holy men to write them. Hundreds of times the Scriptures own themselves to be the word of the Lord. They are the singular record of God, His ways and His will from eternity before time as we know it, and on through the ages to come.

From creation through the fall, through God's history with man, to the Jewish nation and to everything that pointed towards the coming of the deliverer—these writings stand alone as the word of God.

The books from Genesis through Malachi are referred to by Paul and the other New Testament writers as the Scriptures. The New Testament is the record of the fulfillment of what the Old Testament foreshadowed and promised.

Jesus said that the Scriptures testified of Him. He came and completed the revelation and fulfilled the promises. The Scriptures are the word of His grace which is able to build us up and give us an inheritance among all those who are sanctified.

In this day of much deception and a multitude of devious voices, where can one turn for sanity and truth and absolutes? Jesus is the way, and the truth and the life, and the Bible alone contains the sacred revelation of Him who was and is and is to come.

Fill yourself with the riches of His word. Let His word abide in you, and learn of Him through this unique source of revelation. The difficulties of the last days can be faced confidently with the knowledge of God and the comfort of the Scriptures.

Moreover, I will give you a new heart and put a new spirit within you, and I will remove the heart of stone from your flesh and give you a heart of flesh. Ezek. 36:26

A Completely New Heart

By our natural birth we were part of the kingdom of darkness. Corruptible nature inhabited our mortal bodies. Lusts and passions dominated our self-indulging, darkened minds and hearts. We were unfit for the kingdom of God. Our temperaments were unsuited to the rule of the Lord. The righteousness of the kingdom of God was not only beyond our ability to achieve, but also beyond our willingness to have. Men actually love darkness rather than light because their deeds are evil.

Although sin is a mystery, we do know that there was a time when there was no sin. Sin entered through Satan, the fall in heaven preceding the fall of man on earth. However, God has now dealt with sin, Satan and the kingdom of darkness in what He has done through Jesus Christ His Son. So conclusive is God's answer in Jesus, that when this age is concluded, the kingdom of darkness will be no more.

To all who repent from their sin and receive Christ and His redeeming work, God gives a new heart and a new spirit. The new birth is from God, by His Spirit, and creates new creatures with new hearts, new minds, new appetites and new motives.

Our new longings are for the Lord and His righteousness, for purity and holiness. Pride gives way to humility, and hatred and anger to love and kindness. Service to others replaces self-serving as we begin to honor others before self. Our ability to live according to the kingdom of God comes from a heart birthed by God, making us children of the Kingdom of God, joint heirs with Jesus, our Head.

I urge you therefore, brethren, by the mercies of God, to present your bodies a living and holy sacrifice, acceptable to God, which is your spiritual service of worship. Rom.12:1

Presenting Ourselves by Mercy

We can present ourselves to God only by His mercy. Apart from His mercy, we could present ourselves only as objects of judgement and wrath; but God, who is rich in mercy, because of His great love, has forgiven us our sins. We who were dead in trespasses and sins have been crucified, buried and raised with Jesus Christ to walk in newness of life. We must present ourselves to God as those alive from the dead and our bodies as instruments of righteousness. No longer must we be conformed to this world.

Our heart has been changed. We have been given a spirit of power, of love and of a sound mind. The translation into His kingdom from the kingdom of darkness has taken place. The transformation has begun. God is at work in us to conform us to Christ. Our new and true identity—and therefore our fulfillment— is to be found in Jesus. God is working in us at this very moment to enable us to grow up into Christ in every area of our personality. Our happy employment is the giving of ourselves to working out what God is working in.

When we neglect our great salvation, we impair our growth in the process of transformation, and we remain unchanged in our ways. Stagnation and decay are the only alternatives to growth and change. If we do not serve our gracious Master, who kindly attends us with loving care so that we will partake of His nature, then we serve the old taskmaster who hates us and will destroy us.

Sin ruined man and robbed him of his identity in God. How can we who are dead to sin live in it any longer? Present your body in worship to God.

Blessed are the pure in heart, for they shall see God. Matt.5:8

Purity of Heart

All men are born with a need to be purified. Sin defiles and makes unclean, and all have sinned. Our righteousness is as filthy rags in the sight of a pure and holy God. Our consciences are defiled, and our uncleaness comes from within our hearts. We can do nothing to cleanse ourselves from our impurity, but God who is rich in mercy has provided the means of our purification.

Jesus Christ, God's Son, came as the Lamb of God who takes away the sin of the world. He shed His blood for the remission of our sins and to cleanse us from ALL our unrighteousness. Our hearts and consciences are purified by the redeeming blood of Jesus.

God purifies to Himself a people who are on fire from within to do His will. The new purity is not superficial, but radical, for He purifies our very hearts by faith. Our cleansed consciences make us sensitive to God's will, and our new, pure hearts make us inclined to do it. The new birth produces a new creature of the new covenant who has a new heart. Instead of indwelling sin we now have the indwelling Christ who dwells in us by His Spirit.

Sin brought the curse, but Jesus was cursed for us. To those who repent and receive Him God gives the inestimable blessing of a pure heart. Only those who have a pure heart can ascend the hill of the Lord, stand before Him and see Him.

Those who have been purified are responsible to keep themselves pure. Paul's goal was to present Christians to Christ as those who comprise a pure virgin, those who love with a pure heart and have a good conscience and a sincere faith.

For a child will be born to us, a son will be given to us. Isa. 9:6

Unto Us a Child Is Born

The pursuit of the elusive source of life has occupied men of every generation. Scientists who reject the existence of God as creator are totally bankrupt of an explanation for the origin of the material universe and all living things. Man cannot generate life from anything other than what is already living, nor can he make matter from nothing.

Mary was visited by the angel Gabriel and was perplexed at his announcement of her bearing a son, because she had known no man. The angel explained the dilemma by telling her that the agent of conception would be the Holy Spirit. God is the living God, and He gives life to all living things. The Spirit of life came upon Mary, and the power of the Most High overshadowed her, resulting in her bearing a holy offspring, the Son of God.

In the depths of Mary's womb was the marvel and mystery of the incarnation. The dividing of the egg into its fetal growth occurred by the power of the Holy Spirit.

The Holy Spirit does not produce fallen nature, but rather God's nature. In Jesus, divine nature was now in flesh and blood. He was not just a living soul, but a life-giving spirit. In Him is life, and to as many as receive Him, He gives spiritual, eternal life. All other men trace their lineage from their first, fallen father, Adam, but this child could not be traced back to Adam through His Father, for His Father was God.

He was in the beginning with God and was God, and now He was to be called Emmanuel, or God with us. This Jesus was given to us that through Him we might share God's life.

That you may not be sluggish, but imitators of those who through faith and patience inherit the promises. Heb.6:12

Do Not Be Sluggish

When a car is sluggish it is difficult to start, and even when it starts it does not run smoothly. There is also a fear of it stalling because of its unreliability. Christians can become sluggish in starting and difficult to keep running smoothly. The word for sluggish is the same word used to describe those who have become "dull" of hearing.

We are given a powerful start in the Christian life, for we are quickened by the Spirit and made alive from the dead. We are not born again by a sluggish spirit. Neither are we born dull of hearing. We become sluggish and dull through lack of obedience. Instead of walking in the obedience of faith, we ignore the voice of the Spirit.

The exercise of faith by obedience increases discernment. Neglect makes us lose our edge as when a sharp blade becomes dull. God promises His people that He will transform them from being a worm into being a sharp threshing instrument with teeth. There are not many things more dull than a worm, especially if you want to thresh the mountains. "Be transformed!" says Paul.

Jesus warns about the slothful servant. Paul exhorts us not to lag behind in diligence but to be fervent in spirit, serving the Lord.

Are you a cold starter? Is your battery run down? Have your plugs lost their spark? Has your oil of the Spirit been mixed with the water of compromise? Have you lost your edge? True repentance can cleanse you from all filthiness of the flesh and spirit. The Spirit of the zeal of the Lord can jump-start you to run powerfully. Arise and shine and thresh.

The integrity of the upright shall guide them. Prov. 3:12

Integrity Shall Guide Them

The definition of integrity includes wholeness, soundness, uprightness, honesty and purity. He who walks with integrity may abide with God and dwell on His holy hill. He will be guided because he walks with the light of life. The heart of integrity repels seduction as a filthy garment. The new, pure heart that we receive when Christ becomes our life is a force that resists even the devil. However attractive sin was to our old man, it is repugnant to the new man.

The process of maturing includes facing temptations, all of which are within our power to resist through the integrity of Christ who dwells in our hearts. When we resist we overcome, and the power to resist grows greater until, like the young men addressed by John, we become strong, the word of God abides in us and we have overcome the wicked one.

We must believe the truth about ourselves as brothers of Christ, born of the same Father. We will never be tempted beyond what we can resist; therefore, as we come to believe who we are we become unassailable. Walking by faith maintains our integrity. Integrity means walking with the Lord having a conscience void of offense. We may be perplexed and at times unable to understand, but we will not falter as long as we maintain our integrity.

Consider Job, who maintained his integrity under immense pressure and worshiped the Lord. Conflicting choices will be no problem for the upright, because their integrity will guide them. Integrity never settles for the wrong way. Our choices are a reliable test of our how truly upright we are.

There is an appointed time for everything...a time to give birth and a time to die. Eccles.3:1,2

There Is a Time to Die

There is an appointed time for everything, and it is God who does the appointing. Jesus came in the fulness of time and died when His time had come. His Father's timing governed His life. He was able to pass through the midst of those who sought prematurely to kill Him. When wicked hands finally nailed Him to the cross, it was by the predetermined will and counsel of God.

It is appointed for man once to die and then the judgment. Death is the result of sin. The fear of death holds man in bondage all the days of his life. No one can put off the day off his death, but Jesus came that we might have life and be delivered from the bondage of the fear of death and judgment for our sins. Jesus said that if we believe in Him, though we die yet shall we live. Because He gives us His eternal life, physical death is not even considered when He tells us that those who believe in Him shall never die.

The Scriptures tell us that the day of one's death is better than the day of one's birth. Who believes that? Paul considered death far better. He preferred to be absent from the body and present with the Lord.

Man is born to trouble as the sparks fly upwards, but Jesus said that He would wipe our tears and that there would no longer be death, mourning nor crying. Physical death for the believer ushers him into the presence of the Lord where he will never die.

Ultimate bliss is to receive God's welcome as good and faithful servants when we enter into the joy of our Lord. Instead of the fear of death there can be an exciting anticipation.

The word of the cross is to those who are perishing foolishness...
because the foolishness of God is wiser than men.   1 Cor.1:18-25

The Foolishness of God

The gospel of Christ is to the Jews a stumbling block and to the Greeks foolishness, but to those who believe, the gospel is the power of God and the wisdom of God. God's foolishness is wiser than man's wisdom, and His weakness is stronger than man's strength. The world in its wisdom did not know God, yet God was pleased through the foolishness of the proclamation to save those who believe.

When we consider those who have been chosen of God, we see few who are mighty or noble. God has chosen the weak and foolish, the nobodies of this world, to confound the strong and the wise, the esteemed of this world.

Jesus told the Pharisees that prostitutes and tax gatherers would enter the kingdom of God before them. In the face of the arrogance of man, puffed up in his own imagination, God has compelled the lame and the poor and the blind to come into His kingdom. He has done this so that no man can boast in himself.

God has used the foolishness of preaching to transform the foolish into the wise, the weak into the powerful, and the poor into the rich in God.

The wise of this world are the truly foolish because in their wisdom they have rejected God. Their wisdom, strength and values are all deceptions, and the day of reckoning will declare as much. Let the wise of this age become foolish that they may become wise.

God will appraise the values of every man, and many will find that they trusted in straw. Their laughter will be turned to weeping and gnashing of teeth, but those who believe the foolishness of God will weep no more and will enjoy the Lord forever.

*We may offer to God acceptable service with reverence and awe.
Heb. 12:28*

Acceptable to God

God made clear as far back as Cain and Abel what was
acceptable and unacceptable regarding offerings. Abel offered a
lamb, pointing to the substitutionary sacrifice of the Lamb of God,
the Lord Jesus. Cain offered the fruit of his labors, which was
unacceptable.

The Father testified that He was well pleased with Jesus.
Jesus was so well pleasing that He became the acceptable offering for the sin of the whole world. We were all unacceptable to
God because of our sin. We could not justify ourselves by the
works we performed, because our righteousness was as filthy rags
in His sight. However, God delivered us from our inability to be
acceptable by making us accepted in Christ.

Having been accepted in Jesus, we should now be grateful
and live acceptably. Those who are justified are to live by faith.
Without faith it is impossible to please God.

When Christ becomes our life we can live acceptably, but it
is not automatic. We have the grace to deny ungodliness, but we
can fall short of that grace and insult to the Spirit of grace.

The true disciple is one who follows His Lord. It is not we
who are to lead, but He. Doing our will instead of God's is unacceptable. Therefore, we must listen to the Lord if we are to know
His will and do it. Obeying what we know to be the will of the
Lord trains us to discern good and evil.

Getting older does not necessarily mature us in the Lord.
Maturity comes to those who live acceptably. The Lord will reveal Himself and His purposes to those who gratefully and hum-
bly live acceptably in His sight.

For here we do not have a lasting city, but we are seeking the city which is to come. Heb.13:14

No Continuing City

The hostile environment of the world contrasts with the church, which is in the world but not of it. Jesus was a stranger to His own, for they did not know Him. They not only rejected but also despised Him. He faced the hatred and persecution of a contrary society. He warned the disciples that they too would incur opposition for His name's sake.

The New Testament writers continue the theme of contention between those of the flesh and those of the spirit. A true Christian is a stranger to this world. Paul speaks of being unknown, and with Peter, he designates Christians as strangers and pilgrims who have no lasting city here. We have a tendency to want to settle down, but we must always hold ourselves in check with the view that our citizenship is above. We seek a city that has foundations built of God.

All that is material will be dissolved and burnt up. We are aliens, from another world, temporary residents. Jesus said that we are not of this world as He is not of this world. He instructed us to pray that His kingdom would come. It has come, but will come in its fulness, so we must not settle down in an unfinished kingdom.

In the parable of the nobleman who went off to a distant country to receive a kingdom, he commanded his servants to "do business" until he came. We must not merge into the world as part of it, but rather go into all the world and do God's business with His resources. If we are no longer a challenge to the world, we have probably settled down and thereby settled for less. Does the prospect of the return of the Lord make you a little sad that you will lose what you have hear on earth?